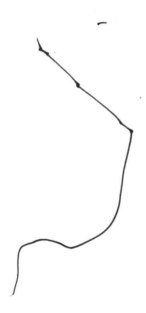

A Work of Heart

Understanding How God Shapes Spiritual Leaders

Reggie McNeal

A Leadership Network Publication

JOSSEY-BASS
A Wiley Imprint
www.josseybass.com

Published by Jossey-Bass
A Wiley Imprint
989 Market Street, San Francisco, CA 94103-1741 www.josseybass.com

Scripture taken from the HOLY BIBLE, NEW INTERNATIONAL VERSION. NIV. Copyright 1973, 1978, 1984 by International Bible Society. Used by permission of Zondervan Publishing House. All rights reserved.

Readers should be aware that Internet Web sites offered as citations and/or sources for further information may have changed or disappeared between the time this was written and when it is read.

Jossey-Bass books and products are available through most bookstores. To contact Jossey-Bass directly call our Customer Care Department within the U.S. at 800-956-7739, outside the U.S. at 317-572-3986, or fax 317-572-4002.

Jossey-Bass also publishes its books in a variety of electronic formats. Some content that appears in print may not be available in electronic books.

Library of Congress Cataloging-in-Publication Data

McNeal, Reggie.
   A work of heart : understanding how God shapes spiritual leaders /
Reggie McNeal.—1st ed.
      p.   cm.
Includes bibliographical references and index.
   ISBN 0-7879-4288-X
   1. Christian leadership.   I. Title.
   BV652.1 .M433   2000
   248.8'92   dc21

Printed in the United States of America
FIRST EDITION
HB Printing   20 19 18 17 16 15 14 13

Other Leadership Network Titles

Leading from the Second Chair: Serving Your Church, Fulfilling Your Role, and Realizing Your Dreams, by Mike Bonem and Roger Patterson

The Way of Jesus: A Journey of Freedom for Pilgrims and Wanderers, by Jonathan S. Campbell with Jennifer Campbell

Leading the Team-Based Church: How Pastors and Church Staffs Can Grow Together into a Powerful Fellowship of Leaders, by George Cladis

Organic Church: Growing Faith Where Life Happens, by Neil Cole

Leading Congregational Change Workbook, by James H. Furr, Mike Bonem, and Jim Herrington

Leading Congregational Change: A Practical Guide for the Transformational Journey, by Jim Herrington, Mike Bonem, and James H. Furr

The Leader's Journey: Accepting the Call to Personal and Congregational Transformation, by Jim Herrington, Robert Creech, and Trisha Taylor

Culture Shift: Transforming Your Church from the Inside Out, by Robert Lewis and Wayne Cordeiro, with Warren Bird

A New Kind of Christian: A Tale of Two Friends on a Spiritual Journey, by Brian D. McLaren

The Story We Find Ourselves In: Further Adventures of a New Kind of Christian, by Brian D. McLaren

The Present Future: Six Tough Questions for the Church, by Reggie McNeal

A Work of Heart: Understanding How God Shapes Spiritual Leaders, by Reggie McNeal

The Millennium Matrix: Reclaiming the Past, Reframing the Future of the Church, by M. Rex Miller

Shaped by God's Heart: The Passion and Practices of Missional Churches, by Milfred Minatrea

The Ascent of a Leader: How Ordinary Relationships Develop Extraordinary Character and Influence, by Bill Thrall, Bruce McNicol, and Ken McElrath

The Elephant in the Boardroom: Speaking the Unspoken About Pastoral Transitions, by Carolyn Weese and J. Russell Crabtree

CONTENTS

To Cathy (soul mate and wife)

*Jessica and Susanna (two daughters who have
shown me the heart of God for his children)*

*And God, whose designs on me
extend from eternity to eternity*

ABOUT LEADERSHIP NETWORK

SINCE 1984, Leadership Network has fostered church innovation and growth by diligently pursuing its far-reaching mission statement: to identify, connect, and help high-capacity Christian leaders multiply their impact.

Although Leadership Network's techniques adapt and change as the church faces new opportunities and challenges, the organization's work follows a consistent and proven pattern: Leadership Network brings together entrepreneurial leaders who are focused on similar ministry initiatives. The ensuing collaboration—often across denominational lines—creates a strong base from which individual leaders can better analyze and refine their own strategies. Peer-to-peer interaction, dialogue, and sharing inevitably accelerate participants' innovation and ideas. Leadership Network further enhances this process through developing and distributing highly targeted ministry tools and resources, including audio and video programs, special reports, e-publications, and online downloads.

With Leadership Network's assistance, today's Christian leaders are energized, equipped, inspired, and better able to multiply their own dynamic Kingdom-building initiatives.

Launched in 1996 in conjunction with Jossey-Bass (a Wiley imprint), Leadership Network Publications present thoroughly researched and innovative concepts from leading thinkers, practitioners, and pioneering churches. The series collectively draws from a range of disciplines, with individual titles offering perspective on one or more of five primary areas:

1. Enabling effective leadership
2. Encouraging life-changing service
3. Building authentic community
4. Creating Kingdom-centered impact
5. Engaging cultural and demographic realities

For additional information on the mission or activities of Leadership Network, please contact:

Leadership Network
www.leadnet.org
(800) 765–5323
client.care@leadnet.org

ACKNOWLEDGMENTS

SO MANY PEOPLE have been used by God to shape my heart—

The communities of my family of origin (H. T. and Nadine McNeal, Royce, Nancy, Randall, and Patricia); my wife's parents, Bob and Gerri Bowen; Ravenwood Baptist Church, Columbia, South Carolina; First Baptist Church, Kaufman, Texas; and Trinity Baptist Church, Mt. Pleasant, Texas

Ananiases—Randall, Royce, and W. L. Collins

Barnabases—Carl George, Bob Buford, Bill Mackey, Lyle Schaller, and Ray and Anne Ortlund

Jethros—Earl Oakerson and Carlisle Driggers

Marys, Marthas, and Lazaruses, who have provided us refuge and community in their homes—Cliff and Mariguinn Butler; Joel and Patty Chapman; Ron and Jeanette Couch; Bill and Norma Fortner; Bill and Nezza Howard; Mike and Amy Kessler; Brian and Judy Lee; Earl and Jewel Oakerson; Karen Oakerson; Stan and Betty Stokes; Bob and Delois Stolusky; Ron and Vicki Waisath; and Bob and Susan Witherspoon

Pharaohs, Philistines, and Pharisees—names withheld to protect the guilty

I am grateful to Carol Childress (Leadership Network) and Sarah Polster (Jossey-Bass) for their vision regarding this project and for their patience as it took shape. Sarah teased out the ideas behind fuzzy speech and together with her assistant, Johanna Vondeling, helped translate the ideas into text. My life has been made rich by hundreds of contributors who show up on every page. Though I cannot acknowledge them all here, I look forward to an eternity with them to talk over things of the heart.

R.M.

INTRODUCTION:
LOOKING FOR GOD IN
ALL THE RIGHT PLACES

I COULD HEAR IT in his voice. He wanted out. After only a year in his new pastorate, Frank was ready to throw in the towel. In fact, he was not sure he even wanted to remain in the ministry. This was his third church. At first, it had seemed to be a fresh opportunity. Now it felt all too familiar. He had been here before—but in another location. The names, faces, and scenery had changed but not the plot. The people were good people. They treated him well, but they differed in ministry values and agenda. Frank wanted to reach out to the community; the church seemed content to look after its own. The knowledge that it would take three to five years to shift their thinking, accompanied by resistance and pain, further discouraged him. He could not stay at it that long, he said. His emotional reserves were depleted. Now, in his mid-forties, Frank questioned whether he wanted to do this the rest of his life. In short, he had lost heart. The lesson: when a leader loses heart, he loses.

Terry had enjoyed a long winning streak. The church he had previously served as a staff member had grown like a weed and had attracted attention for its innovative ministry from people outside the church culture. All of that changed with the move across country. The new assignment brought him into direct conflict with the old leadership, who denied the fact of the congregation's decade-long decline. Innovation not only was considered a threat but also was perceived as disloyal to Terry's long-tenured predecessor. To make matters worse, Terry fought a debilitating and deteriorating medical condition. Yet, in the face of these enormous challenges, Terry maintained energy and focus. He refused to succumb to discouragement or to give up on the situation. His determination inspired others around him. The situation turned around. Against all odds, Terry refused to become an unintentional interim. In short, Terry kept heart. The lesson: leaders who do not lose heart become champions, not victims.

Spiritual leadership is a work of heart. This truth escapes many spiritual leaders. Caught up in helping other people maintain their hearts, they frequently ignore or neglect their own. They suffer for this oversight.

Symptoms stemming from this inattention range from spiritual power-lessness to lackluster leadership to spiritual bankruptcy. The failure to pay attention to fundamental issues eventually leaves the leader, at the very least, bewildered and discouraged, or in the worst cases, devastated. The continuum of loss moves from the deferment of the leader's life dreams to the shattering of a future no longer attainable.

Only in rare instances, it seems, do we run across spiritual leaders who genuinely understand that their leadership is ultimately a matter of the heart. Because they know this truth, they intentionally look after their own hearts in the midst of dealing with the hearts of others.

Leadership development efforts aimed at spiritual leaders all too often have neglected these issues of the heart. With the now decades-long emphasis on ministry as mechanics (how to counsel parishioners, how to grow a church, how to prepare a sermon, how to raise money, and the how-to list goes on and on), attention to the core being of spiritual leaders has gotten squeezed out in favor of more glamorous pursuits, or at least pursuits that would make the minister and his ministry "successful." Certainly leaders can and should add to and improve their set of microskills. I would never argue against learning all one can about leadership. However, all the leadership insight and expertise on the planet cannot, in the end, overcome a case of spiritual heart disease or "heart failure."

The operating assumption has been that spiritual leaders already understand spiritual formation and automatically apply these disciplines into their own lives. Only recently have seminaries begun not to take this for granted. Many are now focusing on the process of the seminarians' spiritual development. Before this, a course or two in one of the spiritual disciplines would be offered and thought to have filled the bill. Leadership development offerings by denominational agencies, parachurch organizations, and consulting firms have also largely focused on information and skill enhancement. Again, the center has been assumed.

My years in personal leadership in local congregations, and now my chance to work with thousands of church leaders across the United States and Canada in their own leadership development, convince me that these assumptions are wrong. Even worse, the conspiracy of neglect has contributed to the problem. Functionalism has replaced spiritual formation. Program manipulation and methodological prowess often serve as mere stopgap strategies to substitute for genuine spiritual leadership.

Empty spiritual leaders flock to conferences that tell them "how to _____" and go home just as empty. The truth frequently goes unrehearsed, which is that great spiritual leaders are great not just because they are great leaders but because they are great *spiritual* leaders. This truth gets lost in the shuffle between the airport and the hotel.

"If we do what _____ did, we can see the same results" is the prevailing mantra. Maybe so, but probably not, because what _____ did grew out of their own walk with God and ministry assignment. Their own leadership journey has more to do with heart issues than most imagine. Capturing and mimicking their techniques will not deliver spiritual breakthrough. That happens only on the heart level. No long-term spiritual gains can be posted unless they show up in the box scores of the leader's own heart development.

These misassumptions have implications that go beyond just the leader's own life. They affect those in the leader's constellation. What we see on the American religious landscape are scores of institutionalized expressions of Christianity that lack spiritual vibrancy or a sense of mission that moves beyond mere survival needs. These congregations and ministries frenetically search for new ways to "do church" or to accomplish their vision without attending to the fundamental heart issues of their constituency. No methodological fix can stir these groups into being spiritually prepared to practice an obedience that will bring them into an active partnership with God in his mission in the world.

The all-too-typical stylistic emphasis does not create communities of faith. It _can_ power a mechanical operation that harnesses activism and materialism to build churches that obscure the agenda of God. Although we have the best churches humans can build, God remains conspicuously absent in many of them. Only renewed attention to genuine spiritual preparedness can guarantee the church a legacy in America. Christian organizations focus on the externals, the material, and the political for one main reason: their leaders choose to. No wonder that millions of Christians in our culture have no idea what God is up to in their personal lives.

In this volume, I am arguing for a return to center, a return of interest and investigation into God's activity in his primary target—the human heart. We will never see a genuine spiritual renewal on this continent until we get down to some serious heart business. The only chance for this agenda to capture Christian energies lies in Christian leaders' reclaiming this focus as legitimate and of primary importance to them. For this reason, this book targets leaders. What leaders do and what they reward gets done. They are the solution, not just the problem.

Heart-shaping is the term used throughout this volume for what some would call spiritual formation. The term _spiritual formation_ may be confusing and without clear meaning to many. It conjures up mystical processes and practices that defy investigation or categorization. To overcome this confusion, this book employs a warmer and more intuitively understood phrase.

Heart-shaping involves both divine and human activity. God does not unilaterally mold and sculpt passive human beings who exercise no role in scripting their life development. Humans can and do make choices as part of the expression of the image of God given to them. God will not override the power to choose, which he grants to humans. On the other hand, God is no passive observer. The Christian doctrine of providence maintains that God lovingly superintends every part of our lives. Our choosings never render us helpless or beyond divine intervention.

A marvelous and mysterious interface of divine and human choices conspires and contends in designing a life and in shaping the heart that lies at the center of it. This divine and human interplay is what this book is about. These pages are an investigation of the heart-shaping process, an attempt to understand the crucible that shapes a leader's life.

The motif of a story or drama lends itself to this investigation. A great story is not just one story but a set of stories. The subplots all contribute a particular element to the development of the major story line. None of the ministories by themselves yields the whole plot, yet taken together they form the drama.

Leaders' lives are great drama. They have a plot that can be separated into several story lines. These subplots reflect different arenas of the leader's life in which God is at work.

We can isolate these dramatic elements for exploration. However, heart-shaping does not progress linearly. Its dynamic reflects more of a layering process, similar to the process used in music studios in recording various sound tracks that are then mixed together to create a single piece. The substories within the leader's life are going on simultaneously and are interacting with one another. Sometimes one is pushed more to the foreground of attention, but no chapter in the leader's life story stands on its own.

Basic heart-shaping occurs in six significant arenas. These divine-human interchanges provide the six major subplots of the leader's heart-shaping process. The development and convergence of these story lines script the leader's life message. These six subplots are *culture, call, community, communion, conflict,* and the *commonplace.*

Culture. Culture is the first major player in the leader's heart development. It creates the backdrop for all the rest of the story lines. In this book's investigation, culture will be broadly defined to include all the environmental influences that shape the leader's life and ministry context. These include the historical period, political situation, societal mores, and traditions. All of these create the cultural milieu in which the leader operates. Culture is not neutral; it contains both positive and negative forces. Nor does it serve merely as a background. Culture creates a story line in itself, for the leader's heart cannot be explained apart from its cultural influences.

Call. Every leader will admit to having some sense of destiny, whether great or small. In spiritual leaders, we can refer to this as the awareness of a call. The call is the leader's personal conviction of having received some life assignment or mission that must be completed. The call orders the leader's efforts, affecting decisions in every area of life. How the leader comes to an understanding of the life mission and how to pursue it provides a significant subplot for the leader's life drama.

Community. Leaders do not develop in isolation. They emerge within a community that plays a vital role in shaping them. Actually, we should speak of multiple communities in the leader's development. The family of origin, or initial life community, provides a beginning place for understanding this subplot in the leader's story. However, other key communities come into play. These may include the leader's friendships and faith-ministry communities.

Communion. This aspect of heart-shaping reflects the leader's conscious cultivation of a relationship with God. Spiritual leaders deal in spiritual currency. The value of this currency depends directly on the strength of the leader's deposits into the relationship bank with the Almighty. The communion subplot opens the door to the intimate interaction between the leader and the Leader.

Conflict. One could naively suspect that because spiritual leaders focus on healing, grace, peacemaking, restoration, forgiveness, and reconciliation, they escape from a lot of conflict. Just the opposite is true. The nature of the work places the spiritual leader in a combative position against destructive powers, the dark side of spiritual forces. Spiritual leaders find themselves thrown into the thick of the fray. These conflicts, whether personal, interrelational, demonic, or organizational, are not tangential developments. Rather, they are central heart-shaping events and episodes.

The commonplace. A lot of heart-shaping activity goes on in the everyday, run-of-the-mill, when-nobody's-looking activity of the leader. The defining moments in leaders' lives rarely offer a study in discontinuity. Usually leaders come to believe that all of life served to prepare them for that crystallizing event. The ordinary and routine serve to shape the leader's character. How the leader responds to everyday challenges and opportunities reflects a basic predisposition toward God's work in the leader's life.

My experience as a minister, a leadership consultant, and a minister to ministers has led me to conclude that many Christian leaders do not understand their own developing life story. They do not have a clear picture of the heart-shaping subplots that in the long run create their life and leadership legacy. They sometimes see individual or significant events as important, but they often fail to connect the dots of their life experience. As a result, they miss the learnings that such understanding yields.

Sometimes we can see the process of spiritual development in others more easily than we can perceive it in our own hearts. Once we learn to see God at work in others, we can then learn to look for these patterns in our own lives. For this reason, Part One of this volume investigates the heart-shaping dramas of four major biblical leaders, two from the Old Testament and two from the New Testament. The development of Moses, David, Paul, and Jesus provides us some clues as to how God works in every leader's heart in every era. Studying these well-known leaders will give us a common language and a storyboard to work from. The six subplots emerge as we rehearse the stories of these heroes of the faith. A few implications for contemporary spiritual leaders are mentioned, but for the most part, the treatment focuses on the dramas of the biblical characters themselves.

Part Two moves into the categorical investigation of the six subplots of the leader's heart-shaping drama. Having discussed these dynamics at work in Moses, David, Paul, and Jesus, Part Two explores these same heart-shaping dimensions in today's leaders. Some specific applications and suggestions offer readers a chance to identify these themes in their own lives and leadership experience.

This investigation pursues one additional agenda, prompted by pondering the question of why God creates leaders anyway. With all of the options available to him, why has he chosen to work through leaders in spiritual enterprises? The answer may at first seem too simple, but it is the best answer I can offer: God creates leaders in order to share his heart with his people. This observation can be verified when we consider what we have come to know of God through the lives of our biblical heroes. This means that the spiritual formation in the life of the leader is not just a private matter. God does not work in the leader's life in a vacuum, apart from the leader's role and life context. God's objectives may (and often do) extend beyond the leader's own life and lifetime. Part of the exploration of the heart-shaping drama considers its impact on the leader's constellation of followers.

As you read, please keep two questions in mind: What is going on (or has gone on) in each subplot of your own life that affects your current heart condition? and What is being revealed about God's heart through you in each of the six key story lines of your life?

This volume does not aim to help you figure out some new methodological approach to your leadership, nor is it designed to remediate flaws or deficiencies. The goal is to get you acquainted with the most important information you will need as a leader—*self-understanding*. This is a different issue than self-preoccupation. Self-preoccupation shows up in leaders who use others in order to achieve their own ambitions. Self-understanding begins and ends with God. This takes time and reflection. However, I am convinced that the most effective leaders are those who take time to ponder what God is up to in their own lives. Those who understand their own hearts will be better prepared to lead amid the growing discontinuities at the dawn of the third Christian millennium.

A few things about the book's format bear mentioning. First, real names in illustrations are never used. Many illustrations are also altered to prohibit easy identification. The reason for this (besides protecting the privacy of individuals) is that my experience teaches me that spiritual leaders categorize others' experiences too quickly, particularly if they know the person or situation. This would get in the way of the intent of this volume, which is designed to coach an inward journey, not to draw comparisons with others.

The reader will also notice a lack of references. In the treatment of biblical leaders, I have not surveyed the literature on these men. I have attempted to stay with the biblical material to demonstrate some connections that readers, working with the same sources, can build on in their own development. Many fine books have been written on the various themes covered here. Again, my intent is to reflect on these themes, not to provide a critical commentary on the subjects. I avoid excessive psychological terms and analysis. My goal is to prompt reflection, not to provide therapy, though I do hope the book has therapeutic value for the leader's soul.

Leadership emphases tend to cycle. Perhaps twenty to thirty years from now, the great need will again be "how to _____." Then someone, maybe me, will write about the limitations of leadership that is too introspective and inward focused. But this heart-shaping emphasis does not currently seem to be in oversupply.

I hope that reading this book will leave you with two major impressions. First, I hope that you marvel at the mystery of God's designs on your life. The writing effort will have been worth it if you become more attuned to the frequency of God's work in you. Second, I hope that your sense of your own leadership task will change. You may discover that God's greatest adventure for you involves far more than making you a great leader. He wants to make you a great person.

You are, after all, a work of heart.

PART ONE

HOW GOD SHAPED MOSES, DAVID, PAUL, AND JESUS FOR LEADERSHIP

WE TEND TO see things in others with greater clarity than we see them in ourselves. The first part of this volume seeks to use this power of observation to our advantage. We begin the exploration of God's heart-shaping work by examining its dynamic in the lives of the four most prominent biblical leaders (the ones that garner the most biblical material). The quest takes us over some familiar ground. Moses, David, Paul, and Jesus provide some well-rehearsed biographies for spotting the signs of divine heart-shaping. Their stories require no introduction for the reader. Because their lives are so well-known, they provide a quick connection for illustrating with real-life examples the thesis of this book: spiritual leadership is a work of heart.

The following exploration into the leadership of these four biblical characters will begin this course on divine heart-shaping. Learning to see God at work in *them* sets the stage for seeing him more clearly at work in *us*.

MOSES

A HEART ON A MISSION

HOLLYWOOD WOULD HAVE had to invent Moses if God had not created him. His story contains all the elements of great epics. The guy with everything going for him blows his advantage. Noble dreams of great accomplishment apparently fall victim to immaturity. However, the potential career detour provides an offstage recovery program. Unexpected turns of events thrust the hero back into the limelight. Deferred dreams come true. And this is only two of the three acts! Moses' drama holds us mesmerized, whether acted out by Charlton Heston in a Cecil B. DeMille production or drawn out by the imaginative talents of a Dreamworks animator.

Spiritual leaders find Moses especially engaging. They identify with much that he endured. High expectations. Public confidence accompanied by private self-doubt. Humiliation. Fickle followers. Draining conflicts. Exhilarating revelations. Miraculous divine interventions. Tedious and debilitating trivia. Fear of failure. Decisive victories. Ambivalent triumphs. Loneliness. Privileged relationship with God.

Moses stands as the colossus of the Old Testament. The legacy of his leadership, the Exodus, occupies center stage as the central event of the nearly fifteen hundred years of Old Testament history. He has commanded the admiration of millions for his mission to liberate oppressed slaves and for his contribution of the Decalogue to human civilization.

Our interest in Moses grows out of the remarkable case study he presents for studying divine heart-shaping dynamics. The subplots of culture, call, community, communion, conflict, and the commonplace present themselves with rare clarity. The Hebrew scriptures give us unusual exposure to so ancient a figure. Our hearts go out to him from the moment of his birth. We find ourselves strangely forgiving of his youthful impetuousness and fits of anger. We cheer for him against Pharaoh. We envy his mountaintop meetings with the Almighty. We wonder to ourselves if we would have endured so much (some of us think we already have) without similar disqualification in the end from entering the Promised Land. Not a few of us secretly wonder if Moses got the shaft or the royal treatment at Nebo.

We feel such kinship with Moses in his leadership challenges. We feel admiration for him because of his accomplishments. We feel challenged by him without being intimidated. His obvious flaws make him approachable but do not take away from his achievements. We too want to succeed in spite of our own flaws. That is why we eagerly search for clues in Moses' own heart-shaping that will instruct our own.

Beginnings and Family Relationships

Before Moses could leverage leadership or even speak a syllable, his life was being providentially superintended in order to prepare him for his unique assignment. Miraculous deliverances and Moses began a very early association. While other Hebrew slave parents were grieving over their losses, Jochebed and Amram were successfully hiding their baby boy from Egyptian authorities and subsequent death. The bulrushes plan worked beyond their wildest dreams. Pharaoh's daughter could not possibly have imagined the events she set in motion when she responded to her maternal instincts. Miriam too proved equal to the moment. Moses would be raised as an adopted Egyptian prince in Pharaoh's court. However, he spent his early months in his Hebrew home, where his mother could whisper into the young prince's ear the things she wanted in his heart. To the ancient Hebrews, nothing happened outside the will of God. Jochebed would believe that God had spared her son for some special reason. She would surely pass this belief on to her son.

This early scripting of a "great expectations" mentality figured prominently in God's heart-shaping preparation of the leader of the Exodus. From his earliest moments, Moses would have a sense of destiny cultivated in him. Robert Clinton (*The Making of a Leader*, 1988), professor of Christian leadership at Fuller Theological Seminary, identifies this "sense of destiny" (p. 238) as a key insight into leadership effectiveness. He defines this awareness as a belief that God has his hand on the leader for a very special purpose or purposes. This belief is tied to an event or set of events that confirm to the leader that he or she has been chosen by God for a life mission. Yahweh made sure that Moses, the future deliverer, would grow up with the knowledge that he himself had been delivered through divine intervention.

Moses apparently enjoyed a significant connectedness to his family of origin. At some point, he discovered that he owed his life to Miriam, insight that forged a special bond between them. Miriam played a leadership role in the Exodus experience, particularly the early wilderness wanderings. She generally supported her younger brother. When she rebelled against Moses' leadership, Yahweh judged her by immediately giving her leprosy. Moses pleaded for her life and forgave Miriam quickly despite the seriousness of her rebellion.

Similar dynamics also characterized Moses' relationship with Aaron. They apparently enjoyed enough time together for Moses to gain respect for and confidence in his older brother. At the burning bush, Moses implored Yahweh to let him recruit Aaron as a leadership partner. Aaron would come in handy for at least two reasons. First, he apparently knew how to talk in front of a crowd. Second, Moses needed someone who still had connections with the folk back in Egypt. Aaron did serve Moses well as a contact person with the Hebrew slaves and as his right-hand man. He, like Miriam, received grace from his younger brother on several occasions. The golden calf episode alone raised serious questions about Aaron's leadership. However, God and Moses honored Aaron by setting his tribe apart as priests.

Although Moses was the undisputed leader of the Exodus, he was not alone in leadership. Many treatments of his leadership ignore this significant fact. Miriam and Aaron formed part of a family triumvirate giving leadership to the liberated nation. The three became a leadership community that faced together the critical challenges of the wilderness sojourn. Despite their failings, Aaron and Miriam contributed to Moses' success. For his part, Moses remained faithful to his brother and sister till their end.

The Prince of Egypt

Yahweh secured arrangements for Moses to grow up the child of two cultures, both of which he would need to understand in order to fulfill his unique role in history. His family of origin provided his Hebrew grounding.

His experience of Egyptian culture would be very different from that of his kinsmen slaves, thanks to none other than the daughter of the same Pharaoh that wanted Moses never to grow up. Why did this boy capture her heart? What prompted her to defy her own father's wishes about this child? What price, if any, did she pay to give Moses his head start in life? Surely Moses' savior told him of the day she had rescued him from the bulrushes along the banks of the Nile. What expectations did she add to those of Jochebed?

Moses, then, developed personally in an atmosphere that heightened his uniqueness. The dynamic of his childhood and early adult years would set most young men to wondering about their destiny. In Moses' case, his unusual circumstances almost certainly conspired to make him feel "different" from the others.

An interview with any great leader will often uncover this same insight into their self-perception. Like Moses, they feel somehow different from others. This awareness often begins in childhood and continues throughout adolescence and young adult development. The sense of apartness signals part of the heart-shaping activity for leadership. It affords the necessary self-differentiation that one needs to provide effective leadership to others. (Leadership is the healthy expression of this dynamic. A sense of being different taken to extremes leads to pathological behaviors wherein people become disconnected from those around them.) In Moses' case, the confluence of these forces predisposed him for leadership.

Pharaoh provided the training that fashioned the future emancipator of the Hebrews. As a prince of Egypt, Moses would be schooled in leadership practices. He would study law. He would learn to express himself and to handle responsibility and authority. He would be expected to become adept in problem solving and project management because the royal building projects were superintended by members of Pharaoh's house. Moses would become versed in Egyptian religion.

All of these fundamental elements of training prepared Moses for different aspects of his assignment to be leader of the Exodus. God spoke his Ten Commandments to a legally trained mind. Moses the expert in law served as judge and eventually established a system of lower and upper magistrates when the stress of his handling each case himself became too great. His familiarity with Egyptian religion elevated his effectiveness as ambassador of Yahweh, God of the slaves. Each plague demonstrated the superiority of Moses' God over the gods of the Egyptian pantheon. Moses' understanding of the royal priesthood of Egypt provided a rich background to the covenant he would receive from Yahweh at Sinai (Exod. 19:1–6). The Israelites were to serve a role that Moses had observed in the halls of Pharaoh from his youth. The ex-slaves were now to be Yahweh's royal priests, carrying out his will and serving as his ambassadors.

We have no clue as to how Moses fared in Pharaoh's court. Was he ostracized as a foreigner? Was he made to feel second-class? Or did he stand out as a symbol of slave-class achievement and become a celebrated prince? At some point, he learned how he had been brought to Pharaoh's household. He obviously maintained some contact with kinsmen. Every sight of a Hebrew slave served as a reminder of his special reprieve in life. The constant personal observations of his people's plight apparently grated on Moses' soul.

A False Start

One wonders how long Moses' anger seethed about the treatment of his fellow Hebrews at the hands of their Egyptian taskmasters. He probably witnessed Egyptian brutality to Hebrew slaves more than once. He may have harbored notions as a young man of redeeming his people. Maybe he lobbied unsuccessfully for reform, hoping to use his influence to change slave treatment. Perhaps Moses intervened many times on behalf of the slaves. But one day he snapped. In a blind rage, he killed the Egyptian oppressor whom he had caught mistreating a Hebrew slave. His opportunity to work within the system to better his people's lot ran out with his victim's blood into the Egyptian sand.

Whatever fantasies Moses might have entertained about being heralded as a hero among his own people were crushed the next day. His attempted intervention into a dispute between two Hebrew slaves proved to be a mixed bag. It probably saved his life, because he learned from them that his crime was known. But the rebuff he received from the slaves introduced him to an ingratitude that he would experience time and time again on the part of those he was trying to lead. This type of scenario may not have been covered in the "leadership curriculum" at Pharaoh's court.

Moses experienced what all leaders ultimately fear—rejection by the people they are called to lead. Part of his internal scripting had come true. As already noted, Moses' uniqueness had set him apart from those around him from the beginning. He was a child of two cultures, who never completely belonged to either. Moses would always stand apart from his people. More than any other biblical leader, Moses seems profoundly alienated from his leadership constituency most of the time. He was never quite accepted by the Hebrews.

These dynamics would play out over the succeeding decades. For the moment, whatever disillusionment Moses had suffered from his initial attempt to deliver his people had to be temporarily ignored. He had to get ready for the escape into the desert.

Flight into the Desert

Within a dozen verses after Moses' birth narrative, we find him in danger from Pharaoh again. The prince had become avenger (Exod. 2:11–12), then would-be judge (2:13–14), then fugitive from justice (2:15). Moses' struggle to liberate, to rescue, to make right of wrong, to champion the oppressed had erupted in lethal fury. It cost him his privileged position and could cost him his life if he stayed around. He did not.

The fleeing fugitive became immediately embroiled in another combative situation. Not far into the Midianite desert, Moses encountered seven young women in distress at a local watering hole. The women's attempts at drawing water were being thwarted by some ruffian shepherds. Moses must have been an intimidating figure. Singlehandedly, he rescued the women from the harassment of the hoodlums. He further attended to their plight by personally drawing water and distributing it to their flock. His bravery and kindness landed him a dinner invitation, a wife, and a job. It turned out to be a productive afternoon.

Some significant themes emerge in the early Moses. These themes reflect similar realities for many spiritual leaders. Moses had a strong internal sense of right and wrong. This compass propelled him into personal intervention on behalf of others, even if it involved conflict. He was particularly sensitive to the needs of the underprivileged. Standing up for slaves and women did not "enhance one's résumé" in the second millennium before Christ. The crusader, liberator heart was unmistakable in the young prince.

Leaders often become leaders because of the same internal drive evidenced by Moses. They are driven by causes and willing to personally risk involvement. As with Moses, the leader's early attempts often end in frustration and even failure. Many leaders' life stories bear remarkable resemblance to this early part of Moses' saga. Consumed with their passion, they frequently overplay their ambition, abuse their position or power, and get into trouble with some authority. Their early mistakes threaten to derail their life missions.

Some spiritual leaders are sent into exile for their leadership blunders. Fortunately, not all of these accept their desert exile as the final chapter of their lives. They learn from their early conflicts. Most important, their hearts remain connected to and energized by their earlier passion.

Moses' heart certainly did. He could have sat at the Midianite well and watched the plight of Jethro's daughters with a detached passivity. However, he overcame whatever reticence his previous intervention efforts may have engendered in him. His refusal to let early failure quell his heart's passion kept him in the game. Moses could not have known that at the time. He did what he did because he obeyed his heart. That conflict at the well revealed the mettle of leadership resident in the young man's heart.

This story reveals another aspect of leader heart-shaping. The subplot of conflict often appears early in the spiritual leader's life script. The leader's response becomes formative for leadership potential. If the leader resists risk after early skirmishes, the heart is stunted by lack of courage. Passion fades. Early promise gives way to mediocrity and lackluster performance. Personal vision shrinks to fit life circumstances rather than creating tension for realization of a preferred future. On the other hand, if leaders decide to continue the personal pursuit of passion, they put themselves in a posture of openness to continued heart-shaping by God.

Perhaps you have your own story of early tragedy and subsequent exile because of some conflict or misjudgment on your part. You may still be in the exile period of your life. What will keep this from being the final chapter for you will be your decision to play out your heart dreams in the desert. You may think you have lost your position, or platform, or power, but if your pursue your call, you can still be a player. You may not be able to see past your past, but do act out your future. Do this no matter how small the situation or how seemingly insignificant the encounter. You can never know the ramifications of your courage for your reentry and your contribution to the world.

Gifts of the Desert

Moses owed a great deal to his wilderness sojourn. If Egypt had provided leadership training for royal sons, Midian served as graduate school for turning an outlawed son into the leader of a slave liberation movement. The Midianite culture and experience shaped Moses in profound ways.

Chief among these influences was Jethro, the Midianite priest. Besides providing Moses with a daughter to marry and a job, Jethro served as the key male figure in Moses' midlife. Perhaps Jethro fulfilled the role of the father Moses never had. Cut off from his natural father at an early age, and significantly distanced from his adoptive father, Moses needed a father figure to make the transition from leader "wanna-be" to real leader of God's people.

Jethro's involvement in Moses' life became a heart-shaping relationship through his support of Moses' call. When Moses returned from the burning bush, he was at a decidedly vulnerable spot. He had to convince others of his need to redirect his life. Jethro could have made life difficult for Moses or could have crushed his new passion if he had failed to support Moses' experience. Fortunately, the Midianite immediately released Moses from his clan responsibilities. The priest blessed him in his new endeavor. Moses probably had never experienced the blessing of a father before. Jethro took care of Moses' own family during the Exodus period when Moses confronted Pharaoh in Egypt. When the Exodus had been accomplished, Jethro came to Moses at Sinai to deliver his family back to him. At the reunion, Moses recounted for Jethro all of the events of the Exodus. The priest genuinely celebrated the accomplishments of his son-in-law. He also gave Moses some good management advice about establishing a legal system. Moses had created a huge bottleneck of justice by trying to handle all of the disputes on his own. Jethro's fatherly advice kept the Exodus from stalling early on.

Moses' eager acceptance of Jethro's advice reflected how strong the sense of trust had grown between them. This trust had been forged in community. We are not told at what point Jethro discovered that the Egyptian he had taken in was really a Hebrew fugitive from the law. We do not know when he became aware of Moses' incredible life story. We can wonder at what point Moses confessed to being a prince on the lam. Obviously when the truth came out, it did not jeopardize his standing with Jethro. Moses was fully accepted and not cast out or turned over to Pharaoh.

The recounting of leaders' life journeys usually turns up a Jethro or two. These individuals are God's gifts to the leader to provide extraordinary affirmation, encouragement, and guidance. They frequently, but not always, arise from outside the family system. They typically surface during times of the leader's self-doubt and at points when the leader's life mission is crystallizing. These God-sent Jethros offer almost unconditional acceptance of the leader, yet they maintain an accountability of presence that implicates itself into the leader's choices. They invest heavily in the leader, believe in the leader's potential, and provide real help at just the right time. Some, like the Midianite priest, provide financial assistance, a support system, and spiritual guidance. They do this without "owning" the leader. They release the leader to his or her life's work and celebrate the leader's accomplishments. In short, they are a heart-shaping instrument of God.

The Midianite clan of Jethro probably provided Moses the strongest community of his life. They nurtured him during his middle years. Their impact can be seen in the names of Moses' children. The name of his first-born, Gershom, signaled that though Moses had become an alien in a foreign land, he had found a home (Exod. 18:2–3). The law of Moses would eventually reflect a high value on showing hospitality to strangers. Moses' naming of his second son, Eliezer, reflected his gratitude at being rescued from Pharaoh's sword (Exod. 18:4). God had delivered Moses *from* Egypt but had also delivered him *to* Jethro's family.

The Desert School of Leadership

We can wonder how Moses evaluated the first forty years of his life in Egypt as he reflected on them during his shepherding years. Had he given up on his people? Could he ever trust the Hebrews? Did he long to be vindicated with them? Did he still want to punish the Egyptians for their oppression?

The torture of unrequited dreams rivaled the torment that the wilderness inflicted on shepherds. To fulfill their assignments, the shepherds had to search for water, watch for predators, and patiently deal with the animals in their care. The unrelenting application of these skills built into Moses the instincts he would need to shepherd a slave people through the unfamiliar territory of not only the desert, but also of freedom.

Shepherding leadership differed significantly from the Egyptian style of leadership that Moses had been taught, a model of authoritarian power and whiplash persuasion employed by taskmasters, princes, and Pharaohs. The desert school of leadership built accountability and stewardship into Moses' character. He tended someone else's flock. He was responsible for his father-in-law's assets. He had to demonstrate not only trustworthiness but also resourcefulness to ensure the sustainability of the flock. Moses' Exodus leadership would draw from these wilderness lessons. He would tend Another's flock, assuming responsibility for food, water, safety, and flock perpetuity. These commonplace activities of shepherds shaped Moses' heart into the heart of a shepherd leader.

Moses demonstrated another quality that was honed during these four decades. He developed a remarkable attention to detail. Shepherds learn to look for signs that could spell the difference between life and death, gain or loss. Hundreds and thousands of daily decisions shaped Moses' capacity to pay attention. Scanning the sky, scanning the horizon, looking carefully at individual flock members built powers of observation.

Moses' attention to detail would serve him well. He had to recall extensive private conversations with Yahweh. He took care to repeat God's instructions precisely to Pharaoh. He relayed to the Hebrews intricate laws, concerning a wide spectrum of behaviors, ranging from hygiene to Sabbath observance. He laid out the directions for construction of the Tabernacle in exquisite detail. The lawgiver and judge had to rely on keen powers of observation that related to people as well. He knew motives and consequences of attitudes and actions. Most of the law he related from God dealt with interactions among people.

One additional benefit from spending years in the desert would pay off during the wilderness wanderings. Moses had to learn wilderness survival techniques. The searches for food and water led him to know the area like the back of his hand. He would pick up valuable information about the tribes of the region. He would learn to be at home in the desert so he could teach others to do the same.

Moses probably never would have imagined that these daily, commonplace struggles of the shepherd were training him for a great life work. He had the heart of a prince and developed the heart of a shepherd, the heart of the privileged free, and the heart of the disenfranchised. He had the heart of a leader shaped by God to play the central role in Old Testament history.

Recalled from Reserves into Active Duty

What a difference a day can make. At the bush that burned but would not burn up, Moses accepted a "person-to-person call" from God that would establish the legacy of his life. Whatever Moses had made of his life was now going to come under reevaluation. Broken dreams, disillusionment, fear, insignificance were all going to be gathered up, not for discarding, but for reshaping in the fire of the call.

The voice from the bush identified himself as the God of Moses' ancestors. This revelation had to be thrilling to Moses. This meant that the ancient patriarchal stories he had heard, presumably first told to him by his mother, were true! Moses would later commit the stories of Abraham, Isaac, Jacob, and Joseph to writing.

Yahweh then tapped into Moses' heart hunger, identifying himself with Moses' own yearning for the deliverance of the Hebrews. Moses seemed reluctant to let old passions be stirred. His excuses were counterpunches to protect himself from vulnerability and even more from disappointment. He let God know that he had dialed up the wrong man. His "who am I?" was rhetorical. Possibly for years, Moses had answered his own question with a resignation that he was a nobody, a failure, having disappointed both his mothers' great expectations for him.

God stripped away Moses' initial objection by telling Moses that he would not be representing himself in Egypt but that he would be representing Yahweh. "Well, then, who are you?" Moses fired back. God's answer gave Israel a proper name for the God of their fathers. Yahweh assured Moses that he would get a hearing with the Hebrews. Remembering the last time he had tried to help Hebrews in trouble, Moses told Yahweh that they probably would not believe him. Even God's miraculous signs still were unconvincing to Moses. He told God that he was not a good speaker, and when God answered this objection, he finally flatly asked God to go get someone else for the job.

At this point in the encounter, God's patience with Moses' self-absorption and pity ran out. He got angry with Moses (it would not be the last time) for his whining and excuses (these would also continue). Yahweh had providentially protected Moses from Pharaoh twice—at birth and when he killed the Egyptian officer. Yahweh had carefully shepherded his life so that Moses was uniquely qualified for this assignment. He understood Hebrew hopes. He understood Egyptian court culture. He was at home in the wilderness. God had plans for a mission that no one else could accomplish. Moses was the man!

Only God knows how many would-be leaders turn away from the burning bush. Having decided their own destiny, they close themselves off from the call of God on their lives, or their preoccupation with themselves prevents them from being open to a mission larger than their own definition of possibilities. They have "shrinkwrapped" God down to the size of their personal frailties and limitations. They fail to allow for divine contingencies. Not willing to risk or to explore a world that has something besides themselves at the center, they never make it onto God's stage. Often waiting for the big break, they are counting on something other than the voice of God to give them a leadership role. They live out their lives in the desert of reserve status.

Moses finally acceded to God's commission. Thus began a remarkable relationship between a human being and God. Moses had to be closer to God than any other human of his day. Moses would have to deliver the word of God to Pharaoh. He could not misspeak words of such import. Moses would take down the very law of God for his people. The scribe of God had to know the One speaking and understand him clearly. Moses' writings would present the world with knowledge of creation, the Flood, the great stories of Abraham, Isaac, and Jacob as told to him by God himself. These revelations would be entrusted by Yahweh only to someone familiar with him, a great friend, a man accustomed to audience with God.

Moses would come to find his greatest sense of belonging in his communion with the God of the burning bush. His constant sense of being an alien among those he lived with and served had carved out in his heart a huge place for God to inhabit. Maybe this deficiency established in Moses a heart hunger to establish community with God. God frequently targets the dark places, the holes in the leader's heart. When God works through deficiencies, he frequently increases the leader's awareness of dependency on him. Moses' reliance on Yahweh became a signature of his leadership style.

Perhaps the notion that God works through weaknesses represents a liberating idea for you. Some of your great heart hungers may still be unsatisfied. God may be using these to create space for himself in your heart. As long as you look to others, to achievement, or to anything but God to fill the void, the hunger will be your master, fueling your drivenness or discontent. Many leaders, unaware of or unwilling to face the holes in their own heart, wreck their lives trying to plug the gap with more work, more attention, more power, more . . . whatever. God desires to fill the heart spaces with himself.

Power Struggles

Moses' appointment with destiny landed him in an adversarial position with the most powerful person in the ancient world. By the time of Moses, pharaohs had ruled Egypt for centuries. They had achieved a godlike status, considered by many to be a divine incarnation. The pharaohs had patronized and surrounded themselves with a powerful group of priests who enforced their reign and ensured that their divine will was accomplished. Pharaoh's wishes were law and not open to dispute.

Pharaoh sniffed in disgust at the demands of Moses and Aaron. He would not countenance the demands from the God of the Hebrew slaves. Just to drive home the point that he was not to be messed with, he issued the famous make-brick-without-straw order. This cunning and cruel move was designed to do two things. First, Pharaoh demonstrated his disregard for any god other than those in his service. Second, his tactic placed Moses' leadership in jeopardy with his own people. In one stroke, the king of Egypt figured he had nipped any slave uprising in the bud, demoralizing the Hebrews and destroying their leadership team's credibility.

The Hebrews played their part just as Pharaoh expected. They immediately buckled, blaming Moses and Aaron for their increased burden. Under normal conditions, up against standard-fare agitators, this would have been the end of the story. But Pharaoh miscalculated on two scores. First, Moses was not an ordinary man. His passion had been set on fire by the fire of the burning bush. Despite his initial reluctance, he had reentered Egypt as a man on a mission. Second, Pharaoh thought he had a problem with Moses. In fact, he had picked a fight with a bigger Adversary. The contest was over before it started. Pharaoh just did not know it yet.

Neither did Moses. Apparently he counted on either one knockout blow or Pharaoh for some reason granting his request. However, the situation immediately deteriorated. One has to wonder if the old tapes of his early attempts at being a rescuer began to play in Moses' head. His early efforts at exodus were fast shaping up to be another failed attempt. Moses took his insecurities to Yahweh. "Since I speak with faltering lips, why would Pharaoh listen to me" (Exod. 6:30)? This was Moses' way of reminding God of his objections back at the bush, a refrain of "I told you so."

Yahweh's response to Moses was to inform the disheartened leader that he was in for a fight. Things were going to get worse before they got better. Pharaoh would resist every request from Yahweh. But, Yahweh assured Moses, Pharaoh would eventually yield after suffering for his refusal to let God's people go. Yahweh repeated this assurance during each of his encounters with Moses during the early days of skirmish. The certainty of Yahweh steeled Moses for battle.

Many spiritual leaders identify with this part of Moses' experience. Leaders, believing that they are operating on clear instruction from the Lord, sometimes run into early opposition that throws them a curve. Rather then responding positively to their efforts, the situation actually worsens. What seemed like a good idea suddenly appears to be a foolish endeavor. "What could I have been thinking?" leaders ask themselves. Sometimes a leader's internal doubts find an external echo in the opinions of others who question the leader's ability. If the leader has made public promises of deliverance or of a better tomorrow, that leader is particularly vulnerable to criticism.

Without exception, all great spiritual leaders throughout history have found themselves in circumstances in which their leadership is both challenged and imperiled. They also have experienced situations in which they have no recourse but God, times when conventional wisdom called their convictions into question, times when even those they seek to serve ridiculed them for their attempts. All of these circumstances established thresholds of pain that they had to tolerate to pursue their mission. Spiritual heroes learn that pain and conflict are part of the package. It just goes with the territory.

In some cases, God will clue leaders in to the conflict they must endure. The powers that keep people in bondage do not relinquish control very easily. Whether it is addiction, or dysfunction, or sin habits, or economic-political control, the Pharaohs of this world scoff at the claims of Almighty God. Leaders delude themselves if they think victory comes without conflict.

This discussion does not intend to glorify the spiritual leader who relishes combat. Some leaders incite conflict through immature power plays. Others create contests purely for self-aggrandizement. Still others do not even know that they themselves bring on persistent conflict through their own unresolved issues with authority or lack of people skills.

The leaders who grow through conflict learn to reflect on their own actions. They take responsibility for their contribution to the situation. In doing so, they allow God to carry on his heart-shaping activity in the pressure cooker of conflict. Maturity begins to be in evidence when leaders who find themselves arrayed against the enemies of God worry more for God's reputation than for their own. Not seeking conflict, they nonetheless refuse to shrink from it if obedience to his call places them in the arena.

Yahweh's predictions to Moses proved to be accurate. In a series of confrontations, God proved his superiority over all other gods and leveled judgment against Pharaoh. Throughout the contest, Moses never asserted his own agenda. He refused to become the issue. He did not focus on his own personal sense of rejection. Moses knew the struggle was not about him. The battle was between Yahweh and Pharaoh. Moses played the role of messenger. God used Moses' confrontation with Pharaoh to teach Moses that the battle rises or falls on obedience. If the leader champions God's agenda, spiritual breakthroughs redraw the spiritual landscape. Captives are set free. God is declared the winner.

A Love-Hate Relationship

Moses' initial confrontation with Pharaoh set up another, more challenging contest, especially in terms of emotional and spiritual wear and tear on him. Moses would endure protracted criticism and opposition from the Hebrews. One of the reasons that spiritual leaders of all ages admire Moses is their identification with his struggles at this point.

Just a few examples of the fickleness of the Hebrews suffice to chronicle the rocky relationship between them and their leader. When Moses delivered whatever was the going request of the day (water, food, and so forth), the people tolerated him and even went along with him. But his line of credit was forever short. Any failure on his part to deliver brought swift criticism, murmuring, and rebellion. When they faced hunger, they charged, "You have brought us out into the desert to starve this entire assembly to death" (Exod. 16:3). When thirsty, they whined, "Why did you bring us out of Egypt to make us and our children and livestock die of thirst" (Exod. 17:3)? When tired of manna on the menu, "If only we had meat to eat! We remember the fish we ate in Egypt at no cost" (Num. 11:5).

Moses, like every spiritual leader since, had to marvel at the capacity of people to idealize or to reinvent the past. "What have you done to us by bringing us out of Egypt? Didn't we say to you in Egypt, 'Leave us alone; let us serve the Egyptians'? It would have been better for us to serve the Egyptians than to die in the desert" (Exod. 14:11b–12). The leader, of course, is to blame for all difficulties encountered en route to the Promised Land. And sometimes, at the very door of God's delivery on his promises, the spiritual leader hears what Moses heard, "We should choose a leader and go back to Egypt" (Num. 14:4).

God's people exasperated Moses. Of interest to us is how the heart of Moses was affected by this wilderness community of liberated slaves. "What am I to do with these people?" he frequently complained to God. Moses' own feelings toward them expressed the ambivalence that he felt coming from their side of the relationship. At times, he was so angry at them that he had them punished, even to death. At other times, he interceded for them before Yahweh, who more than once threatened to kill them himself.

The ongoing dialogue between Moses and Yahweh about the Hebrews offers rare glimpses of heart-shaping at work. Both Moses' passion for righteousness and his shepherd heart bleed through the conversations. It is interesting that Moses often displayed one face to the people—usually that of judgment and threats. But when he was with Yahweh, listening to God's intentions to do just what he himself had threatened to do, Moses often presented a different attitude. He begged Yahweh not to abandon the people. Moses knew that if God did abandon them, it would mean certain death, as well as a negation of Yahweh's intervention in Egypt. When Yahweh afflicted the people, it was Moses who pleaded their case. Moses' heart grew each time he interceded for the people. Constant intercession seems to be the prescription for retaining a shepherd's long-suffering heart. One mark of genuine spiritual greatness is compassion for one's tormentors.

Moses cast his lot with the people, once asking that he be punished himself instead of them. On another occasion, Moses refused Yahweh's proposal to start a new line of people through Moses, thus cutting off the rebellious Hebrews. God's dialogues with Moses about the fate of Israel helped draw out Moses' own heart about the people. These encounters stand as witness to the greatness of the man Moses had come to be. He would be counted with the Israelites even when they would not receive him. He would plead for their forgiveness when they sinned. Moses sacrificed his own chance to forgo the trials of the wilderness, choosing instead to identify with the people he had led out of bondage. He would suffer their same lot—death—instead of entering the Promised Land. His overriding concern focused on preserving the link of the people with Yahweh.

Spiritual communities are sometimes burned by leaders who have not cast their lot with them. Some leaders use people to further their own positions. Some spiritual leaders have not developed the shepherd's heart of sacrifice for their people. Even in doing spiritual things, or building great ministries, they reflect more the heart of Pharaoh than the heart of Moses.

On the other hand, some spiritual communities give their leaders a taste of what the Hebrews gave Moses. They never fully embrace the leader. The leader experiences rejection. The people's attitude and actions may simply reflect a spiritual immaturity on their part. The leader represents the tension of demands placed by God on his people. The people may refuse or resist the responsibility to grow. Sometimes the community wants the leader's blessing, but fears the leader's connectedness with God.

This dynamic between Moses and the Hebrews reveals one of the mysteries of heart-shaping. Moses' yearning for the belonging that he never fully experienced caused him to fight for it on behalf of the people he led. They were to be a people "belonging to God" (Exod. 19:5). Sometimes God creates within leaders a desire to experience something they themselves have been denied. This desire fuels a passion in them to make sure that others experience something that they themselves yearn for.

Face to Face

The character of the communion that Moses enjoyed with Yahweh proves unique among Bible figures. "The Lord would speak to Moses face to face, as a man speaks with his friend" (Exod. 33:11). Sinai summits, tent meetings, glowing countenance, private burial with God as the lone pallbearer—these are images of Moses' personal interaction with Yahweh. They provide venues for intense, divine heart-sculpting activity.

God conducted a lot of business with Moses at Sinai. When Yahweh commissioned Moses at the burning bush, he also instructed Moses to bring Israel back to the mountain once the Exodus was accomplished. Moses obeyed. Israel camped at the base of the mountain while Moses made several trips up the rocky slopes to meet with Yahweh. Aaron sometimes accompanied him, as did Joshua. The elders were allowed only partway up. Most of the time, Moses met with God by himself. Probably no one minded. God's presence was accompanied by lightning and thunder, clouds of smoke, and fire. Moses could approach and disappear into the cauldron of divine presence. Twice he spent forty days sequestered with Yahweh. No other mortal has ever experienced such prolonged exposure and audience with Almighty God on location planet Earth.

The initial Sinai summit occurred between two and three months after the liberation from Egypt. At that meeting, Yahweh revealed to Moses his master plan. Yahweh covenanted with Israel to be in partnership in his redemptive mission in the world. God designated them a "kingdom of priests" (Exod. 19:6), signifying their special status with him. The Hebrews and their descendants were his personal representatives on earth.

The ex-slaves would hear this covenant imagery in the light of their Egypt experience. Royal priests were powerful figures who partnered with Pharaoh in ruling the kingdom. This announcement provided a huge promotion for the house of Jacob from the bottom of the social order to the lofty position of royal priests.

The importance of this covenant can hardly be overstated. Its impact reached well beyond those first recipients. When searching for words to convey the mission of the Christian movement, the apostle Peter chose these same words and imagery: "But you are a chosen people, a royal priesthood, a people belonging to God" (1 Pet. 2:9a). Followers of Jesus inherited the mission that Israel received from Yahweh at Sinai. In the vision of the apostle John on Patmos, the gathered church at the end of history is celebrated as "kingdom and priests" (Rev. 1:6; 5:10). This idea, first enunciated by God to Moses at Sinai, stretches across time and into eternity.

Moses became the first to grasp this part of the heart of God. At Sinai, he "received" the picture of a God on a mission in the world. He captured the heartbeat of a God intent on creating a people who would join him in his redemptive efforts.

This insight not only would shape Moses' heart but also would frame the subsequent understandings of God in Judaism and Christianity. Moses would later cast the patriarchal narratives to reflect the revelations at Sinai. He would highlight the theme of a God in search of relationships with people. The story line he developed in Genesis recounted the beginnings of humanity in general and Abraham's seed in particular. The drama of human beginnings would be staged against this backdrop of a God determined to establish a missional partnership with part of humanity in order to establish a relationship with all creatures bearing his divine image.

The pair of forty-days-and-forty-nights Sinai sojourns gave the world the Ten Commandments. The first set of stones, written in the hand of God, shattered when an angry Moses flung them down at his sight of the golden calf. The second set survived, and humankind became the possessor of its initial set of laws expressly grounded in divine will.

Another feature of Moses' communion with God on Sinai was his fascination with the name and glory of God. Both of these elements figured prominently at Moses' call experience. The glory of God caused the bush to glow, attracting Moses' attention. During the ensuing exchange, Moses asked for God's name. The fact that Yahweh disclosed his name to Moses and through him to the Hebrews confirmed their special status. Moses responded to this with a jealousy for the Lord's name, or reputation.

He did not want it tarnished by the actions of the people or by Yahweh himself. Moses considered God's presence a physical sign of God's commitment to Israel. This is why Moses pleads with Yahweh, "If your Presence does not go with us, do not send us up from here. How will anyone know that you are pleased with me and with your people unless you go with us? What else will distinguish me and your people from all the other people on the face of the earth" (Exod. 33:15–16)?

Moses also continued to be fascinated by God's glory. In his boldest request, Moses asked for a full view of Yahweh's glory (Exod. 33:18). The Lord granted his request. Yahweh gave Moses the gift of his glory in such a profound way that Moses' face glowed even after he left Yahweh's presence.

The huge failure of Moses' leadership, the famous striking of the rock, proved so disastrous for him precisely because of the close communion he had experienced with God. In the Numbers 20 episode, God appeared to Moses in his glory and gave explicit instructions about how Moses was to perform the miracle of causing the rock to yield water. Moses crowded in on God's glory by seeming himself to procure water. Yahweh called the action a lack of trust and a failure to honor God before the people.

Every spiritual leader faces this same test. The stewardship of intimacy with the Almighty carries with it a heightened sense of accountability. Obedience to do what is disclosed provides the only continued guarantee of enjoying all God has in store. God does not want his spokespeople relying on past techniques or methodologies (previously, in Exodus 19, the rock issued water when Moses struck it). He wishes the leader to rely on him.

This episode diminishes but does not erase the legacy of the great liberator of the Old Testament. Moses serves as the great archetype of the Deliverer. It is not enough to be delivered *from* something. The trick is to be delivered *to* something. At 40 years of age, Moses could have gotten the Israelites out of Egypt. Not until he was 120 years old could he deliver them to the banks of the Jordan. He could accomplish his call only by his constantly submitting to God's heart-shaping activity. And having gotten his people ready for their next chapter, Moses moved on to his.

The graduation ceremony at Nebo was attended by an Audience of One.

2

DAVID

A HEART AFTER GOD

ISRAEL'S GREATEST KING is one of those larger-than-life characters who captivates our imagination. The David described in Hebrew scriptures reveals many fascinating and sometimes contradictory characteristics. Humble birth. King of the most extensive empire in the Middle East a millennium before Christ. Courageous. Conniving. Loyal. Self-serving. Hero. Fugitive. Military strategist. Architect. Adulterer. Protector. Brutal. Sensitive. Vengeful. Forgiving. Murderer. Lover. Warrior. Musician.

No wonder we find so much in David to admire and so much we wish we could ignore. Yet David's nobler qualities win out and earn him three thousand years of prominence. David's saga reveals a person obviously and genuinely open to the heart-shaping work of God in his life.

Rise of a Nation

The cultural backdrop of David's early years provided the stage for his entrance into Israel's history. Born the youngest of eight sons to Jesse of Bethlehem of the tribe of Judah, David grew up in a time when the identity of people in Israel revolved around their tribal affiliation. Upon entering Canaan, the twelve tribes of Israel settled in territories assigned to them. This parceling out was done after initial warfare had generally established Israelite dominance in the region. Once secure, the Israelites began to tame their new land for their own use through animal husbandry and farming. Life centered on the village. Threats to peace from the surrounding hostile populations were addressed with the help of neighboring villages and sometimes villagers from other tribes.

Leadership for the loose tribal confederacy was the province of the elders of each tribe and village. They administered routine matters of justice and village operations. Occasionally, special challenges arose that called forth judges, a unique set of individuals anointed by Yahweh to deal with these situations. The judges, because of their anointing and heroic performances, enjoyed a transtribal authority.

The last great judge was Samuel the prophet, a rather mysterious figure who played a crucial role in the selection of Israel's first two kings. The uncertainty and instability of tribalism and regional judgeships gave rise to a yearning for a more centralized government. The elders persuaded Samuel (against his better judgment) to anoint a monarch. He did, being drawn to the charismatic, handsome Saul of the tribe of Benjamin.

The young David suffered the plight of all Israel during Saul's reign. Saul sabotaged his initial success through his impetuousness, pride, and impatience. He ran afoul of the powerful Samuel, so much so that the prophet announced that God would take the kingdom away from Saul. Obviously, Saul suffered from mental and emotional illness. His dementia, decline, and demise provide the prologue to David's rise. The destiny of the boy shepherd of Bethlehem was inextricably tied to the fortunes and failures of Israel's first king.

A Secret Anointing

Some leaders' calls are gradual. They almost steal up on the person. Rather than an immediate and dramatic burning bush episode, the call for them is progressive. Perhaps it initially comes quietly with little shape to it. It may first be perceived as just a direction toward some major assignment. Clarification may come only after the journey has begun. Sometimes this clarification process takes years. The dynamic of David's call fits this description. It was a long way from Samuel's mysterious and secretive anointing in Bethlehem to the public anointing of David as king over Israel by the elders at Hebron.

The second go-around for Samuel in anointing kings barely resembled the first. Even though the prophet had recently delivered the words of doom to the imploding Saul, he took no pleasure in it and still grieved over the king's condition. His trip to Bethlehem occurred only at God's prodding and chiding for his languishing in grief.

Samuel was the closest thing to a national celebrity in those days in Israel. His visit to the village of Bethlehem caused some stir. The question of the town elders, "Have you come in peace?" (1 Sam. 16:4), reflected their anxiety at his sudden appearance. They knew of no reason for Samuel to visit them. The prophet allayed their fears. Samuel convened a feast as a cover for his secret mission. Saul's discovery of the prophet's real intentions could have rendered the act futile. Saul was, after all, still king, even though his successor was about to be anointed in a revolutionary act by the prophet of God.

In this episode, we are treated to the mystery of God's call. Even Samuel is perplexed and a bit slow on the uptake. He is quite certain that Jesse's tall and good-looking firstborn son, Eliab, is the chosen one. God instructs Samuel not to rely on the outer appearances, because the heart is the most important qualification for service to God. Wasn't Saul enough of a lesson here? His physical prowess and good looks, which provided him a head start, had not been enough to secure a good finish. At the feast in Jesse's home, God demonstrated that he was looking for inner qualities that might not be readily apparent to human perception. David came in last in nominations by his own father, but first in the call of God.

Every age and every organization develop their own list of qualities that form the selection criteria for their leaders. In recent years, personal charisma, motivational prowess, and marketing savvy rank near the top of those qualities that are rewarded by large followings in ministry. But God defines the search parameters of what he is looking for. Future ministry models will increasingly return to a renewed emphasis on models that value heart integrity and spiritual presence for those who lead spiritual communities.

To his credit, Samuel waited for the Lord to give him the right cues at Jesse's house. We do not know what David thought of Samuel's actions that day. What did the prophet say to him? Whatever David thought of the proceedings, two impressions seem to have powerfully shaped his heart. First, he shortly became propelled into the concerns of the young kingdom. A sense of personal responsibility would not let him remain an observer. A lunch run to his brothers turned into the famous encounter with Goliath. The shepherd boy emerged from obscurity to begin building his reputation as a warrior.

Those who experience progressive call dynamics as David did respond similarly to the way he responded. They sense a growing responsibility that propels them personally into leadership arenas. And as with David, early victories help build the leader's reputation and confidence. The call begins to solidify. Obscurity often begins to give way to recognition, perhaps even notoriety.

A second theme emerged in David's life that reflected the significance of Samuel's actions at Bethlehem. David developed and maintained enormous respect for the office of king, which he often referred to as "the

Lord's anointed" (1 Sam. 12:3; 26:9). This reverence influenced David's treatment of Saul, even when the king pursued David to have him killed. David refused to raise his hand against Saul, even when twice he had the chance to kill him. He even put to death the Amalekite who killed Saul after the king's botched suicide attempt. David could not understand why the young man would not be afraid to lift his hand against the Lord's anointed (2 Sam. 1:14).

David possessed a reverential awe of the significance of the anointing. His perspective proves instructive for those who give spiritual leadership today. All of those who have ever experienced the anointing of God to do the work that God has called them to do have encountered a profound mystery and reality. The anointing is the God-part of the leadership equation. It accounts for the leader's effectiveness that reaches far beyond what the leader alone brings to the table. The leader's efforts become multiplied and remarkably sufficient to the challenge. A few fishes and loaves feed five thousand. The experience of the anointing is truly humbling to the leader, who knows that unless God shows up, the crowd goes away hungry.

A case can be made that God never removes his call on a person's life. But he definitely withdraws his anointing. One of the horrors of not following the will of God is the leader's awareness of the lack of anointing. The leader may go on functioning in the leadership role, but minus spiritual power. The leader's heart cannot rest fully. No amount of human exertion or ingenuity will compensate for the loss. The only remedy is a return to obedience, a plea for mercy, and a hope that it is not too late, that the window of opportunity to get in on what God is up to has not closed.

Saul pleaded too little and too late. He played the fool with the call of God. Following his breach with Samuel, the king began to deal with long bouts of depression. Some of Saul's servants knew of David's musical skill, and thinking the shepherd's music might soothe their monarch, they made arrangements for David to play at court.

Saul's "palace" resembled more a fort. His throne room was no larger than a large-sized great room in a contemporary home. David could thus observe at close hand the ravages of Saul's unstable emotional condition. The pathetic state of the king was widely attributed to the withdrawal of the Lord's Spirit from him after Saul had disobeyed the Lord's instructions. David learned that the capacity to rule depended on spiritual power as well as military might. Years later, after his transgression with Bathsheba, David's prayer reflected this early lesson. His plea, "Do not cast me from your presence or take your Holy Spirit from me" (Ps. 51:11), represents far more than mere personal piety. The thought of ending up like Saul terrified him. David's early glimpses into Saul's torment convinced him that as king, he must depend on God and maintain fellowship with him.

David decided not to play loose with God's call but to order his life around it. This decision showed up in his determination and patience. The road to being king would lead through the territory of being a hunted fugitive, disenfranchised from home and family. Yet even when circumstances seemed to militate against the call's fulfillment, David remained undaunted in his belief that he would be king. God had promised it. David had been anointed to that purpose. He trusted God to deliver on his promise.

Christian leaders certain of their call allow it to become the center of gravity for their life experiences. They order their lives around the call of God on them. They exhibit patience and determination to pursue God's call when, as in David's case, circumstances would dissuade them or threaten the call's fulfillment. They are convinced that life will eventually line up with the reality of the call. God has anointed. God will deliver on his promise.

The Fight with Goliath

God's anointed one rose to national prominence through a spectacular conflict involving David's defeat of Goliath, the Philistine's great champion. Several leadership lessons emerge from this event. The first is obvious, yet it cannot be overlooked. It took raw courage, significant "chutzpah," for David to go up against Goliath. Saul had promised to reward Goliath's slayer with the king's wealth, the king's daughter, and a tax break. David inquired about the reward, but no amount of reward could engender by itself the courage it took to face Goliath. This character quality had to come from within; it could not be generated from extrinsic motivations.

Many spiritual leaders do not lead from courage. They lead from fear. Fear drives many ministries. Fear of being disliked, fear of losing income, fear of failure, fear of conflict—these and a hundred other fears form a giant that calls the leader out to a contest. Often the leader resembles more the rest of the Israelite soldiers, who were held hostage by Goliath's threats. Those who are fear dominated may even suit up for battle each day and visit the battlefield to skirmish. However, they are playing not to lose rather than playing to win.

We also learn about the heart of a champion from David's response to his reception at the battle scene. First, he has to contend with the scorn of his older brother. When he heard of David's interest in fighting Goliath, he questioned David's motives, ridiculed his character, and treated him as an embarrassment to the family. Second, David had to persuade Saul to let him fight. The king obviously lacked confidence in David's warrior capabilities. He knew David as a musician. However, Saul did not have many options, so he relented from his objections and wagered the kingdom in a duel between David and the giant. Third, when David approached Goliath, he once again endured scathing remarks.

David refused to accept others' low estimations of his ability. Though we might consider David boastful in his attempts to persuade Saul, he did prove his abilities with the sling and his courage when confronted by danger, just as he said he would. David set out to prove that others' low expectations or belittlement would not be the book on him.

Many great leaders face the same challenge to their self-esteem. Their family of origin may be unaffirming or downright discouraging of their abilities. Early circumstances may not be sufficient to demonstrate the full range of the leader's talent. Authority figures may pigeonhole the leader in ways that constrict the leader's development. The leader faces a similar choice of having to risk, to throw off the lid of others' diminished expectations. David learned what every leader-who-would-be-king must also learn. All the leader's cues cannot come from the external environment. The drive has to be fueled by the call and not dependent ultimately on the opinions of others, even significant others.

David's confrontation with Goliath illustrates another key leadership principle. David chose his weapons and manner of attack. He refused Saul's armor, preferring instead to engage the giant with a strategy built on his own strengths. The shepherd's prowess with the sling had been honed. This was his best skill. He refused to allow the conflict to force him to abandon his best chance at winning. He did not want to give up the advantage of delivering a preemptive strike from a distance. He could not have prevailed in a toe-to-toe sword fight. His approach caught Goliath off guard, and it brought the giant down to size so David could finish him off.

Spiritual leaders sometimes abandon their strengths when facing conflict. Smart leaders choose to employ weapons that are comfortable and proven to them. Perhaps prayer, or people skills, or persuasion are talents that a Christian leader possesses. Then these are the best weapons in the leader's arsenal against hostile forces. Some leaders mistakenly abandon their spiritual leadership during trials or challenges, to exert power over people or to pummel people to secure victory.

One final leadership lesson presents itself in the story of David and Goliath. For David, the overriding issue was God's honor. Though he inquired about Saul's rewards and was partially motivated by them, his pre-eminent concern was a jealousy for God's reputation. He did not want the Philistines to conclude that the God of Israel could not be feared or could not win over their giant. God's reputation was at stake.

David had a personal stake too in the confrontation. The God of Israel had called him. Part of their relationship involved God helping David defeat his enemies and the enemies of God's people. The challenge and defeat of Goliath secured the honor of the God of Israel. God's intervention and deliverance also established David as a leader who did battle in the power of the Lord.

David's life project involved living out his call. He did not adopt the goal of becoming the greatest king in Israel's history. His goal was to live out his call, not to have the call serve him. His own reputation would be bound up in his faithfulness to his call. God's purposes, not his own, captured his life efforts. A couple of examples of David's behavior reflect this attitude. When the ark made its way into Jerusalem, David danced before it with abandon. His dance signified to his people that their king had yielded to an even higher King, whom he delighted to praise (1 Chron. 15:25–29). He was in the service of God, not vice versa. Nor did he think the call entitled him to personal fulfillment at others' expense. He refused to drink the water from the well at Bethlehem even though some of his men had risked their lives to get it (2 Sam. 23:13–17). He did not want to signal a belief that his mission was about getting his personal whims attended to. He would not allow the call to become subservient to personal convenience and comfort.

David lapsed on this perspective occasionally. Such instances proved costly. The sordid episode with Bathsheba was set in motion when David sent others to fulfill his assignment (2 Sam. 11:1). He eventually repented but unleashed a family dysfunction that plagued him the rest of his life. On another occasion, he ordered a numbering of his fighting forces, an action that ran counter to trusting God. Though David was pricked in his conscience, the lapse of obedience cost him seventy thousand men, an immediate reduction of troop inventory with no victory to show for it (1 Chron. 21:1–30).

Leaders who are gripped by a call from God do well to remember that they serve the call. The call is not given to serve them. The initiative and substance of the call belong to God. The leader is an instrument in the Lord's hand to help others have the opportunity to live their lives with greater significance and in relationship with God. By following their call, leaders establish kingdoms that enjoy secure borders and domestic tranquility. Those in the kingdom's realm are able to live peacefully and fully.

The Cauldron of Conflict

David had to fight to become king, not just against Goliath, but against Saul's family, with and against the Philistines, against the Jebusites, and eventually against his own son. Without question, David's life was bloody, so bloody that he was not allowed to construct the Temple. Yet the demands of his situation required gruesome solutions. Kings fought to become and remain kings in those days. Any attempt to retrofit the cultural mores of David's time with those of today will obscure the larger picture. For David to have shied away from these conflicts would have meant an abdication of his life mission. Our interest focuses on how these conflicts shaped David's heart.

David's protracted struggle with Saul played a significant role in shaping his heart into the heart of a king. He determined not to challenge Saul's authority. He could have reasoned that the Lord would deliver Saul into his hands. David could have ended his exile and avoided the anxiety of being hunted by assassinating the reckless king when he had the chance. By refusing this course of action, David elevated the position of king to a level beyond that of simply being a strongman. Had David killed Saul to secure the throne, he would have established a dangerous precedent for succession by bloodshed in Israel.

David's most painful struggle involved Absalom's revolt. The victorious warrior against Israel's enemies was most vulnerable in his own house. David learned the exquisite pain of being betrayed by those closest to one's heart.

David played by different rules of engagement with Absalom than when he confronted others. He was reluctant to fight against his son. He actually abandoned Jerusalem and went into temporary exile. When Absalom was ultimately killed, David despaired as at no other time in his life. His judgment became clouded to the point that he temporarily demoralized his followers by failing to honor their victory over his enemies. Only Joab's sharp rebuke helped David regain his leadership composure to look beyond his own grief to the needs of his followers (2 Sam. 19:1–8). Their sacrificial efforts needed to be legitimized and appreciated.

Like David, today's spiritual leaders face many different kinds of conflict. Some challenges to their leadership come from the outside. The most challenging always arise from within. Many understand the situation of being exiled from their own kingdoms because of a betrayal from within the closest circles. Yet those who follow the leader need for the leader to keep heart. Joab's prescription to David, to "go out and encourage your men" (2 Sam. 19:7), still needs heeding. The need to encourage the followers in the leader's constellation can sometimes, as in David's case, pull the embattled and disheartened leader out of lethargy and despondency.

The cauldron of conflict shapes the heart of the leader. Each instance forces a redefinition of the leader's mission, values, and actions. Through conflict, the leader's heart can grow haughty and hard, ruthless, even punitive. On the other hand, conflict can enlarge the leader's dependence on God for deliverance.

David gained some significant heart lessons through conflicts in his life. Many of them still apply to contemporary spiritual leaders. First, the weak of heart need not apply for leadership. The tumult of these times calls for stout hearts and courageous leaders for the Christian movement. Second, the leader must expect conflict to come as part of the territory. The conflict-allergic leader who shrinks from all conflict and gives in to fear will fail to preside over an expansion of the kingdom. Third, leadership must be earned. Enjoying leadership by virtue of position is increasingly rare. Fourth, betrayal poses the greatest emotional threat to the leader and the leader's followers. The battle can be lost over disappointment and heart failure. Fifth, the leader needs to secure the blessings of God for the followers. The benefits of David's conflict extended beyond him. His victories brought peace and blessing to those who lived under his leadership influence.

Community of the King

David did not fit the leader-as-loner model. He apparently craved community. As the baby boy in his family, he had been surrounded by older brothers. He was never really alone, except on shepherding assignments. He kept people around him always, people who were close to him, beginning with Jonathan, then Abner, then Joab. These relationships stand out, but scores of others, including the thirty mighty men of valor, created for David a web of people connections.

God used the community around David as a powerful tool to shape his heart. The foundation of David's community grew out of his security in himself. He had been anointed by God. He took this as a sign of favor and blessing. The appointment by God framed David's self-perception. Even when he blew it, David fell toward God. Whether it was with the horrific actions regarding Bathsheba and Uriah or the haughty numbering of the army, whenever David sinned, he repented, learned, and moved on. He did not let his tragic mistakes define him in a negative way.

Contrast David's personal perception of self-confidence to that of Saul's sense of inferiority. Saul's lack of ego strength bred paranoid and schizophrenic behavior. Saul never saw himself as king. He told Samuel the prophet that he had chosen the wrong man because Saul was from a small tribe and an undistinguished family. When Samuel anointed Saul as king, Saul did not tell anyone about it. He had to be coaxed out of hiding on the day of his presentation. This action should not be mistaken for humility. It revealed a self-image problem that eventuated in Saul's incapacity to establish solid relationships. Saul's public failures were perfectly consonant with his internal view of himself.

Spiritual leaders who are fairly intact in their self-esteem can build community. They breed health in their relationships because they themselves possess psychological health. The opposite is also true; dysfunction breeds dysfunction. The contrast of David and Saul teaches us that people can commit themselves to leaders who are not threatened by them. Healthy people tend to avoid being trapped in the leadership constellation of paranoid kings. Sick kings can, however, usually attract those whose own needs for approval keep them tied to dysfunctional systems and relationships. Consequently, sick kings have no one around them who has the strength of character to oppose or to challenge them. Those who do are usually exiled or driven from the king's presence. Insecure leaders make supporting them a litmus test of their followers' devotion to God.

David's security in himself did not lead him into believing more about himself than he should. He did not ever fully believe his press. He knew where his real source of strength resided. His confidence grew out of the security of his own relationship with his King.

David's security in his relationship with God allowed him to entertain others' notions and ideas without feeling in competition with them. He had the benefit of wise counsel because of the community he enjoyed. He did not always have to be right. He was willing to trust others' judgments. He relied on Jonathan's insights early on. He frequently consulted with military commanders in combat situations. Nathan's access to David extended beyond one incident. The prophet's ability to challenge the king proves the point. David avoided a haughty heart because he did not insulate himself against the community he served. David forged a great kingdom because he captured the people's own dreams and served them.

David created a wonderful legacy in part because he lived an open life that allowed others to find their own destinies in his. He developed a heart after God's because he had a heart that had room for others.

A Man After God's Own Heart

David's passion to pursue God's heart fostered a communion between him and God so powerful that the very words of their conversations still inspire the communion of millions seeking after God's heart themselves. The psalms of David serve as a journal of divine heart-shaping. From them, we learn several key insights into how God molded David through their intimate encounters. First, David's communion with God supported his sense of destiny. Second, David was transparent in his relationship with God. The full range of emotions poured out in David's discourse with his King. Third, he reflected on commonplace experiences of his boyhood shepherding to create new insights into God's heart. Finally, David saw God everywhere he looked.

A Sense of Destiny

Throughout the psalms, David revealed a strong sense of personal destiny. He combined two major sets of imagery to express this theme—warrior imagery and regal imagery.

The God of Israel made David a successful warrior. God revealed himself to David in military terms. Warrior and battle language in David's heart talk include *refuge, rock, shield,* and *stronghold,* among others.

Psalm 18 serves as an example of how these military themes express David's connection with God. In this song, David says that God trains him for battle (v. 34), arms him with strength (v. 39), and exalts him above his enemies (v. 48) by allowing him to rout those who oppose him (v. 40). David viewed his success as a soldier as clear affirmation of God's favor: "He gives his king great victories; he shows unfailing kindness to his anointed, to David and his descendants forever" (v. 50).

David's claim as "God's anointed" reflects his sense of connection to God more than any other phrase. David was king because God wanted him as king. His position of being king over Israel represented a personal favor to him by God because the Lord liked David. "He brought me out into a spacious place; he rescued me *because he delighted in me*" (Ps. 18:19, emphasis added). David not only had ascended the throne over Israel but also had become a significant ruler in the ancient world.

David treasured his position at God's "right hand," a recurring phrase in the psalms (Pss. 16:8; 63:8; 110:1). Eastern kings granted this place of honor and distinction to someone they trusted. Those in this position of prestige and power carried the authority of the king himself. Being at God's right hand secured audience with him. David delighted himself in the presence of his King. (Eastern rulers would have expected the same from those who were privileged to be in their presence in their court.) David did not take this relationship for granted, but he used it to exalt and praise, to petition, and to receive instructions.

God still shapes leaders' hearts with a sense of destiny. They have a place and a role assigned by God in his work on the planet during their lifetimes. They also carry a sense of legacy. They believe God is working through them to influence the generations following them.

So many things vie for the leader's attention. To the degree that Christian leaders nurture their communion with God, they keep sight of the best contributions they can make. If the communion suffers, the mission of the leader is placed in jeopardy, in danger of being lost to trivialities or distraction.

The leader's sense of mission is not a matter of pride. It is a point of privilege and responsibility. If the leader's heart remains in communion with God, then humility graces the leader's life. The leader maintains an absolute awareness of owing the leadership role to God. The leader is king by the design and pleasure of the Almighty.

Heart to Heart

David was honest with God. He did not pretend in his conversations with God, playing games to avoid confronting the truth about life, about his circumstances, and about himself. He felt he had nothing to hide from God; rather, he viewed his life as an open book. For this reason, David did not feel a need to sanitize his prayers. He brought to God the raw stuff of his heart, uncensored, untidied up. He was not afraid that God would be repulsed by his heart, because God, knowing his heart, still wanted communion with David.

David teaches us that honesty is the real currency of heart-shaping communion. "Search me, O God, and know my heart" (Ps. 139:21a) expresses a plea with God to conduct a thorough investigation so that the leader can grow. Humans can be tricked and deceived. They can be misled, and the result can be cancerous to the relationship. Humans can also demand that their leaders present themselves in certain ways in order to unlock the door for approval or sanction. God does not reward posturing. No attempts at wiggling out of the truth will succeed.

This truth has both frightening and thrilling implications. The real breakthrough to heart-shaping communion occurs when the fear of this truth gives way to the thrill of this truth. The leader is set free in God's presence to deal with the hardcore truth without fear of being misunderstood or of suffering negative consequences for sharing true thoughts. The freedom of such heart-to-heart discussions with God are afforded by few human relationships.

Understanding that his life was transparent before God, David enjoyed the full spectrum of emotional release to God. Opening up his inmost thoughts to God proved therapeutic for the king of Israel. In a single psalm, David would sometimes display a huge assortment of emotional expression.

Praise frequented David's communion. "Praise the Lord, O my soul; all my inmost being, praise his holy name" (Ps. 103:1). David celebrated God's goodness, his righteousness, his character, his mighty deeds, and his creative activity. "My soul will boast in the Lord" (Ps. 34:2a) signals this desire to rehearse God's attributes, much as a lover would extol the virtues of his or her beloved.

David also pleaded for deliverance when he was anxious or afraid. "O Lord, do not forsake me. . . . Come quickly to help me" (Ps. 38:21–22) was a theme that took several variations. David counted on God's deliverance from the slimy pit (40:2), from guilt of sin (53:14), from his enemies (56:1), from his distresses (55:17). Pride did not get in the way of David's asking for help: "Cast your cares on the Lord, for he will sustain you" (55:22).

The psalms contain passionate outbursts of the hatred David had for his enemies. He wanted God to punish them: "May the table set before them become a snare; may it become retribution and a trap. May their eyes be darkened so they cannot see, and their backs be bent forever. Pour your wrath on them, let your fierce anger overtake them. . . . Charge them with crime upon crime, do not let them share in your salvation. May they be blotted out of the book of life and not be listed with the righteous" (Ps. 69:22–24, 27–28). And these verses are not even the most explicit in David's prayer arsenal against his enemies!

Many Christian leaders today might feel uncomfortable praying against others with this much zeal. Perhaps the leader's prayer would be more healing if, like David, the leader were not afraid to say the first thing that comes to mind or bubbles up from the gut. The process of sanitizing prayers cuts God out of the healing loop. God can handle emotional outbursts. He has heard it before. From David.

David also was not above some self-congratulations in the psalms. He exulted in his own performance: "Vindicate me, O Lord, for I have led a blameless life" (26:1). He was also quick to admit his failures and to beg for mercy: "O Lord, do not rebuke me in your anger or discipline me in your wrath" (38:1).

In short, David's psalms are chatty, reflective, celebratory, morose, lofty, punitive, hopeful, dark, loud, quiet—whatever state or states of mind David found himself in as he came to God.

Christian leaders can find a psalm of David to match any mood. David's honest expression still helps the leader give release to thoughts and feelings that are at times immature, contradictory, and even embarrassing to look back on. David depended on communion with God. He was not just developing a discipline. He clung to God because fulfilling his life destiny depended on it. David would not have been David without his singing.

The Shepherd King

Like Moses, David had a leadership curriculum that involved shepherding. Shepherding provided David with some of his richest imagery about God. The commonplace experiences of his boyhood afforded him new ways to talk about the God of Israel. The notion that God looks after us in protection and provision, that we are the sheep of his pasture, provides an incredible dimension to the Old Testament revelation of God. In Moses' time, God lived on the mountain, in fire and smoke. He was unapproachable. No one looked on him lest they die in their tracks. David painted a picture of a God intimately involved with and concerned for his people.

Shepherding themes invoke deeply instinctual human heart emotions. Hope, security, rest, contentment, care—all these categories find expression in the pastoral images of the Davidic psalms. Psalm 23, rife with shepherding imagery, provides the clearest expression of the impact that commonplace boyhood work made in David's heart in terms of understanding and appreciating God. In this psalm, the sheep is nurtured, provided for, and protected. Green pastures, still waters—these are optimum conditions of provision. Paths of righteousness lead to security. When danger threatens, even shadows cast in the valley of death, the people of God can live without fear, for God protects them. And hope is the final word. The promise of dwelling with God forever represents a powerful statement of belief and faith one thousand years before Christ.

God Is Everywhere

The shepherd of Bethlehem also developed a deep appreciation for the handiwork of God. Waterfalls, mountains, valley streams, still-water ponds, lush vegetation, craggy hillsides, caves, open vistas, snow-capped peaks—all and each of them inspired David and caused him to worship God.

The capacity to see God at work in the common things of life is a hallmark of great spiritual leadership. David serves as a model for turning life assignments into windows for viewing God's heart. The ultimate responsibility of the spiritual leader is to share the heart of God with the people of God. This cannot happen if the leader does not know the heart of God.

This kind of intimacy comes from an intentional and frequent cultivation of a personal relationship that draws from every life experience.

David felt very close to God. That was because he looked for God all of the time and in every situation. He lived up to God's assessment voiced to Samuel. He truly was a person who sought after God's heart. His mission reflected God's mission. God has honored his pledge to him. David's kingdom has been established. One from David's line will occupy the throne forever.

3

PAUL

A HEART CAPTURED BY GOD

FOR MANY, PAUL epitomizes the quintessential spiritual leader. For this reason, scores try to emulate him. Others find him intimidating. His intellect, giftedness, and commitment to Christ combine to make him alone in his class. Few dare to believe they can achieve peerage with him in terms of influence. The apostle surely is the most quoted Christian leader of all time. And despite the dark side that some see in his performance orientation, drivenness, and boastfulness that borders on conceit, his achievements and obvious passion command almost universal respect by spiritual leaders.

The Christian movement cannot be understood apart from its premier missionary. No one took more seriously the Great Commission uttered by Jesus before his ascension than did Paul. The converted Pharisee personally and permanently planted evangelism and missions into the character of the Christian church. Paul's vision for the church created an understanding of how Christian community should be practiced, not only in the first century but in every century since. His preeminence and accessibility nominate him as a good candidate for viewing the heart-shaping work of God. The heart of the Christian champion beat with a message that God surgically wrought in its inner chambers.

Cultural Layering

Saul of Tarsus entered Christian history at the stoning of the first Christian martyr, Stephen the deacon. Eager to please his teachers and anxious to make his own mark, Saul served as an accomplice to the brutal killing.

Apparently fired up by the event, Saul determined to personally begin a program of persecuting Followers of the Way. He targeted Damascus as first on his list, because many disciples had fled there in the wake of heightened harassment by Jewish authorities. Saul sought and obtained permission from "upline" religious authorities for his campaign. He may have believed that he was about to realize his ambitions for leadership. However, God had been superintending Saul's training agenda with a different mission in mind. He had prepared Saul to be the first cross-cultural missionary for the very movement he was intent on destroying.

God secured the influences of three cultures in the heart-shaping of the apostle. Paul would need to be well acquainted with Roman, Greek, and Jewish cultures in order to carry out his life assignment. All three cultural streams converged in the home of Saul of Tarsus.

Saul's father, apparently a man of some means, had become a Roman citizen before Saul's birth. This meant that Saul possessed Roman citizenship by birth, a significant distinction that played into several events during his missionary days. His citizenship protected him in Ephesus and Philippi by granting him special legal status. Most notably, Paul's Roman citizenship allowed him to appeal to Caesar in his trials before Festus and Agrippa. This legal right cinched for Paul the chance to preach the gospel in the world's capital city. This privilege of Roman birth enabled Paul to fulfill his commission to carry God's name "before the Gentiles and their kings" (Acts 9:15).

Being brought up in Tarsus, Saul also learned to speak, read, and write Greek, the international language of commerce in the first century. A few centuries earlier, Alexander the Great had established the Greek language throughout the ancient world through his conquests. This move did for the first-century world what the Internet has done for the twenty-first century in terms of facilitating information exchange across national lines. The ubiquitous presence of the Greek language created the world's first global village. Paul was quite at home in the Hellenistic world of Asia Minor. He could communicate the Christian faith to people in the many cities established by Alexander.

By far the most significant cultural conditioning Saul received for his life calling occurred in his family of origin. God placed his future apostle into a Pharisee home. For Saul's father to be a Pharisee meant that young Saul would absorb Pharisaism's comprehensive worldview and political-religious orientation. By his own admission, Saul took to Pharisaism with a noticeable zealousness. Arrangements were made for him to move to his father's sister's home in Jerusalem at about age thirteen, so he could study under the great rabbi Gamaliel. By this time, the rigidity and discipline of

Saul's upbringing would be showing up in drivenness, self-righteousness, and bigotry toward all others who did not share his views.

The Heart of a Pharisee

The origins of the Pharisees remain somewhat obscure. During the post-exilic period, after the rediscovery of the law books and the revival under Ezra, a contingent of Jews emerged who devoted themselves to the restoration of the law to its proper place in Jewish life. Convinced that the Exile had been God's punishment visited on Israel for their lack of attention to the Torah, they wanted to prevent another such episode. This determination gave rise to the teaching of the law throughout the synagogues of Israel. A group of men who were the scribes and teachers of this movement at some point became the original Pharisees.

By the time Saul moved to Jerusalem, the Pharisees had become the most significant religious-political party in first-century Judaism. They controlled the teaching in the synagogues. Young men who showed promise, like Saul, were recruited into their ranks and trained at rabbinical schools. The Pharisees maintained a controlling majority in the Sanhedrin. Their influence, once thought to reside mostly in rural villages, is now known to have been significant in Jerusalem as well. In short, the Pharisees largely defined first-century Judaism. It is important to understand them, their teachings, and their practices as the cultural backdrop not only for Paul but also for Jesus and those he called on to form the leadership nucleus for the Christian movement.

Though the Pharisees do not fare well in the New Testament, their doctrines helped prepare the Jewish people to receive Jesus' message and Paul's teaching. Unlike their political rivals, the secular Sadduccees, the Pharisees emphasized the supernatural. Their study of the Torah led them to ancient stories of angelic appearances to Abraham and Moses and miracles performed by Yahweh during the time of the Exodus. These accounts signaled to them that a spiritual world existed beyond the physical, material one. Their teachings emphasized that spiritual realities influence people's lives and destinies. Paul's and Jesus' references to angelic and demonic forces would have made little sense to Jewish listeners before Pharisee theology had reshaped the spiritual landscape.

A related theological development involved the Pharisee belief in personal survival after death in a conscious, individual form. Those who effected their salvation through proper observance of the law could look forward to being resurrected. This resurrection would take place at the end of earth history at the dawn of the Messianic era when God's Anointed would inaugurate the restored kingdom for the faithful in Israel. As these soteriological and eschatological beliefs evolved, the Pharisees came to believe that the keeping of the law and the epiphany of God's Messiah were interrelated. If enough Jews would properly observe the law (the core of which was Sabbath observance), then God would send his Messiah.

Hope for surviving the grave runs throughout ancient literature, but it is generally associated with corporate existence with one's fathers (family) or nation. The Old Testament itself is not specific about afterlife experiences. The Pharisees created a hope for a realized personal spiritual existence, a resurrection of the body unto eternal life. Paul's teaching on these matters built on the foundation of his initial theological education.

The Pharisees maintained two emphases that became obsessions. The first had to do with the proper observance of the Sabbath. Keeping God's Sabbath provided a clear opportunity for a Jew to demonstrate obedience to the law. In addition to the original Mosaic commandments introducing and instituting the Sabbath, the Pharisees added hundreds to build a hedge around it.

The Pharisees' other grand obsession involved ceremonial cleanliness. Concerned with becoming defiled by unclean things and thus being disqualified from salvation, they kept huge water pots in their homes. Over time, they altered their lifestyle to become more and more insulated from unclean people. By the time of Saul's conversion, the Pharisees had restricted their dealings with people other than other Pharisees. When traveling, they stayed with other Pharisees. They ate with other Pharisees. The thought of eating with "sinners" revolted them. (Sinners was the Pharisee designation for the common people. In some Bible translations, this word appears in quotation marks to connote its source. This was a Pharisee evaluation of people, not God's.)

A sign of the depth of Saul's conversion can be seen in his discussion of eating meat offered to idols (1 Cor. 8). Nothing could have been more repulsive to a Pharisee than reclining with unclean pagans to eat unclean food. Paul's remarkable shift in attitude and behavior reflected his life-changing experience on the road to Damascus.

A Blinding Light

The preceding rehearsal of key tenets of Pharisaism provides significant background for understanding the dynamics of Saul's call experience. The voice that would change Saul's life belonged to a person who had played loose with many things that the young Pharisee held dear. Jesus had hung around with sinners, even eating with them, a total disregard for purity and ritual cleanliness. He had violated the Sabbath, even claiming to be doing God's work on that day. The Nazarene had been an avid party goer, mixing it up with people of all social classes. He refused to judge people for their obvious sins. Even though he aroused Messianic expectations, he refused to challenge the Romans' authority. Instead, he saved his scathing remarks for the Pharisees. Jesus was perceived as extremely dangerous by the Pharisees. He threatened the hope for God's deliverance from Rome and the reestablishment of the kingdom of Israel.

Jesus called the Pharisees "blind guides." Saul the Pharisee literally experienced the truth of that judgment. Saul's call began in the dark. The blindness that struck him in the presence of so great a light provided a commentary on his earlier blindness to the truth. In the hours and days without physical vision, the apostle could contemplate the Light that had arrested him. The awful brightness of truth called to question all he had understood previously. The restoration of physical sight would come only after an internal vision had begun to come into focus.

On the road to Damascus, the self-proclaimed Pharisee of the Pharisees suddenly encountered the hope of his faith—personal and bodily resurrection. Saul never expected to meet a resurrected person until the Messianic age. Here was incontestable truth validating the Pharisee belief in resurrection! That was the good news—the Messianic age had arrived. The disturbing news for Saul was that the resurrected one was Jesus. This meant that Saul's colleagues had conspired to kill the Messiah of God! Saul himself was undertaking a mission to suppress the Messiah's followers. This placed Saul in a precarious position, lined up on the wrong side of God. No wonder Saul did not eat or drink for three days. Suddenly all that Saul had lived for was shown up for what it was—a misguided zeal without real knowledge.

Christian leaders who report blinding light call experiences will often report dynamics similar to Paul's. The call encounter with God provides them with a new clarity of vision to see previous efforts as unenlightened pursuits. Their view of God sometimes undergoes significant revision. They testify to being brought to a point of helplessness in their own strength. A dramatic change in lifestyle occurs to mark a clear departure from previous values and life goals. Like Paul, they evidence a zealousness to their new call typical of late-in-life converts.

God could have restored sight to Paul without outside intervention. He had, after all, struck the Pharisee blind with no outside help. Yet God chose to mediate Paul's healing and anointing through a human instrument in the person of Ananias. The most courageous believer in Damascus played out a parable of grace. Saul had hoped to imprison Ananias, yet it is Ananias who came to set Paul free.

The acceptance and touch of the obedient disciple of Jesus introduced a new spiritual reality to Paul. The Pharisee had persecuted Jesus, yet was rescued by him. Even though Saul's original intentions in Damascus were to harm Ananias, the follower of Jesus immediately accepted Paul as a new brother. Paul experienced through Ananias something new—grace. Paul would come to see his previous efforts to attain righteousness as being revolting to God. He could only be acceptable to God through Jesus. The gift of grace restored his sight. Paul woke up to a brand new world of relationship to God and others based on the grace he had received.

Throughout Christian history, God has used Ananiases as part of his heart-shaping strategy for many leaders. The story of spiritual leaders often includes encounters with a significant person who intersects their lives with powerful spiritual truth. Sometimes the messenger takes great risk in dealing with the emerging leader. In some instances, these human messengers sense a divine urging to intersect the leader. The latter-day Ananiases often see something in the leader that others do not. They are able to open up the leader to new understandings of God on the basis of their affirmation. Frequently these special emissaries drop out of the leader's life once they have completed their mission with the leader.

Paul's call experience defined the rest of his life. The apostle recounted his Damascus road experience in his apologia to the crowd in Jerusalem and in his trials before Festus and Agrippa (and surely before Felix, though not recorded). Paul argued that he could not have done anything other than what he had done with his life since Christ blinded him and restored him to sight. Paul contended that his life could not be understood apart from his call.

Women and men who have similarly received a life-changing call consistently live out the same truth. The call provides them with their life direction. It informs their decisions by reorienting their priorities and establishing a new set of core values. The call provides a content that becomes their life message. They would not be who they are without it.

During times of great testing in the leader's life, the call serves as an internal-navigation beacon of hope and reassurance. When Paul's life was on the line, he resorted to retelling his story. Christian leaders of all ages have done the same thing. When the going gets tough, when doubts crowd in, when fear and uncertainty threaten, the called return to the experience of their call. When tempted to quit, to run away, to hide, the memory of the divine intervention beckons them to renewed determination to live up to their call.

Paul never expressed regret at having failed to heed his life mission. On the contrary, what he said was just the opposite. In public, he proclaimed that his life had been one of integrity because he had lived in accordance with the call he had received. In his magnificent last letter to his protégé Timothy, Paul likened himself to a spent boxer or runner who had endured to the end to receive the prize (2 Tim. 4:6–7).

Modern-day Pauls and Paulines who live out their call also model a similar life mission integrity. Confronted with other options, they consistently choose the life path that will bring them closer to the realization of their call. They live fulfilled lives because they live lives of *intentionality* in obedience to the mission they receive from God. Their hearts are captured by God's designs on their lives.

Paul's call experience yields one further lesson. The apostle saw the call as integral to his relationship with God. He could not separate his obedience to the call of God from his ability to enjoy a deepening personal relationship with him. For Paul, knowing God meant experiencing the power of Christ's resurrection and the fellowship of his sufferings (Phil. 3:10). Both of those elements figured into Paul's call experience. Paul encountered the resurrected Christ on the Damascus road. During the three days of blindness, Paul acquired the specific knowledge that he would suffer for Christ.

Christian leaders captured by the call of God cannot separate their relationship with God from this unique aspect of their life together. How the leader experiences God is colored by the character and content of the call. Leaders are bound to God by a special contract that the Almighty has on their lives. Discussions that press a dichotomy between who the leader is and what he or she does seem artificial to them. Such a distinction flies in the face of the mysterious and profound spiritual reality of God's call at the center of their hearts.

Those in the leader's constellation of influence find their view and experience of God also to be shaped by the leader's call. This is precisely why God uses the call to shape the leader's heart. Through the call on the leader, God reveals himself to his people. God writes his message on tablets of flesh in the leader's heart.

The character of New Testament Christianity significantly reflects God's dealings with Saul the Pharisee–Paul the apostle. The evangelistic and missionary spirit of Paul's writings and life has challenged believers for two millennia to join him in the mission of sharing the good news of God's grace through Jesus Christ. The conversion on the Damascus road permanently imbued Christianity with the understanding that God is in the life transformation business. When Paul answered the call, all Christians heard from God.

A Long Interim

As soon as Paul yielded to God's call, things immediately got worse. As his internal turbulence gave way to peace with God, his external world suddenly filled with turmoil and animosities directed at him. When news leaked out about Saul's conversion, he suddenly became a marked man. Perhaps some of the very people that Saul had brought with him to Damascus to ferret out Christians for prosecution now sought to end his ministry before it got started. One of the remarkable testimonies to the Spirit of Jesus in the early Christian community took place at this point. The followers of Jesus in Damascus immediately came to Paul's assistance. They recognized in him the Spirit of their Lord and now protected him against the very harm he had wanted to inflict on them. They smuggled him out of town.

The Christian movement was still centered in Jerusalem at this time. The apostles there legitimized any new developments in the young faith. An event so public as Paul's conversion would require the comment of the Jerusalem leaders. Any efforts of the Pharisee-turned-gospel-preacher would remain suspect until the church fathers gave their approval. Not surprisingly, some leaders received the news of Paul's conversion with a mixture of skepticism and hope.

God raised up Barnabas for the task of sponsoring Paul. Barnabas carried sufficient clout with the church leadership to secure a blessing for the upstart disciple. We do not know why Barnabas believed Paul so readily. We must see in this the work of God, because without Barnabas's urging, the Jerusalem church might have welcomed Paul with much more guarded approval. However, with Barnabas paving the way, Paul convinced the senior leaders of Christianity that he had experienced a genuine conversion to belief in Jesus as the Messiah. Ten years later, when the work of God needed leadership in Antioch, it was Barnabas again who recruited Paul away from Tarsus to join him. The Antioch church launched the Christian missionary movement with Barnabas and Paul as the initial team.

Many Christian leaders throughout history have had their own Barnabas figures, or sponsors. Often they serve to give the leaders the "break" they need. These Barnabas heroes buy into the leader's possibilities when others ignore them. They follow the progress of the young leader and serve as encouragers. Sometimes they promote the new leader by bringing the protégé alongside themselves in ministry efforts. Often the sponsors never achieve the status of the ones they broker into a place of significant ministry influence. In some instances, a very painful break occurs between the early sponsor and the Christian leader, just as happened between Paul and Barnabas.

God's first assignment for Paul did not involve immediate fulfillment of the vision of his new life. The promise that he would preach to Gentiles and kings would take years to be fulfilled. A long interim, beginning in the wilderness, would relegate Paul to relative obscurity for a decade.

In his letter to the Galatians, Paul alludes to a desert sojourn. Scholars debate the exact length of its duration and when it occurred. However, the significance of the desert experience seems clear. In the desert, a close communion between Paul and God brought into focus the elements of Paul's mission and his message. The church leaders in Jerusalem also affirmed the conclusions that Paul had reached in the desert about his ministry. "These men added nothing to my message. . . . They saw that I had been entrusted with the task of preaching the gospel to the Gentiles" (Acts 2:6).

Paul wound up in Tarsus, hardly a glamorous assignment. The fate of hometown prophets is well-known. But in Tarsus Paul could be protected from his detractors through family connections. Here he could attract little attention, thereby posing less threat to his enemies and avoiding their attacks. We are not privy to Paul's conversations with God during the Tarsus years. Perhaps he chafed over not seeing his life mission take shape as fast as he thought it should. Maybe he feared that his early success in Damascus and Jerusalem would turn out to be his career pinnacle, that he would be a flash in the pan. He may have thought he was spinning his wheels. Whatever he thought or prayed or wrestled with, he grew through the commonplace assignment God had given him in his hometown. When he emerged from Tarsus, it took very little time for Paul to assume a lead role in the development of Christianity for the A.D. 50s and 60s. Had Paul pushed for earlier, "better" assignments, he may have had his ministry shortened by a too-early martyrdom, or he may not have emerged prepared enough to be the leader he became.

Many Christian leaders report the same dynamic and challenge that the early Paul did. At some point, they gain a vision for their lives that is compelling to them. The normal tendency is to go out and make something happen. Sometimes the temptation is to manipulate situations and assignments to try to get positioned for a better platform, so God can "use them" in a "bigger" way.

Too early promotion can mean too short a ministry. Unseasoned leadership wreaks havoc in Christian organizations. However, many leaders are not willing to accept the ministry posts that seem out of the way or unglamorous or too small for them. The lure of the limelight has caused many leaders to miss the maturing of the commonplace. By fast-tracking themselves into premature leadership, they get into situations that are over their heads.

God's career path for his leaders does not seem to be informed by the same standards that guide many Christian leaders in making choices. An antipathy toward the commonplace has left many wanna-be spiritual leaders impoverished. God uses the commonplace to build character, to expand the leader's heart by layering experience and learning that must be available to the leader for larger assignments.

God uses a preparation model for developing leaders, not a planning model. Leaders who give their best efforts to their current assignments from God are prepared for their next level of influence. Those who plan their ministries in advance often get where they want to go, but along the way they lose the anointing that comes only with radical obedience and trusting in God to fulfill the dreams he gives. Leaders of great legacy look back over their lives and see that in every ministry assignment, God was preparing them for the next. Trusting God with their destiny, they wound up with influence they never could have pulled off on their own.

Paul obviously proved himself in Tarsus. Faithful over little, he was eventually given influence over much.

Shaping a Movement by Shaping a Heart

The conflicts Paul faced, recorded in the historical narrative of Acts and in his own letters, shaped both the apostle's thinking and the character of the Christian movement in its formative century. His challenges came from those who shared his theological background as well as from those he introduced to his newfound faith.

The consuming struggle throughout Paul's ministry involved the Judaizers. Part of the Judaizer conflict was theological. The new grace theology that Paul began teaching after his conversion was antithetical to the old theology of justification through observance of the law. Paul was seen as a particularly dangerous opponent by the Judaizers because he understood their system so well. The Judaizers' concept of God revolved around the special revelation of his law to Israel. If the law could be set aside somehow, or if another basis for justification with God could be demonstrated, then the unique position of Israel (not to mention Judaism's spiritual leaders) would be jeopardized.

Paul proved himself a heretic to the Jewish religious establishment when he departed from traditional Jewish monotheism. Monotheism was the cardinal tenet of the faith. The Shema declared: "Hear O Israel, the Lord our God, the Lord is one" (Deut. 6:4). Paul's insistence on ascribing deity to the crucified teacher from Nazareth brought him into direct conflict with his former teachers and associates.

Paul's detractors and the conflict generated by them served to help him articulate his experience with Jesus and the Spirit of God. The debates forced him to crystallize his own thinking and enabled him to communicate more precisely and forcefully his understanding of Jesus. The magnificent passages of Christological hymnody in Colossians 1, Ephesians 1 and 3, and Philippians 2 may never have been penned without the pressure to explain Christ's place in the Godhead and in the created universe. In addition, Paul lived with such constant awareness of the Spirit of Jesus that he identified him as a third person of the Trinity. The apostle maintained his monotheistic view, but now cast in a Trinitarian understanding of the person of God. His writings provided the early church, particularly Augustine, the bulk of the scriptural argument for the development of Trinitarian theology as the cardinal tenet of the Christian faith.

Challenges from the Jewish establishment extended beyond verbal sparring and theological debate. More than once, Paul's enemies tried to kill him. They succeeded in having him stoned, getting him thrown into jail, and breaking up his preaching services by various means.

Paul's response to these attacks profoundly affected the character of the Christian movement. His strategy did not involve handing himself over to his enemies. The apostle hid in baskets, demanded armed escorts from his jailers in order to escape assassination, and in general looked out for his own safety. Nor did he flinch in the face of their threats. Fear for his own life, fear of pain, fear of being rejected or ridiculed did not prevent him from sharing the truth of what he knew.

The apostle's pain became others' gain. Paul became a hero to the first-century believers because he endured such enormous persecution. His appeals to his chains, his stigmata, his trials and tribulations established his credibility. He inspired the courage of other brothers and sisters who suffered similarly. Not only did he encourage the persecuted Christians of his day, but the legend of his life has emboldened every Christian martyr during the last two thousand years. Paul has helped many fight the fight, keep the faith, and anticipate the reward of enjoying Jesus' presence in heaven. God used the persecution that Paul endured to strengthen his message.

The persecuted apostle did not resort to physical force to fight physical threat. In this regard, he reflected Jesus' attitude of refusing the sword and rebuking Peter for using it in his defense in Gethsemane. Had Paul rallied believers to fight for him, the history of Christianity would be very different. At his conversion, Paul not only turned his back on his previous misguided theological zeal but also eschewed his former methodology of employing force to compel religious compliance. His participation in Stephen's stoning and his trip to Damascus proved that he was not always averse to backing up his religious convictions with force. The fact that Paul laid down the sword in the Damascus dirt reflected a significant change of heart that shaped the heart of Christianity itself. Military force and political maneuvering done in the name of the faith constitute aberrations of it, not its true nature.

Paul's challengers did not all come from outside the church. He had his detractors inside the church as well. The Corinthian church has long stood as a symbol of the kind of grief that followers can dish out to their spiritual leaders. Some of the Corinthian congregation did not care for Paul's preaching, his personality, or his ministry program. In the Corinthian correspondence, we can feel the pain of someone who has to defend his authority and position even though he has paid a high price for it.

If Paul's external conflicts toughened and steeled his heart for the cause, these internal conflicts softened the apostle's heart. Sometimes they broke it. But in his brokenness, Paul learned that God's strength is made perfect in weakness.

Many spiritual leaders know exactly how Paul felt. The apostle exposed his problems and conflict in his letters. In them, he revealed his impatience, his woundedness, his astonishment, his ego, his bewilderment, even his pep talks to himself. These open-heart discussions have instructed many leaders facing similar trials. Not every leader can identify with Paul in his assertiveness, in his passion, in his intensity, in his accomplishments. But every leader can identify with Paul when criticized.

Paul also dealt with problems in the churches not related to him personally. If the early church had been as ideal as some think, the New Testament would be much shorter. Problems gave rise to many of Paul's letters. The Corinthian church had factions; the Colossians flirted with incipient gnostic philosophy; the Galatian church seemed determined to reinstate law over grace; Timothy needed some encouragement for pastoring in Ephesus; Titus struggled with Cretan parishioners; the Thessalonians had some deadbeats sitting around waiting on the Second Coming; Philemon was called on a personal debt.

In the very common issues facing the churches, God molded Paul's heart and through him instructed the entire church. If Paul had never been forced to declare on some of these issues, we would not have the benefit of his insights in the love sonnet of 1 Corinthians 13, his instructions on spiritual leadership in the pastorals, the information about the Second Coming given to the Thessalonians, or the earliest written record of the words that Jesus spoke at the Last Supper, shared with the Corinthians as part of their worship instructions.

From the small inconveniences of first-century travel to the perils of shipwreck and imprisonment, Paul learned that common human needs and wants become ways that God conditions the inner person. Paul did not drift into Stoicism or asceticism. He included both plenty and want in his famous statement on contentment (Phil. 4:11–13). He knew both and received both as tools of God's heart-shaping activity.

Finally, God used Paul's community of coworkers as a heart-sculpting process. Although he was not always with the same team every time, from the commissioning at Antioch forward, Paul was almost always in the company of ministry colleagues. His journeys and itinerant preaching efforts not only planted and nurtured churches but also created a phenomenal ministry team. Silas, Luke, Timothy, Titus, and John Mark are just a few of the luminaries that became part of the apostle's leadership constellation.

Paul took the team approach very seriously. For him, practicing teamwork went way beyond meeting a need for companionship; it represented a key piece in his strategy for spreading the faith. The apostle told Timothy to make sure that he passed along to others the things he was learning himself (2 Tim. 2:2). Paul knew that ministry reproduction would be necessary for the movement to survive. He also knew that effective leadership development included the chance for leaders to debrief their ministry experiences with others who faced similar ministry challenges. In this approach, Paul followed Jesus' model with the Twelve.

Each and all of these companions enriched Paul. His letters contain warm references to his coworkers, both the ones with him as he traveled and the ones in the congregations to whom he wrote. Paul took obvious joy in the spiritual growth of those he knew. He had been converted to genuine knowledge of God through a relationship with Jesus Christ. He came to understand that one's relationship with Jesus Christ is lived out in the relationships with other believers.

Close Encounters

In the quiet places of blindness in Damascus and hiddenness in the Arabian desert, Paul discovered his new life mission. In jail cells, ship holds, and mission posts, Paul received personal visitations from the divine to strengthen him for the demands of his call. Paul's close encounters with God stretched throughout his ministry. Apparently the apostle took his own advice to "pray without ceasing" (1 Thess. 5:17). No other explanation can be given for Paul's miraculous ministry.

Paul sometimes received clear directives in his close communion. While Paul was in Jerusalem during one of his early postconversion visits, the Lord appeared to him in the Temple. He directed Paul to "leave Jerusalem immediately, because they will not accept your testimony about me. . . . Go, I will send you far away to the Gentiles" (Acts 22:18). In this way, the Lord continued to steer Paul to place his greatest ministry efforts on the Gentiles. In Acts 16, Paul received the famous Macedonian vision that directed him to Troas. Paul's obedience introduced the gospel to Europe.

Paul's communion also sustained him for his task. At those critical moments when Paul was discouraged or driven to despair, Jesus showed himself again to his apostle. The Lord's appearance to Paul in Corinth encouraged him to stay in that city, though he faced stiff opposition: "Do not be afraid; keep on speaking; do not be silent. For I am with you, and not one is going to attack and harm you, because I have many people in this city" (Acts 18:9, 10).

Jesus also visited Paul in the tumultuous days surrounding his arrest in Jerusalem after the apostle's stormy meeting with the Sanhedrin. "Take courage! As you have testified about me in Jerusalem, so you must testify in Rome" (Acts 23:11). This communication convinced Paul that he would escape the plot to kill him and would survive his trials before officials in Caesarea.

When Paul was on the ship bound for his Roman trial, Jesus again visited his apostle. This time Paul received assurance that he would survive imminent shipwreck. He passed this along to the ship's crew to stiffen their own courage. This vision saved not only Paul's life but his traveling companions as well.

The apostle admitted to being actually transported to heaven itself on one occasion. There he beheld "inexpressible things that man is not permitted to tell" (2 Cor. 12:4). Such privilege carried a price. As a souvenir, he was given a thorn. Paul expressed ambivalence about the thorn's origin. It seemed to be both a gift of God to keep him humble and a messenger of Satan to torment him. Whatever its origin, Paul knew who had the power to remove it. He pleaded for relief. Yet God refused the plea of this close companion, choosing to increase Paul's experience of grace.

Perhaps you have not been struck blind, nor had personalized visitations, nor spent three years in desert retreat. Maybe you as a leader have not been permitted into the throne room of heaven. Whether or not you have experienced these communion experiences, you probably have one thing in common with Paul. You have picked up a thorn or two. At times you believe Satan has conspired against you. Yet you also sense the overarching determination of God to shape your heart through the pain. You have taken up your hurt in communion with him. And you have received grace.

The Free Slave

Jesus rescued Paul from the road to destruction and allowed him a chance to know the truth. The apostle's heart, consumed with serving God from his earliest recollection, found an object of affection in Jesus. His zeal without knowledge as a Pharisee became a personal relationship with the resurrected Messiah of God. His desperate attempts to win God's favor through keeping of the law were replaced with a sense of acceptance through Christ.

Paul's life message of grace grew out of his own intense heart connectedness with Jesus, who himself had shown Paul mercy. Saul, the enemy of Jesus, had been arrested and conquered by Jesus. Instead of receiving what he deserved, Paul received a pardon. Paul willingly indentured himself to Jesus. He never got over the thrill of being captured.

4

JESUS

THE HEARTBEAT OF GOD

JESUS CONTINUES TO captivate people even after two thousand years. Despite the population-at-large's declining sentiment for the institutional church in North America, it gives its founder rave reviews. Jesus makes the cover of *Time* or *Newsweek* (or both) annually, generally around Easter. He shows up on most everyone's list of the most influential leaders of all times. He would remain an appropriate entry in a volume on divine heart-shaping even apart from his claims to share in the divine nature itself. The fact that he did makes studying him even more compelling.

The treatment of leadership themes in Jesus' life often focuses on some particular aspect of his ministry style. Some commentators champion servant-style leadership based on his ministry efforts and life relationships. Others see in him insights appropriate for business executives responsible for managing employees and corporations. Still other investigators focus on spiritual leadership principles that inform personal character development.

This volume investigates how Jesus' heart was shaped for his leadership mission. Some theological presuppositions about the person of Jesus guide this inquiry. First, Jesus was fully God. This means that he could tap resources unavailable to mere mortals. Second, Jesus was fully human. This means that he went through life developmental stages, including a growing awareness of who he was and what he came to do. To grow up without having to struggle with basic identity issues would make him less than human. To grow up without absolute commitment to his mission would make him less than divine. Less divine is not divine at all. Less human is not human. Jesus was fully God and fully human.

Setting the Stage

"When the time had fully come," Paul observed, "God sent his Son" (Gal. 4:4). God meticulously arranged the cultural backdrop for his unique interface with humanity. He built a custom-designed stage for the divine-human drama, complete with backdrops never before on display. Put another way, the confluence of cultural phenomena occurring in Jesus' time prepared the world for his advent.

Several key cultural components significantly frame Jesus' life and earthly ministry. The Greek culture, imperially exported by Alexander the Great, gave the world a common language for the first time in human history. The vast extent of Alexander's empire, coupled with this language standardization, made possible commercial relations and cultural exchanges among peoples and countries previously isolated from one another. The former empires of the Egyptians, Babylonians, Assyrians, and Persians had not linked so vast an area nor afforded a lingua franca throughout the regions under their hegemony.

A second important development along the same lines came from the Romans—their marvelous road system. The empire's subjugation and centralization of Europe, North Africa, the Middle East, Near East, and parts of central Asia ushered in the development of a transportation infrastructure never before seen. The Roman highways linked together cities along trade routes and promoted urban development.

The combined impact of the Greek and Roman empires gave the world its first global village. The significance for Jesus' mission is enormous. If Jesus had come only a relatively short time before, his story would never have made it out of Palestine. As it happened, the gospel messengers fanned out along the Roman roads to take the miraculous news to key urban centers all over the world in a language that could be universally understood. With Greek manuscripts appearing at about the middle of the first century, the story of Jesus' life could be read all across the world. At the first moment in history that God could ensure widespread knowledge of his earthly intervention, and not before, the Incarnation mission commenced.

God also crafted the spiritual environment for Jesus' advent. Traditional religion had collapsed. In the century before Christ and during the apostolic era of the first century, energy shifted away from the institutional expression of religion to the search for personal salvation. The discussion of Pharisaism in the last chapter pointed out its belief in a personal resurrection to the kingdom of God. This degree of individual consciousness after death represented a more advanced notion than earlier Hebrew thought had entertained.

The quest for soul survival during this era extended beyond Jewish culture. This search would inspire the rise of two of the biggest challengers to Christianity during its early years—Gnosticism and Mithraism. Even though Jesus himself did not deal with these contenders during his lifetime, their later development signaled the spiritual hunger already present during his time that made the world susceptible to new concepts of spiritual truth.

Gnosticism, a Greek philosophy, maintained that the soul entered the material world from the spiritual world (a Platonic notion), remaining captive in this existence until enlightened by the appropriate knowledge *(gnosis)*. A soul in possession of this gnosis would be released back to the spiritual world free from the limitations and travails of the material, physical dimension. An elaborate cosmology and elements of reincarnation spiced up the appeal of this philosophy as a means of attaining personal salvation.

Mithraism, an ancient Persian cult imported into the Roman empire through military contact, reflected a search for personal salvation through ascetic and moral pursuit. Its appeal centered around an ethical emphasis in a world of declining morality (a theme commonly rehearsed by New Testament writers). Mithraism was called a mystery religion because its teachings, its "secrets," were known only to its adherents. Believers entered the cult through a baptism of blood (typically that of bulls) to live a life of high personal morality resulting in personal salvation. Cult members enjoyed close fellowship, meeting frequently to eat together.

The old gods had failed. People of the early Christian era were primed for a spiritual experience that was personal and transcendent. Jesus made his entrance in a time ripe for harvest.

Within Judaism, important spiritual dynamics were also occurring that would make way for Jesus' immediate impact on his initial followers. None of the prevailing options for first-century Jews proved satisfying to people who were spiritually hungry. The Sadducees, the most exclusive and elitist religious-political party, enjoyed more favor with Rome than with the people at large. They mostly promoted a civil religion centered around Temple services. The Sadducees' religious beliefs allowed little credence for the supernatural. Spiritual vitality proved a lesser passion than gaining material wealth and political influence. The Sadduccees' party collapsed with the destruction of Jerusalem and the Temple in A.D. 70.

The Essenes, another religious group in first-century Judaism, viewed the traditional and institutional Judaism of the Sadducees and Pharisees as irredeemably corrupt. The Essenes' monastic, communal approach made their movement limited in its appeal to common people. However, their eschatological teachings probably raised the level of discontent with contemporary Jewish leadership and created a climate for a spiritual renewal apart from institutional Judaism. The Essene community was short-lived.

The Pharisees had advanced several key ideas that promised spiritual fulfillment. However, in their hands, these ideas had soured. By the time Jesus entered the scene, the Pharisees had alienated most people from being included in their group or from being able to enjoy the prospects of participating in the kingdom of God when the Messiah came. Keeping Sabbath ordinances constituted the litmus test for earning divine favor. Those who did not have the education in the law that the Pharisees and scribes enjoyed did not have much chance of winning God's approval. The Pharisees' elitism, along with the accompanying sociological cocooning they practiced, characterized the synagogue leadership of Jesus' day.

The Jews had given the world a major religious contribution, a monotheism that offered humans a chance to enjoy two extraordinary relationships. One was community with one another by virtue of every person's being created in the image of God. The other was the privilege of being in a covenant relationship with the God of all creation. This covenant carried with it the responsibility of sharing Yahweh with the rest of the world, so that others could also establish a relationship with him. Israel received this mission at Sinai when Moses delivered the law to them. Throughout their history, the prophets had thundered this message time and time again. God intended to bless the whole world through his covenant people. However, Israel tended to neglect an inclusivist strategy in favor of an exclusivist one. They preferred to keep Yahweh to themselves.

The missional aspect of Judaism suffered from neglect in the years preceding Jesus' arrival. The Sadducees had tied their fortunes to political favor with Rome. The Essenes had devised an exit strategy from the current age based on an end-of-the-world scenario. The Pharisees had reduced the faith to lifeless legalism.

Jesus reacted against this bankrupt religious culture. He tapped into people's aspirations for a personal relationship with God. He again called attention to Israel's mission by his vision of an expanding kingdom of God. In truth, he led a revolt against misrepresentations of God's heart as taught by the religious authorities of his day.

The drama of Jesus' life played on a set carefully laid out for the unique intersection of divine and human. Both the opportunities and the challenges he faced were partially shaped by the cultural milieu of the first-century world. Jesus' heart would be fashioned by his response to his culture, in what he accepted as well as what he rejected.

Growing Up as God

God could have sent a full-blown adult to be the savior of the world. Instead, the Son of God entered history inside a tiny human frame bound by time, space, and a baby's survival needs. By placing his son in a family, having him progress developmentally as a human child, giving him opportunities to engage in business dealings with people and be on the receiving end of contemporary Jewish religious instruction, God ensured that Jesus would be shaped by community and the commonplace. In short, Jesus would come to the realization of his divinity through the ordinary routines of commonplace human experiences.

At some point, Mary and Joseph told Jesus of his very special arrival. One wonders how many times he must have asked his parents to retell the stories of his birth, exactly what the angels said, what the wise men did. These questions had to be followed by hours of conversation between the child and his earthly parents. Even though we are not told of these, we would be misguided to assume that Jesus was left on his own to figure out who he was. He obviously had made significant progress by the time of the episode at the Temple at age twelve. Mary and Joseph's frantic search revealed that Jesus seemed quite at home in his Father's house, already aware of his unique relationship with the God of Israel.

The youngster from Nazareth, able to spellbind the teachers as a youth, would grow up to be their nemesis. One gets the feeling that this early sparring match served as a key developmental episode in Mary's mind, as she later recalled the scene to Luke so vividly. Jesus' relationship to his earthly parents probably shifted after that occasion, though he remained obedient to them.

As the oldest boy in the family, Jesus trained in his father's work. Carpenters in that society were skilled tradesmen who built houses and fitted oxen for their yoke. Carpenters helped translate ideas and hopes into concrete expression, whether it was creating living space or facilitating work in the fields. Their work involved them in people's lives in order to connect with their physical needs.

Jesus learned a lot about people as he watched them in his father's shop, and as he visited their homes and fields. He saw how they treated the land and how they treated one another. He witnessed their business dealings. He listened to their heart hopes. He haggled prices with them, and had to collect on bad debts. He learned how to judge character. At some point, Jesus took over the family business. He assumed leadership in his home by providing for his mother and younger siblings. The concerns about meeting basic life necessities played an important role in sensitizing Jesus to the life concerns of people.

God's choice of the commonplace as the schoolroom for the spiritual development of his incarnate Son sent a powerful message through Jesus. God did not belong just to the educated few, the learned theologians, or the informed lawyers. He belonged to the people who hammered, fished, and farmed.

Jesus' teachings reflected his common upbringing. He connected with common people because he drew from the commonplace in revealing what God is like. While the scribes and teachers of the law continued creating volumes of commentary on Old Testament texts about God, Jesus related stories about farmers, builders, and fishermen. He revealed a God who is a farmer fervently sowing the seed of truth. He taught about God the vineyard owner, who prunes those he loves in order to encourage their growth. He painted the picture of God as a father preparing a room for his son who is to be married. God numbers hairs on heads, keeps up with sparrows, and dresses lilies in blooms. Jesus' hearers immediately connected with his teaching.

Jesus also watched the people laboring under the heavy religious burdens imposed on them by the religious rulers. The Pharisees browbeat the people about Sabbath, and the Sadducees took advantage of them when they went to Jerusalem on the feast days to offer their sacrifices. More in touch with ordinary life than the elite religious leaders, Jesus himself felt the pressure they put on common people for their institutional religious concerns. He came to see the spiritual bankruptcy of their approaches to religious leadership.

Luke summed up these early years of Jesus with Mary's simple remembrance that her firstborn son grew in "wisdom and stature, and in favor with God and men" (Luke 2:52). The fact that Jesus grew in favor with people signals that he mastered the basic relationship skills that lie at the heart of leadership effectiveness.

The initial task for all leaders is the building of basic human relationship skills. Abrasive leaders who bully, cajole, intimidate, and manipulate have missed the basic competencies that qualify them for effective spiritual leadership. All leaders must take inventory of the stock of their people skills. Effectiveness hangs on it. Sometimes people who try to live out great dreams, convinced of significant calls on their lives, stumble out of the starting block, tripping over this fundamental deficiency. A lack of people skills can be overcome, but not without acute awareness and accountability to a relationship skills coach.

Jesus also grew in his relationship with the Father. His desire to be about his Father's business matured for over a decade and a half between the Temple incident and the public baptism. Jesus patiently waited until the right time to begin his public ministry. He certainly had access to miraculous powers earlier than age thirty, yet he apparently did not evidence this to his family or the townspeople. His mother and siblings came to fetch him shortly after he began preaching, still not clear about who he was. This would hardly have been the case had Jesus grown up performing miracles. When he made his one-time return visit to Nazareth, the locals registered disappointment at his lack of miracle working in their midst. Both episodes reveal that Jesus listened to the Father, obediently waiting for the signal to enter the world stage. He obviously did not debut prematurely.

This dynamic of divine deliberateness has consistently turned up in all the lives of the biblical heroes in our investigation. The leader's life mission is not rushed. Moses' hopes to facilitate the redemption of his kinsmen are delayed for a forty-year stint as nomadic shepherd. David waits for years for the realization of his boyhood anointing as king. Paul's meteoric rise in Pharisaic Judaism did not set the pace for his leadership ascendance in Christianity. In each case, God had work to do—sometimes in the leader's world, always in the leader's heart. These biblical leaders cooperated with the divine timetable. They did not do so with sure knowledge that they were leaders-in-waiting (with the exception of Jesus). They did not practice patience because they knew the rest of the story. They developed a heart discipline of obedience to God that made them particularly effective as spiritual leaders under his supervision.

I Can See Clearly Now

Jesus left his father's business in order to pursue his Father's business. Jesus' act of obedience to submit to John's baptism set in motion an intense period of call clarification. Jesus had sealed his special relationship with the Father (a fact confirmed by the heavenly voice and anointing with the Spirit). Now the time had come to seal his mission.

The Spirit immediately whisked Jesus away from the public eye. The Judaean wilderness served as the backdrop for the most intense call crystallization in all history. Going in, Jesus knew he was called to be on a redemptive mission. He emerged with an unmistakable and unshakable comprehension of the mission's price.

Up until now, in his personal development, Jesus had been coming to grips with his being divine. Now he had to come to grips with being human. The temptation episode provides a clue to the struggle that Jesus would have from that point on through Calvary. Would Jesus' humanity survive the test? Would he misuse divine power for personal needs (turn stones into bread)? Would he arbitrarily use miracles for self-serving ends (leap from the Temple)? Would he compromise his mission to escape the pain of torture and death (acknowledge Satan's rule and bypass Calvary)?

The timing of these temptations was not accidental. They came at the end of fasting and praying. They were the final exam, once Jesus had grasped completely the challenge of being God's Messiah. In each case, the devil offered to Jesus a substitute, a shortcut way to accomplish the mission without enduring the cross. Jesus was urged to use his power in his own service, rather than to depend on the Father's provision. He was given the chance to gain public notoriety short of serving others. He was offered kingship without personal sacrifice.

Preachers for centuries have noted that Jesus' replies to Satan used the words of the Father. "It is written" were insights that emerged out of communion. Jesus had been with the Father when these words were originally spoken to previous Hebrew leaders in previous centuries. Jesus recalled this communion with the Father when he faced temptation. Recalling and respeaking ancient truths bolstered Jesus' resolve. His memory of past communion, reminding him of his divine origin, also preserved his humanity.

Jesus passed the test in the wilderness. The Father immediately dispatched angels to minister to him as affirmation. The temptations constituted the enemy's best shot since the Garden to sink humanity. Satan lost. We won.

The temptations, trials, and testings that spiritual leaders face always challenge their call. Moses faced obscurity and anger; David confronted abusive power in Saul and in himself; Paul wrestled with pride. They did not always win, but they passed the test often enough to gain their place of leadership in biblical history.

No one can calculate how many would-be leaders go down in the wilderness. The leader cannot advance to the next level without passing the entrance exam—the call clarification. The leader cannot emerge from the wilderness until this challenge is met. God is patient in the wilderness. He uses the experience to sculpt the leader's heart. We see the wilderness as something to avoid or to spend as little time in as possible. Ask Moses about spending forty years there. We expect God to pave for us a road to public acclaim. Ask David about being driven into the outback. We believe academic training will route us around the wilderness and graduate us into ministry leadership. Ask Paul about the school of the desert. Some of the wilderness testings will show the face of the devil. Ask Jesus. This remains a profound mystery. God uses wilderness trials, even the devil's wiles, as tools in his heart surgery.

Jesus returned from the wilderness with unswerving intentionality. He knew what his mission was and what it was going to take to accomplish it. From this point on, every action, every decision, was evaluated against the yardstick of the call.

A couple of examples from Jesus' life prove this point dramatically. Early in his ministry, crowds swelled around Jesus, curious about his teaching and hungry for his miracles. One morning, Jesus found a bit of solitude in order to commune with the Father. Peter and the other disciples found him. "Everyone is looking for you!" they exclaimed. Jesus surely astounded the disciples with his response: "Let us go somewhere else—to the nearby villages—so I can preach there also. *That is why I have come*" (Mark 1:36, emphasis added).

Many Christian leaders thrill to hear, "Everyone is looking for you!" Living for the crowd, they die to their mission. Living only for the crowd eventually leaves them emotionally burned-out and empty. Intentionality often yields to the first demands placed on them by those in their ministry constituency. If this dynamic goes unchecked, the lack of focus eventually bankrupts early dreams. Bewildered and broken, spent leaders end up never accomplishing the great task of their life calling. They may claim that their failure is due to having too large a heart for people. This is a self-delusion. The problem is not having a heart *large enough* for God. By not developing the discipline of saying no to some needs that would claim them (and other distractions), they could not say yes to the mission of God's call. Leaders must learn what they can say no to as part of maturing in ordering their life to the voice of God. This tension between human need and divine assignment constitutes a major heart-shaping dynamic.

A second episode demonstrated Jesus' focus. One day Jesus was teaching inside a packed house when his mother and younger siblings showed up. They had come to "take charge of him" (Mark 3:21) because they thought he had gone mad. They sent for him, interrupting his ministry. Jesus chose the opportunity to establish a clear boundary for them and for himself. He refused to go with them. This was not an act to sever ties. However, the family relationship now had to serve the mission in a different way. Jesus' response did not damage his family of origin or nullify his connection with his original community. He later returned to Nazareth for a brief visit (an unpleasant one, as it turned out). Jesus' mother proved faithful to him to the end. His brothers and sisters became members and leaders in the early church.

Without absolute intentionality, Jesus' power and person easily could have been used to serve lesser missions than the one he came to understand

in the Judaean wilderness. None of us can comprehend the challenges he
faced on this score. For instance, he could have spent all his energy in
healing. The more people he touched the more would have been physically restored. His popularity would have soared. Yet he knew that crowd
approval constituted a false measurement of his effectiveness.

Every spiritual leader operates with some decision-making matrix. The
most effective learn to say no sometimes when others push them to say
yes. They are willing to order their life around their calling. The great
temptation and debilitator for many Christian ministers is not moral failure, but compass failure. With no clear call signal constantly guiding
them, they dissipate their energies in lots of activity that does not further
the missional agenda of their call from God. Ministry focus proves particularly challenging when ministry constituents feel as if they "own" the
leader and the leader's services. The most effective spiritual leaders maintain appropriate boundaries with their ministry "family" so they can perform the agenda of their divine call.

As the recipients of his ministry legacy, we were all counting on Jesus
to stay with his call. There are people counting on every leader to do the
same. They usually are not on hand when the leader has to make the
tough call. The effective leader, like Jesus, has to keep a clear view of a
future that will come about only by being faithful to the Father's call.

Leader of the Band

Jesus' original family provided him with community. Father, Son, and
Spirit have lived in eternal relationship with one another. The Christian
doctrine of the Trinity reveals a profound truth, that at the center of the
universe is a God who lives in relationship. This is why love abides. God
is love. He exists in loving community.

Being created in the image of God means, in part, that we have been
prewired by God to hunger for community. Human beings come to discover who we are only in relationship to others. All of us since Adam have
been born into a relationship web. Our species cannot raise ourselves; we
are dependent on others for our very survival from the moment of our
conception.

From eternity past, Jesus had done his work in community. He decided
to do his work in time and space on earth in community. He called twelve
men to himself. Not only did Jesus shape that early community, but he
also was shaped by them. Had this not been the case, the first disciple
group would not have been a true community. It would have been part of

a staged play, with the disciples' role being that of providing mere stage props for the drama of Jesus' life.

The teacher from Nazareth and his band of disciples developed into a learning community. They could question one another's biases and prejudices and tease out one another's thinking and ideas. This heart-shaping process took place in the context of a nonjudgmental environment. The community provided enough security for these men to share their hearts without fear of being rejected or cast away. Jesus as leader established these ground rules, just as leaders always determine the level of community that can occur around them. In Jesus' community, truth acted in love. This combination remains the recipe for an outbreak of genuine community in all leadership constellations.

A few excerpts from the gospel accounts demonstrate the disciples' learning community in operation. After exposing them to his teaching and healing ministry, Jesus sent the disciples out on their own. First, the twelve went out (Luke 9:1–6) and later seventy-two others (Luke 10:1–24). In their pre-mission briefing, Jesus gave them the parameters of their mission and instructions about carrying it out. When they returned, he pulled them aside for a debriefing of their ministry experiences. He would often end a day of teaching by privately rehearsing the meaning of the parables he told to the crowds following him.

Jesus as learning coach often challenged the actions and attitudes of his disciples. He quizzed the group once about a dispute they had had during their travel day. Greeted only with sheepish looks, Jesus addressed their concern about who should be greatest in the kingdom of heaven. He used a child as a teaching prop (Mark 9:33–37). When the disciples tried once to send the children away from Jesus, he was indignant and told them so (Mark 10:13–16). The night before he was crucified, Jesus gave the disciples a lesson in servanthood they would never forget. When no one else was willing to do so, Jesus commandeered basin and towel to wash the feet of his followers (John 13:1–17). The lesson stuck. The early Christian community adopted Jesus' posture with one another and even toward those who persecuted them. This remarkable phenomenon demonstrates the power of learning in community. Such learning changes behavior.

Jesus' band of followers also shaped him. He tried out all his lessons and teachings on the twelve, who served as a microcosm of those he addressed. They reminded him of the enormous challenges that he faced in overcoming the false religion of first-century Judaism. Each of them had been taught by the Pharisees. The racial prejudice, the doctrinal dogma, the legalism, and the sociological cocooning that permeated the Pharisees' religion framed the world for Jesus' disciples. Jesus had difficulty getting his disciples to open their eyes and see the harvest potential (John 4:35), because they had grown up in church (the synagogue)! They had been taught to focus in, not out. They had not contemplated engaging the Samaritans, for example; they had been schooled to avoid them. They heard Jesus' teaching about the kingdom of God through the filters of the myopic vision of first-century Judaism. Even at the Ascension, the disciples asked him, "Lord are you at this time going to restore the kingdom to Israel?" (Acts 1:6).

The disciples also served as a feedback loop for Jesus. After a day of teaching. he quizzed them. Through their own understanding, he could check out how his messages were coming across to others. Jesus wanted to know what people were taking away from his ministry. His great questions, "Who do people say the Son of Man is?" "But what about you?" "Who do you say I am?" (Matt. 16:13–15), cannot be reduced to rhetorical status, designed just to prompt discussion. Jesus genuinely sought out from his learning community the public perception about him and what they themselves thought about him.

This ministry community that Jesus called to himself provided for him a learning curve for redemptive activity. What Jesus did for all humanity, he initially did for that small group of disciples. He shepherded them, attended to their needs, answered their questions, and stirred their ambitions for a better world. He harbored a thief and a skeptic. One would turn on him and sell him out, despite Jesus' best efforts to reach him with love. Still Jesus loved Judas, just as he loves all since who have betrayed him. Jesus' heart for all of us, in part, was developed among the initial followers.

The Bethany Trio

Jesus needed friends who could nurture him. It is no accident that Jesus spent his last weekend before the onset of Passion Week in the home of his good friends Mary, Martha, and Lazarus.

We know little about this intriguing brother-and-sisters team. They apparently had some money. They were significant citizens of Bethany, a village in close proximity to Jerusalem. As a well-to-do family, they would be well connected with local political-religious leaders. And for whatever reason, they were one of the first of the upper social class to follow Jesus. They provided him a place to stay on his infrequent visits to Jerusalem. Certainly they contributed to his ministry treasury. But, and most especially, they just seemed to have a special love for Jesus.

He loved them too. Jesus' obvious affection for this family made his response to the news of Lazarus's impending death a source of curiosity for his disciples. Only later would they understand that Jesus had reserved a very special miracle for perhaps his best friend. At Lazarus's tomb, Jesus wept. His grief was not occasioned merely by the disbelief of the Jews. Jesus registered in his heart the pain of his good friends. Seeing Mary and Martha in mourning moved him to tears, to lament the sting of the enemy of death, an enemy he was growing more familiar with as he himself prepared for Calvary.

The joy of Lazarus's resurrection probably sustained Jesus through some of the pain Jesus anticipated about his own death. The sight of his friend's emergence from the tomb burned into his own mind. Perhaps Jesus recalled that image while on the cross to give him the power to go through the incomprehensible agony of that experience. The reunion banquet in Lazarus's home after Jesus' miracle—the family being together again with Jesus in attendance—foreshadowed the reunion the savior would make possible for many through his death on the cross. As he witnessed the joy of that occasion in Bethany, surely Jesus' mind raced forward to anticipate a much larger banquet with many more in attendance where he would again be the guest of honor.

The Bethany trio provided Jesus friendship. They served as a community of love and acceptance that allowed him to experience what he was providing for others. They strengthened his heart for the work of his calling.

In Jesus, we find reassurance of the eternal value of community. What he experienced with the Father and Spirit, he also developed in his earthly life and ministry. Christian leaders can draw hope from Jesus' attitudes and actions in this regard. Even with the imperfections of all human community, Jesus sought it out and believed in its power to support and change lives. Jesus teaches leaders that community-making is worth the effort, despite its frustrations and disappointments. It serves as one major arena of heart-shaping dynamics for spiritual leaders.

Online with the Father

With appropriate reverence, we open the door to enter the world of Jesus' communion with the Father. After all, these conversations involve the highest levels of authority in the universe. The whispers between Father and Son affect the fate of billions. Some exchanges between them took place before time. During the earth mission, the dialogue involved brand new concerns that were introduced by the sacrifice and miracle of incarnation. Divine communion became challenged by human nature. The Father constantly shaped the Son's earthly experience, including his life and ministry development.

We can enter into this arena only because we have been invited. Jesus deliberately allowed his disciples access to this dynamic exchange between him and the Father for their learnings. They became so intrigued with Jesus' communion that they implored him, "Teach us to pray!" (Luke 11:1). It was not as if they had never prayed themselves. They had grown up in the synagogue and had attended feast days at the Temple in Jerusalem. They had just never seen anyone pray like Jesus did. He would sometimes pray through the night. He would pray before and after big events. He would pray as he walked. He would hike up into the mountains to be alone with the Father. He would commune in worship at the synagogue. In short, Jesus was constantly online with the Father.

With the power Jesus had to influence any situation of his choosing, with all of the needs tugging at him, the Son needed direction. He got it from his constant communion with the Father, who was clearly in charge of the mission. No more telling insight of this dynamic can be found than in the words Jesus spoke to his detractors to explain his actions: "I tell you the truth, the Son can do nothing by himself; he can do only what he sees his Father doing, because whatever the Father does the Son also does. For the Father loves the Son and shows him all he does" (John 15:19–20a).

The link between Father and Son provided a seamless interface to accomplish the work of God during the days of incarnation.

The garden of Gethsemane episode proved, among other things, that this communion did not constitute a mindless march to the Father's drum on the part of the Son. In the agony of what faced him, Jesus raised the possibility of mission redefinition. This kind of interaction probably typified the exchange between Father and Son. However, in each case, including the Gethsemane experience, the Son yielded to the Father's will. In perfect obedience, he committed his will to accomplish his Father's designs. "Shall I not drink the cup the Father has given me?" (John 18:11). Jesus told Peter when he scolded Peter for wielding a sword against Jesus' arresting party.

Jesus could submit to the Father's will for one reason: he knew the Father loved him completely. Willing submission grows out of a secure relationship grounded in love. This theme permeates the exchanges between the two. Their love relationship had been published at the public revelation of Jesus' identity at his baptism. In an audible voice from heaven, the

Father blessed the Son: "You are my Son, whom I love; with you I am well pleased" (Mark 1:11). On the strength of that affirmation, Jesus went into the wilderness, where he would receive an excruciating set of instructions from his Father. When Jesus confided to his disciples on the Mount of Transfiguration that he would be killed, thus publicly confirming the Father's plan, he again received affirmation. The disciples heard a voice: "This is my Son, whom I love; with him I am well pleased" (Matt. 17:5). From that moment, Jesus descended the mountain from his meeting with Moses and Elijah to turn his face toward Jerusalem and Calvary.

On the eve of Jesus' crucifixion, the Father again nurtured the Son through communion. The Father reminded the Son of what was to come, so that he could endure the trials of the moment. Jesus remembered his place in the universe: "And now, Father, glorify me in your presence with the glory I had with you before the world began" (John 17:5). In coming to earth, Jesus had yielded up his shared glory. He now anticipated its restoration: "I am coming to you now" (John 17:11, 13). Jesus acquiesced to the Father's plan in order to obtain the reward he sought: "Father, I want those you have given me to be with me where I am, and to see my glory, the glory you have given me because you loved me before the creation of the world" (John 17:24). That request would be granted in only one way. Jesus got up from communion with the Father to face the devil.

Pentecost granted online capability to connect with God to all believers. The event completed the network connection. The Spirit linked believers to the Son who is connected to the Father. Jesus told his followers that when the Spirit came, he would remind them of all Jesus had taught them. He also promised them that the Spirit would enable them to remain constantly connected to him. By abiding in him, Jesus' disciples of all ages can access his thoughts and will about life situations.

Christian leaders who stay online with Jesus are shaped by the heart of God. However, those who go offline miss the information shared along the network channel. Modern spiritual leaders can be guided in their lives and ministries in the same way that the Son was shepherded through his earthly ministry by the Father. Just as the communion between Father and Son shaped the destiny of all humanity, it can shape the destiny of one.

Nobody Knows the Troubles I've Seen

Nobody knows, that is, except Jesus. He has seen plenty. His life mission brought him head-on into conflict. As a baby, he was hunted to be killed. The beginning of his public ministry involved squaring off with Satan in the Judaean wilderness. Demons shrieked at his presence. He incurred the wrath of the religious establishment. His detractors screamed for Jesus' blood, and in the end, they got it. Bring up the background music from the movie on Jesus' life and ministry. It will not be elevator music much of the time.

Jesus' conflict pitted him against three major enemies—sin, Satan, and the flesh-and-blood enemies of God.

Sin

Most discussion of *sin* in American evangelical circles gets tangled up in morality. The talk centers on *sins*. This predisposition gets ingrained early in evangelicals' lives. In trying to convince children and youth of their need for redemption, many spiritual guides focus on getting them "lost." This is usually accomplished by helping the potential converts admit to having committed sins, a catalogue of their wrongful deeds and attitudes.

Sins certainly have a relationship to sin, and people do stand in need of redemption. But the core issue of Jesus' trek to Calvary is sin, not simply moral behavior, doctrinal purity, or politically correct positions on certain key social problems.

Sin is the propensity for humans to live as if they are God. Sin is the decision to live life away from God rather than toward him. This decision can be subtle or blatant. It involves a contest of wills between humans and God. It is the oldest contest in the world, the pride of life, the saying yes to the temptation to live as if we humans are not accountable for our lives moment by moment to our Maker. Sin is the failure to surrender life, moment by moment, to the rule of God. We sin when we place *ourselves* in charge of our lives.

Morally circumspect people can often be blind to their own sin. This was the condition of the Pharisees. Declaring a certain set of behavioral benchmarks as the test, they passed with flying colors. Religious zealots are often the most sinful of all people. They claim to be close to God, although in effect they have sought to accomplish something only God can do—redeem themselves through their own performance.

Morally depraved people suffer the result of their sin too. They are not able, apart from an admission of guilt, to gain redemption on their own. Their being sorry for the consequences of their sin in and of itself does not commend them to God. Only the act of willful abandonment to any claim of being in charge of their own lives releases them to enjoy God's forgiveness and experience reconciliation with him.

The Scripture teaches that since the Garden, we humans cannot help ourselves. We will to some degree declare ourselves to be God. We corrupt the image of God, the Godlike power to choose, by acting on it inappropriately. We choose to curse rather than to bless. We choose to be selfish rather than to share. We choose to exert power over people rather than to serve them. On and on the list goes. Unlike God, who used his Godness to our benefit, we do not exercise our Godlikeness with the same lack of self-serving. We grab for what is already ours. In clamoring for the throne, we depose the rightful king of our lives. Seeking to actualize our lives, we die. This was and is the persistent paradox of human existence.

Jesus faced the same temptation that every human has faced. Not only did his divine nature not protect him from temptation, but it actually complicated his situation. He surely had ranges of choices available to him that we have never dreamed of and that could have been used in his own self-interest. He chose against sin. His willful disuse of divine power on his own behalf is demonstrated by the fact that he used it to heal and to serve others. In the wilderness trial, he refused to turn stones into bread to feed his own hunger. On the cross, he chose not to save himself as his tormentors suggested. To have done so would have been yielding to sin. In proving himself to be God, he would have lost his humanity. This is precisely what every other human being has done. Trying to be God, we lose humanness.

By his sinless life, Jesus proved that humanity's final definition does not lie in its sin. Jesus defeated sin by refusing it. When he conquered sin, he overcame its child—death. Centuries earlier, God had declared to Adam that to join with sin made one pregnant with death. Jesus removed sin's capacity to carry death to full term in every person.

Jesus' conflict with sin reveals something of the heart of God. It proves that God's disposition toward humanity is beneficent. Instead of leaving humans to suffer the consequences of sinful death, God comes as liberator and redeemer. Jesus *became* sin, the scriptures say. This means that he took its full venom. Sin now holds no ability to erect a tombstone over humankind. Its back has been broken. Humanity won over sin and death through Jesus, who chose to be fully human.

Battling Satan

Another of Jesus' prominent conflicts pitted him against Satan, or the devil. The Hebrew scriptures link the entrance of sin into the human condition with some coaching on the part of Satan. However, never do they suggest that humans can blame Satan for their own sin. The second Adam (Jesus) also faced Satan's temptations. Had Jesus yielded, a colossal fall would once again have barred humans from paradise.

Satan's interest in Jesus stemmed from the fact that Jesus was scoring big gains in Satan's territory. Jesus had invaded Satan's kingdom. The kingdom of light was making advances against the kingdom of darkness. When Jesus healed people and set them free, he pried them from Satan's grasp. When he set them free from lies, bigotry, pride, and so forth, he lessened the clutches of evil on people's hearts.

This shift in the balance of power accounted for the screaming of the demons. The rules of the game were changing. Satan's minions knew perfectly well who Jesus was. If the religious leaders did not believe Jesus' claims, there was no shortage of belief among the evil powers that he met head on.

Satan knew that the new movement of God rose and fell on Jesus. He had to be stopped. During his trials, Jesus surely caught a glimpse of Satan whispering in the ears of Pontius Pilate and Herod. The devil had children that sat on the Sanhedrin (Jesus did call the Pharisees children of the father of lies). And certainly Satan moved among the crowd to incite them to scream at the right moment, "Away with this man! Release Barrabas to us!" (Luke 23:18).

Every hammer blow on Golgotha brought a scream of glee from Jesus' archenemy. Even Jesus' shout "It is finished!" (John 19:30) may well have been greeted with delight by the devils in hell. If so, the evil minions may have miscalculated the situation. Though Jesus' adversary was powerful and crafty, he was not omniscient. Perhaps Satan was the most surprised creature in the universe on Resurrection Day!

Jesus' conflict with Satan demonstrated God's determination not only to overcome sin but also to limit the spread of evil in his created universe. Jesus proved that evil loses. God and good win.

Human Enemies of God

Jesus also battled some flesh-and-blood enemies. The cast of antagonists commenced with Herod the Great, who was threatened at the news of Jesus' birth. However, a later boyhood experience introduced the group that would give Jesus the greatest trouble—the Pharisees. His energetic discussion with the teachers of the law during his Temple visit at age twelve escalated into a public battle in his years of public ministry.

Jesus' harshest words were reserved for the Pharisees. The Pharisaism of the first century proved odious to him. Judgmental, haughty, legalistic, nationalistic, mercenary, power hungry, religiously fanatical but spiritually dead, these characteristics described the leaders parading as representatives of his Father. In fact, Jesus said that they did not even know God, but were children of the devil. Jesus' flagrant violations of the Pharisees' Sabbath laws and purity codes challenged their legalism. He debunked their teaching in most of his sermons. He healed people on the Sabbath right in the synagogue, the seat of Pharisee power. Jesus criticized Pharisee customs and character ("Do not pray as the Pharisees do"). He denounced them as fakes and cursed them seven times as his last public statement ("Woe to you!" Matt. 23:1–39), saying that even cursed publicans and prostitutes got a better hearing with God than they (Matt. 21:31–32).

The conflict between Jesus and other religious leaders of his day demonstrated some significant truths about the heart of God. First, it signaled that God is interested more in relationship than in mere religious observance. Second, God is on a redemptive mission, and those who do not join him disqualify themselves as his true followers. Third, God's basic disposition toward human beings is more informed by love than by law. Fourth, the kingdom of God will not be ushered in by people being good. The gospel is not about being good. It is about grace. People enter the kingdom of God when their hearts are captured by the heart of God. Then, transformed from the inside out, they become salt and light to help the world taste and see that God is good.

Jesus still does battle with religious authorities. Spiritual leaders who believe that the kingdom of God will be established if people will just behave (believe right, dress right, act right, vote right) keep alive the spirit of the Pharisees. Those who attempt to gain or maintain spiritual influence by relying on political clout or social props are disciples of those Jesus despised, no matter how zealous they may be. Spiritual leaders would do well to study Jesus' conflict with the religious establishment of Judaism. Otherwise, like a very famous Pharisee, they may one day be shocked to hear from him, "Why are you persecuting me?" (Acts 9:4).

Jesus was not spared the heart-shaping work that God intends for all his leaders. From eternity past, the heart of the Son was molded for his mission. From the moment of miraculous conception to his ascension, every detail of his earthly life was superintended in order to fashion the heart of the Father in him.

Jesus provides us with the greatest look into the heart of God. Those who want to know what God is like find in him their best answers. "Anyone who has seen me has seen the Father," (John 14:9) he said to his disciples on the eve of his crucifixion. From him, we learn that God is love, that he has chosen to send a redeemer not because he is ticked off with the world but because he is moved with compassion. We learn from Jesus that the heart of God is big, eager to welcome others into relationship with him. And we learn that the heart of God breaks, for he ruptured it for us on the cross. Wonderfully, we also discover that the heart of God is hopeful, for he eagerly anticipates all his children coming home.

PART TWO

RECOGNIZING GOD'S SHAPING WORK IN OUR OWN LIVES

THE INVESTIGATION OF divine heart-shaping in the lives of four remarkable biblical leaders in Part One uncovered some discernible markers of God's efforts. These discoveries prompt our inquiry into God's continuing heart-sculpting of contemporary spiritual leaders.

The leader's life story is informed by six major subplots that God develops throughout the leader's life. They are *culture, call, community, communion, conflict,* and the *commonplace.* No single one of these explains the leader's heart development, nor do they stand alone. Though distinguishable for analysis, each of these six story lines intersects and conspires with the other subplots to fashion the life drama of the spiritual leader. At certain times in the leader's life, the development of one or more of these story lines becomes more apparent than the others. Yet, in the end, each plays a crucial role in the work of heart that defines the leader and the leadership legacy.

5

CULTURE

MEETING THE WORLD

THE DISCUSSION OF CULTURE in religious literature frequently focuses on the need for transforming it. Culture is something to overcome if not downright avoid. In this vein, culture represents the world system as apart from God, the kingdom of human existence acting as a kind of antimatter to God's rule. Culture carries a negative connotation. To be fair, the biblical witness does speak of spiritual realities that are anti-Christ. The "world" stands for the realm that does not acknowledge Jesus as Lord, and the spiritual leader should indeed be careful not to become unduly influenced by it.

Culture also serves God's purposes. He uses it to shape the hearts of spiritual leaders. This means that culture can be appreciated and studied for its contributions as a heart-shaping drama in the leader's life story. Our curiosity about culture proceeds from this point of inquiry.

We are not born into a vacuum. We enter the world into a stream of the human family and human experience. Language, race, geography, demography, and economic status all influence and shape the world we live in and define our connectedness to it and our distinctiveness from it. We depend on culture to give us a beginning point in understanding ourselves. It delivers to us necessary ingredients for life development—language, history, intellectual and philosophical predispositions, worldview, as well as prejudices, varying levels of xenophobia, and difficulties in communicating with and understanding other cultures. We breathe the culture through our minds and psyches, as we breathe the air through our lungs.

The Almighty sovereignly decides where and when our lives become a part of human history. We enter a story already under way, because culture is the story of a particular time and people. For the purpose of our discussion, the term *culture* will stand as a shorthand for all environmental forces that influence the leader. These include the historical period, prevailing societal values, political concerns, and faith community experiences. These all form the backdrop against which we live out our lives. The cultures into which we are born, in which we develop, and in which we carry out our life mission (all of which can be different cultures) profoundly affect who we are and who we become.

God shapes the leader's heart through culture. The life stories of Moses, David, Paul, and Jesus show how God used cultural factors to prepare them for their life assignments. Yahweh providentially arranged for Moses to grow up the child of both Egyptian and Hebrew cultures. Then, at a critical period, he introduced Midianite culture to Moses as a graduate degree program to prepare the leader of the Exodus. David absorbed the heart cry of his people to experience stable national leadership and to be free from Philistine threat. Paul's shaping as the premier Christian missionary included Jewish, Roman, and Greek cultural conditioning. Jesus shared the cultural influences of his fellow countrymen under the bondage of Pharisaic Judaism. The lives of these biblical heroes cannot be understood apart from their cultural context.

Nor can ours. We are in part products of cultural forces. Our self-understanding remains incomplete without identifying and reckoning with these.

But we are also more than products of culture. The development of the leader's heart also affects the leader's culture. The four biblical case studies prove this point. Moses set in motion the Exodus and the subsequent demise of the Hebrew slave culture. David extended Israel's borders and presided over the rise of a true nation. Paul shaped the early Christian movement to be cross-cultural. Jesus revolutionized the concept of God and changed the world.

Spiritual leaders exercise a significant stewardship in their response to culture. Through their choices, they instruct those they lead. What they accept, their followers accept. What they reject, others do too. What they change casts their shadow, through others, through history. This responsibility is particularly challenging for today's leaders. Gargantuan struggles result from the clash of colliding cultures. The world as we have known it for the last several centuries is giving way to . . . we do not know what.

This discussion will not dwell on the decline of a Christian worldview in Western civilization. Those looking for culture bashing will need to look elsewhere. Those who view culture as an automatic evil to be avoided or overcome will find no support for this view in these pages.

However, spiritual leaders who feel they should somehow connect with culture, who choose to engage the culture despite its shortcomings and different values, will find some encouragement here. Those who feel commissioned to influence culture rather than to insulate against it will find affirmation for their approach here.

Understanding the role of culture in the heart-shaping process involves more complex analysis than merely treating the culture as something outside the leader to be accepted or rejected. It also involves learning to appreciate the gifts of culture as one of the forces God has used and continues to use in forming the leader. Ultimately, leaders integrate these insights into their life mission.

This integration occurs through the work of culture in:

- Forming leaders
- Confronting leaders
- Challenging leaders to connect the culture that has formed them with the culture that confronts them, without shutting down

These activities can be restated as a series of heart tasks. These three tasks, or inquiries, form the outline for this discussion of the interface between culture and the leader's heart. The heart's tasks for leaders in relation to culture are:

- Knowing where you come from
- Knowing where you stand
- Knowing where you want to go and take others with you

The leader who is willing to work through these tasks can lead with an open heart. An open heart adopts the presupposition that God works in each culture and wants to use the leader as a transformation agent. With the opposite approach, the leader shuts down. This occurs when leaders refuse to integrate cultural insights into their own life experience and adopt a "hunker-down" mode of dealing with what is going on around them.

God shapes the leader's heart in order to amplify his own heart through the leader. Once captured by God's heart, the leader is positioned to share God's heart with God's people. This divine intention is nowhere more apparent than in the way God uses culture as a method of heart sculpting. The intended outcome of this discussion is that you as a leader treat culture as a gift and lead those you influence to missionally interface with culture.

This attitude can be realized only if the heart has done its work in assessing the three inquiries we have identified.

Knowing Where You Come From

Henry wonders why he struggles with his current ministry assignment. The first part of the answer lies in the fact that Henry has never reckoned with where he has come from. Henry grew up in a rural county in an area long settled and inhabited by his forebears. His first pastorate, in a town close to home, was a smashing success. It was a cultural "fit." Henry managed such church life rituals as covered-dish suppers with ease. He was as much at home in the church members' houses as his own. In fact, he spent a lot of time on their porches and at their kitchen tables.

Henry's second pastorate involved a move to the city. The homogeneity of his first congregation gave way to multiculturalism in his urban pastorate. Henry does not fit. He blames his church members for his frustration. They never have him over for dinner. They lack "commitment," he asserts, because their lives are not centered around the church. "How are you supposed to pastor people who don't want you to be a part of their lives?" he laments. Further conversation reveals that the pastor has no disposition toward connecting with the culture of his new congregation. Instead, he intends to mold his new ministry venue into a congregation like his first. His country pastorate acts as an internal benchmark of how he is to relate to parishioners. Henry will continue to experience frustration until he can sufficiently differentiate himself from his past so that his past does not dominate him.

This real-life example highlights only one aspect of the role of culture in forming the leader. In this case, it was an investigation into cultural factors and influences that we commonly call "roots." We could just as easily have considered other key cultural factors, including geography, ethnicity, socioeconomic variables, and language, all important early-forming heart shapers. An important line of inquiry includes a rehearsal of key early events shared by the leader's particular generation as well as those events unique to the leader's individual life.

The task of knowing where you come from constitutes an important developmental stage in the leader's life. Until this inquiry and analysis is done, the leader runs a constant danger of not understanding personal vulnerabilities. This same dynamic carries some positive implications as well. Knowing where you come from frees you from making blind responses to forces you have yet to understand.

The point of knowing where you come from is not so that you can jettison the past or discover how you are a victim of the past, but rather it is a way to gain insights into your initial and early formative experiences. Early cultural conditioning almost always presents some challenges to overcome. One of the results of a media age is the creation of pronounced generational differences that form the leader's initial cultural frame of reference. This gives the leader a sense of identity but also establishes the challenge of appreciating alternative generational cultures.

Maturity comes when we can learn to appreciate how our hearts were formed, to look at our early cultural development as a gift. Sometimes these experiences and influences have been crippling or harmful. But God can turn the past that we find ugly and wish to expunge into a beauty mark. Conversely, early opportunities and head starts, if viewed as testimonies to the beneficence of God, can inject humility into the heart tempted to practice ingratitude for unearned advantages.

The author of Hebrews exhorts us to run with perseverance the race that is "set before us" (Heb. 11:1). God designs the leader's race. None of us picked the circumstances of our birth and early environments. God sovereignly placed us in formative cultural dynamics that framed our world and shaped our hearts.

Many people fail to contemplate the forces that shape their lives. As a result, they fail to understand themselves and others. Self-understanding forms the fundamental building block for the leader's personal development. Failure to attain this level of reflection destines the leader to attempt to act out a script that will remain unintelligible. Further, leaders who do not know where they come from find it difficult to appreciate where others come from. The current "worship wars" in American churches reflect just such immaturity in the leadership of many congregations. Every generation must find its own heart language for worship, and it must be free to give expression to it.

A group of doctor of ministry students shared their pilgrimages as part of entering their course work. As they offered their life stories, the impact of culture on their heart-shaping stood out in marked relief. The Korean pastor recalled arriving in America as a high school teenager with no English skills. He has a heart for working with misunderstood youth. A young Hispanic pastor rehearsed how his work in the migrant fields sensitized him to the plight of people locked into substandard jobs for lack of other skills. Another pastor told the story of how early, precipitous poverty visited his family and how it profoundly shaped his view of God's care and provision in crisis.

This discussion of knowing where you come from does not mean to suggest that early culture is determinative. Many leaders minister effectively in cultures quite different from their culture of origin, whether this means their capacity to reach cross-generationally or in another demographic group. However, the process of discovering where they come from broadens the worldview of leaders. They come to see that everyone does not begin where they did. Their hearts enlarge to include more of the world.

Do you know where you come from? How did God shape you early? What gifts from your beginnings have you come to treasure? Have you reflected enough on the whole culture of your forming to gain freedom from acting out hidden scripts? Have you come to terms with your past? Do you need to let yourself out of jail? Are you holding others hostage to your own past? Have you grown to respect the heart-forming foundation in others?

Do not stop short of this examination. Your capacity to exercise mature and empowering leadership remains arrested until you make this inquiry.

Some leaders prefer to take this heart journey into their culture of origin independently of other people. Most of us need some company for the trip, both for guidance and for comfort. Companions might be a family member, a trusted friend, a counselor, even a skilled colleague. We all do well to remember that we have a Guide who knows us better than we know ourselves. Because he was there all along, knitting us in the womb and shepherding us before we recognized his voice, he is an indispensable fellow pilgrim.

Knowing Where You Stand

The second task of the heart in its relationship to culture is knowing where you stand. This phrase is often used to mean "taking a stand" on issues. The meaning here is quite different. Here, the emphasis is on the ability of leaders to understand and connect with the culture that God has placed them in as their ministry post. God uses the culture that confronts leaders as a heart-shaping process. Leaders who cooperate with this divine work learn to look for ways in which God is at work in the culture and figure out how to belong to and transcend culture.

Knowing where you stand demands that you become a student of culture. Leaders with the courage and commitment to engage culture want to be culturally relevant. They hold this ambition not for relevancy's sake, but in order to establish and maintain a credible dialogue and connection with those inside and outside the faith. Christian enterprises that engage the culture have leaders who view cultural connectivity as an essential aspect of fulfilling the Great Commission. They hold cultural relevance as a core value.

This observation highlights the truth that whatever happens in the leader's heart affects those who follow. This work of the heart in relation to culture becomes not just an exercise in the leader's personal insight and development. A "heart blockage" in the spiritual leader can cause heart failure for those in the leader's constellation of influence. The unwillingness or inability of leaders to engage their culture cripples the ability of God's people to do so. Conversely, Christian leaders who engage their culture create missional ministry environments where others do the same.

Cultural exegesis has always been important for spiritual leaders. Moses, David, Paul, and Jesus each demonstrated mastery in their understanding of their culture and were effective because of it. Moses could operate equally in Pharaoh's palace and in the Midianite desert. David captured the aspirations of his countrymen for a strong king who would free Israel from foreign threats. Paul was at home in the urban centers that served as his mission "fields." Jesus, as a small business owner, related to the concerns of ordinary people. It was the religious elite who were out of touch with the people. That is why the people were captivated by Jesus. The Pharisees exegeted texts; Jesus exegeted life.

Fortunately, many contemporary leaders have chosen to follow the leads of our biblical case studies. They are developing ministry efforts that target various cultures. One new Generation X ministry recently made its first purchase—a portable cappuccino machine, which they haul out to malls and sports centers as an outreach strategy, to create an experience of community. Another church leader spent nine years in a church transitioning its 1950s-style church program into a vibrant, culturally relevant congregation that targets its community. Still another church leader in an inner city has created a multiracial and multiethnic congregation that reflects its cultural surroundings. Hundreds of new ministries target the unchurched culture, including one that takes young people of Generation Y into high-rise apartment communities. Their "ministry teams" of kids aged nine to sixteen perform street concerts and baptize converts on the spot in a portable water tank they take with them.

Contemporary Christian leaders who have chosen not to withdraw from the cultural arena face white-water rapids. Culture roils and churns in the collision of the old with the new. At the dawn of the third Christian millennium, continuity battles with discontinuity; the emergent dances with what is passing away. Leaders of spiritual enterprises, like many of the adherents of the faith, have oars in both currents. The challenge involves getting as many through the rapids as possible, knowing some will never make it. The success of the mission largely depends on the ability of the leader, the river guide, to know how to "read" the water.

Entire volumes dedicate themselves to discerning the times, and dozens of newsletters and on-line services harbinger what's next. A detailed analysis of cultural trends falls outside the purview of our investigation. The concern here is the leader's perception of responsibility in relation to culture, whatever the culture is, and the contention that culture plays an important role in shaping the leader's heart. Nevertheless, several significant shifts and emerging issues clearly establish the river's run. It helps leaders to know these. This discussion focuses on those trends that influence the spiritual climate of the culture and some implications for Christian ministry.

Heightened Spirituality Across the Board

Secularism has lost. For the most part, people do not see humankind as capable of solving its deepest dilemmas on its own, nor is technology viewed as messianic. Instead, the notion that the world is primarily physical and material is giving way to a view that life is more than what can be seen, touched, counted, or consumed. A basic disenchantment with the rationalism of the Cartesian scientific method creates an atmosphere in which people are willing to look for knowledge and understanding through nonrational, intuitive, and spiritual explorations. People are increasingly engaged in a search for meaning, purpose, love, self-worth, compassion, dignity, transcendence, a sense of unity with others and with the universe, along with a search for a means to express these things. Every sector of society now talks openly of spirituality.

Christian leaders should avoid two misperceptions given these dynamics. The first is to miss this point entirely and still battle secularism. Telling people in the pews that the people outside the church or the faith do not care about God or spiritual things relays a false message and reveals cultural ignorance. To assume that people are not in church because they are not interested in spiritual truth demonstrates denial on the part of church leaders about *their* lack of cultural relevance rather than an accurate reading of people's attitudes about spiritual matters.

Americans remain highly religious. Whereas a week's worth of major network sitcoms and newscasts pretend by their silence on the matter that America is almost totally secular, fewer than 10 percent of the people in this culture claim to be atheistic. Whenever tragedy strikes, like a school massacre or a deadly tornado, a major part of the story involves spiritual expressions that follow immediately in the affected communities. These range from candlelight vigils to community prayer meetings to disaster relief efforts by religious organizations. A noticeable shift has occurred in other media venues. Movies, radio, and cable television series probe angels, the paranormal, the unexplained, and refuse to challenge nonrational and nonmaterial realities.

Christian leaders would also be mistaken to assume that all of this heightened awareness of spirituality and spiritual talk represents outcroppings of a spiritual awakening in a Christian sense. When many people talk in spiritual terms, they should not be perceived as talking about God in the Christian sense. Postmoderns can speak about spirituality without ever mentioning God. They can develop elaborate cosmologies that are inhabited by all sorts of intermediate spiritual beings and gods.

The challenge for the church involves helping spiritually hungry people experience classic Christian truth. This effort will require Christian leaders' getting outside the walls of the church and into the streets. First-century leaders adopted this approach when faced with a similar challenge. Had they chosen to hang around the holy huddle exclusively, the movement would never have exploded the way it did.

The church might fail to capitalize on this heightened spiritual awareness for another reason. Many Christian leaders are uncomfortable with genuine spiritual realities that involve the powerful and immediate presence of God. The truth is, many churches are more secular than the culture. Everything that transpires in them can be explained away in terms of human talent and ingenuity. It would be a huge mistake on the church's part to continue its pursuit of programs and methodological prowess (what "works") when the world desperately seeks for God. Only when something goes on in church that can be explained as a God-thing will a spiritually fascinated culture pause to take notice. Otherwise, those outside the church culture are not impressed with building programs and real estate acquisitions. What church culture people see as evidence of success matters little to pre-Christians.

In the mid-1980s, when seeker-driven churches began to emerge, the seeker-targeted services used nonspiritual language and soft-sell approaches to God in order to connect with nonchurched people. Today's church service had better get God up front, center stage, and in a hurry, or pre-Christians will not take the church seriously as a source of spiritual help. This shift reflects how swiftly this move toward heightened spirituality in our culture has occurred.

I recently visited with a leadership team of a new church. They indicated their target group to be the unchurched. Their Web site declared their goal of developing a twenty-five-acre campus and a membership of a thousand people. They did not understand that these goals reflected church culture values, not the values of their target group. Pre-Christians are looking for God, not for a successful church. Church leaders who believe that building the perfect church will attract pre-Christians do not yet understand the culture that confronts them. The ultimate measure of cultural relevance is what happens in the community, not the church. Don Clifton, chairman of the board of Gallup, convened a group of pastors in Lincoln, Nebraska, around the question, "What would Lincoln look like if churches were doing their job?"

A new pastor in West Virginia demonstrates this idea. Arriving in a small town to a small church, he quickly discovered that the congregation had aged through the years and was no longer connected to the community. He began to pray about how the church could be a significant force for positive community life. He led the congregation to adopt a local elementary school. After securing a list of the children's needs from the faculty, over 60 percent of the church members agreed to help out in one of five specific ministries. The church is experiencing renewal because the community is responding to their efforts to raise the quality of life in that town.

Like this West Virginia pastor, spiritual leaders themselves need to be sources of spiritual insight and strength. This assertion does not argue against leaders developing other competencies. They are also valued. However, leadership skills in and of themselves do not qualify men and women for spiritual leadership. The spiritual component of leaders' lives must be obvious and vibrant. This quality is absolutely critical for spiritual leaders who want to achieve cultural connectivity. People want to see a correspondence between the claims of Christian abundant living and its experience in the lives of its representatives.

The Relocation of Authority and Power

People in this culture grow increasingly hostile to the notion that others know what is best for them or should be able to tell them how to live their lives. One reason for this is the increasing democratization occurring in every sphere, aided in large part by technology. Another factor involves the failure of institutions to deliver solutions to mounting problems. More and more people perceive power and authority as lying in the hands of individuals. Mother Teresa and Princess Diana represent the power of the individual. Their power devolved from their moral authority. Jesse Jackson frees American prisoners of war in Yugoslavia, a personal achievement that could not be pulled off by the United States government.

This relocation of power and authority to the individual extends to how people view family. This came home to me during a seminary class I taught. A discussion erupted about the true nature of family. An older baby boomer offered her opinion that churches should not use the word *family* to describe themselves, because, as she put it, the church could never truly be family to her. A firestorm of conversation ensued. Generation X students argued for the viability of seeing the church as family, but not because the church claimed it. According to them, the decision to view church as family rested with the individual. As one of them put it, "I adopt the church as my family." Another even more boldly asserted, "I choose my family." A baby boomer retorted that people cannot pick their families. "You can't have two fathers," he said. "Sure I can," shot back a man in his young twenties. "I have three men who serve that role for me at different times and in different circumstances."

To the baby boomers in the class, authority still belonged to assigned roles. The radical notions of the Generation Xers, that they had the authority and power to dispense with or create family, demonstrate the shift toward power of the individual.

Spiritual leaders must not miss the significance of this discussion. A growing disaffection for top-down anything extends to ministry structures and congregations. People increasingly will abandon the kinds of ministries and ministry leaders that seem more interested in institutional concerns than in assisting individuals to develop spiritually. People will support leaders who help them discover who they are created to be and then empower them to employ their talents, energies, and passions. Congregation members who feel their primary function involves making the clergy's program a success will exhibit far less enthusiasm and lend fewer resources than those who feel they can serve as ministry entrepreneurs to help the mission succeed.

The flip side to this dynamic also carries enormous implications for leaders. Having a position or title no longer guarantees that people automatically afford leadership to the person in that position. Leadership must now be earned; it is no longer bestowed. Effective leaders grasp this cultural shift and its implications for them. They evidence servant attitudes and focus on building people as the way to missional effectiveness.

Jesus turned the leadership equation around with his emphasis on servant leadership. Instead of establishing leadership positions in his kingdom, he focused on the character of leadership, declaring it to be that of serving others in humility. Instead of their studying rulers for leadership insight, he suggested that his disciples should learn from children (Mark 9:33–37).

The Collapse of the Newtonian Worldview

Since Sir Isaac was hit on the head, we have assumed that learning is linear and analytical. We have believed that if we tore something apart into its constituent components, we would somehow understand the whole better. Analysts and consultants have thus been busy dissecting organizations and corporations in their quest to make them work better. The trouble with this approach is that organizations and ideas are more than the sum of their constituent parts. Creating synergy and systemic change involves coming at things using a more holistic approach. The new world values resource people and leaders who can put things together, not tear them apart.

Effective spiritual leaders in contemporary culture do just that. They understand that people who are overwhelmed with complexity need help in making sense out of it all. These leaders search for ways to uncomplicate life for those in their ministry constituency. In recent decades, church leaders layered more and more activity in their ministry programs. People-friendly leaders now search for ways to simplify life for those they lead rather than complicate it. The messages they teach and preach and the ministry programs they design and implement connect people in a more meaningful way with everything else that is going on in their lives.

This approach requires two things of the spiritual leader. First, the leader must demonstrate competency in systems thinking. This microskill usually does not show up as part of the current ministry credentialing curriculum. More fundamental, this shift requires that the effective spiritual leader achieve an integrated life. People want and need to see models of intentional living informed by biblical values and principles.

A corollary to this cultural current involves a shift in emphasis away from teaching to learning. In a Newtonian world, the teacher drives learning. The teacher transfers information and knowledge to the pupil. Accordingly, teaching has predominated the educational agenda for centuries. Today's technology renders didactic methods increasingly obsolete. Students can access more information on the Internet than the teacher can present. The learner now drives the teaching. Research into learning reveals that it is not necessarily linear or even cognitive. Learning must be continual and extend beyond the classroom for those who want to be competitive. In this environment, teachers serve as learning coaches.

The learning revolution also applies to spiritual communities. Many congregations and their leaders continue to misassume that traditional educational and classroom models are adequate for the pursuit of spiritual formation. However, a growing number of church leaders recognize that information alone rarely changes behavior. Heart-shaping involves the presence and support of community. Effective congregations and leaders are busy creating learning venues for people, not teaching venues. The rise of affinity-driven small groups of all kinds represents one answer to this need. Other congregations employ some sort of mentoring process, as do many spiritual leaders in their own development. This shift registers an end to the presumption that years of sitting in pews and Sunday school chairs automatically results in the development of Christian character.

The Cry for Both Community and Distance

This paradoxical cry for both community and distance results from several factors. The mobility of the population frequently means that immediate family members are sometimes hundreds of miles away. Intergenerational networks rarely get cultivated as they would with the close proximity of family. The increasing number of broken homes militates against the modeling of good relationship skills, thereby ensuring a cycle of continued relationship carnage. The advent of air conditioning and the rise of crime in the second half of the twentieth century exiled people from the streets and into their fortified homes. All of these factors, and many more, have created a culture characterized by isolation. Many people express a growing sense that they need to belong to someone. Recall the seminary classroom discussion cited above. Generation Xers eagerly and proactively seek to find or to create family. This generation particularly values community. This will be a growing issue.

On the other hand, the harried lifestyle of most people and families allows them very little discretionary time for themselves. They yearn for space for the emotional, physical, and spiritual margin to ponder their lives and reflect or renew themselves. They need sanctuary so that personal reserves can be replenished. To secure this, they seek distance from the world around them.

Church leaders in the new millennium will need to consider both of these needs in planning congregational life. The real estate-bound and program-based church models that characterize most expressions of contemporary churchianity do not address these needs. The programming in many churches can actually be counterproductive in that it contributes to these problems. Creating both community and space for people to experience genuine spiritual formation will require an act of courage on the part of spiritual leaders. It will involve significant shifts in the way we currently keep score in churches. We have worked hard to produce church members who show up at the church to demonstrate their loyalty to the church. In the future, less will be more, but it will look like less to those accustomed to keeping box scores measuring the amount of activity at the church.

The Return of Apologetics

Apologetics played an important role in helping people embrace Christianity in its initial growth period. The similarity between the current religious and spiritual landscape and that of the apostolic era calls for a renewal of apologetics. Many commentators have declared Americans to be post-Christian. In reality, they can be described as pre-Christian. Generation X is the first American generation in which over half of its population begin their religious pilgrimage from some starting point other than a Christian worldview. Though spiritual interest among this group is high, their file folders are largely empty of classic Christian theology. The new and needed apologetics will differ from previous apologetic models geared at convincing people solely or even mainly from a rationalistic perspective or that begin with biblical authority. People want to see spiritual power demonstrated by transformed lives expressed in community. This is the great hope people harbor. They will respond to a spiritual belief system that delivers at this point. Jesus said that the proof of discipleship to the world would be his followers' love for one another (John 13:35). Early observers were drawn to the Christian movement exactly for this reason (Acts 2:44–47). Love expressed through community still transforms people and creates an attractive and compelling invitation for others to join up.

The Role of Technology

The growing dominance of technology in every aspect of the culture provides an increasing dilemma as well as an opportunity to spiritual enterprises. Almost any statement written here about technological horizons will sound dated by the time the publishing production cycle gets it in front of your eyes. In general, *high tech* will increasingly have *high touch* as its goal. This will be seen from the development of more and more sophisticated tracking systems for organizations to the creation of more diagnostic tools for medical intervention. We could just as easily talk about the economic impact of technological development, from the burgeoning Internet trade to the rebirth of trade guilds in the inner city made possible by improved labor training. But technology will also continue to create ethical issues related to biomedical breakthroughs. Privacy issues and Internet crime will command more attention. The simplest response to these technological trends also states the challenge. Christian leaders will need to be careful to champion appropriate uses of technology. But to fail to be technologically relevant will limit ministries from being able to intrigue younger generations.

The last information revolution, triggered by the invention of the printing press and moveable type, took only fifty years to put the monks out of their centuries-long monopoly in the information industry. The latest information revolution carries implications just as far-reaching for the church today.

The Collapse of the Church Culture

The single most challenging cultural shift facing many spiritual leaders involves the huge reorientation away from the church, a shift that has accelerated since the late 1980s. This may sound contradictory in light of the earlier discussion about heightened spiritual awareness. Simply put, Jesus is hot, the church is not. Organized religious efforts hold less and less appeal.

The collapse of institutional religion as a driving force in the culture carries several huge implications for spiritual leaders. First, the paradigm of how church is done in a Christianized culture differs significantly from effective missional strategies in pre-Christian cultures. "Come-and-get-it" evangelism or marketing strategies that reflect a "build it and they will come" level of understanding grow increasingly suspect in a culture that no longer pays much attention to what is going on at church.

Some church leaders and congregations wring their hands over this development and obsess over how to stop the collapse. Frequently their efforts get channeled into improving what is already being done or redoubling efforts in programs and emphases that no longer provide a good return on investment, or that may even prove counterproductive. This approach usually accompanies fear and a denial mentality that fails to reckon with what potential customers consider interesting. These church leaders whine that their job is made more difficult by the media, moral decline, the Supreme Court, and so forth and so on. In other words, absent the cultural props they consider essential, they believe the church has a reduced capacity to influence culture.

Church leaders who choose to reconceptualize the Christian expression in light of the church culture collapse adopt a different attitude. They do not peer in fear out of the citadel at an alien world they seek to avoid. Rather, they strategize on how to get beyond the citadel and into the village where people are hanging out. They choose engagement over retreat.

A young minister shared his dream with me over lunch. His vision is to build a community center rather than a church. His center would provide recreational facilities as well as a place where families could receive music lessons, art instruction, and the like. His ideas represent a growing expression of Christianity that will show up in a Christian presence in malls and recreational centers. The goal will be to take the church where the people already are, rather than trying to entice the people onto church property.

This last trend anticipates the third heart-shaping task in relation to culture. Knowing where you come from is usually a trip to the past. Knowing where you stand demonstrates your view of the present culture. Knowing where you want to go involves bundling up the lessons of the past and the challenges and opportunities of the present to create a future for the leader and those in the leader's constellation of influence.

Knowing Where You Want to Go and Taking Others with You

The final task of heart-shaping in terms of culture requires both the integration of the two previous tasks and a transcendence of them. The leader, having achieved a measure of independence from the formative past and a good fix on the realities of the present culture, incorporates these learnings and establishes a direction for a life and a ministry that will interface effectively with culture. Having looked back and looked around, the leader now looks ahead. The choice that confronts the leader precipitates a decision. The shaping of the leader's heart will differ depending on where that leader determines to go.

Soon after Cathy and I were married, we traveled to Colorado for the first time. After spending some time in the eastern part of the state, we headed west to meet some friends. This trip took us through Wolf Creek Pass near the western Continental Divide. Even though it was July, we stopped off for a snow fight in the woods. Our skirmish took us off the path. We came to a place where the water from the melting snowpack obviously trickled off in two different directions. Part of this runoff would eventually find its way into the Gulf of Mexico, whereas the other stream would wind up in the Gulf of California. From the same source, these waters would wind up in very different places.

That episode represents the current cultural dilemma for Christian leaders in North America. The leaders of congregations, denominations, and Christian ministries face choices that will take them to very different places. Their response in terms of how they relate to culture forms a continental divide.

The options can be described in two words—*refuge* or *mission*. The notion of refuge can carry either positive or negative connotations. The biblical teaching that God is our refuge in times of trouble obviously conveys an encouraging and comforting meaning. The use of refuge in the context of ministry paradigms, however, signals an ominous choice. A refuge approach to ministry involves a leader's taking an approach to culture that attempts to insulate against it, to withdraw, to adopt a sectarian mentality. The leader who chooses mission, on the other hand, seeks to interface with culture, to build bridges to the culture for the sake of sharing the heart of God with the people of that culture. Either choice significantly affects the leader's legacy by framing the orientation of the followers.

The Refuge Response to Culture

Leaders who choose a refuge response to culture follow a motivation to preserve a world order that has already significantly collapsed. Its roots reach back to the fourth century with Constantine's decision to prop up the church with cultural reinforcements. As that world unraveled over the last half of the twentieth century, various attempts were made to salvage or protect it. These efforts reflect a growing refuge mentality.

Spiritual leaders who adopt refuge thinking go to one of three places; they also take others with them. The first can be designated as the *withdrawal-reactionary destination*. Some refuge leaders, faced with an increasingly hostile culture, give in to the tendency to withdraw, to protect, to insulate against an alien world.

This response reflects the leader's underlying perspective that "the world" should be avoided as a dangerous sphere of human activity that threatens the Christian culture. Refuge leaders narrowly define the parameters of God's work in the world. For them, a demarcation between believers and nonbelievers circumscribes God's activity. God works in the church among believers. The world outside the faith has spun out of God's control. This view authorizes a withdrawal from the non-Christian culture. God himself has capitulated his providence in this sphere.

A disturbing corollary often accompanies this theological presupposition. Many refuge paradigm leaders believe that the Almighty's basic disposition toward people outside the faith is anger. An unfortunate leap of logic usually follows. Because God is unhappy with pre-Christians, it is okay for Christians to be mad at them too. In fact, being angry with those on the outside becomes a matter of faithfulness to God. This view creates a signature church culture. People usually find it hard to have compassion for those with whom they are angry. We typically do not want to be around people we are upset with. So we withdraw. The anger probably represents a stage of grief. Realizing that the culture is no longer reflective of the church, these leaders and their ministry constituents are just mad, period.

This perspective explains why many North American Christian leaders have adopted a social and political agenda to replace personal evangelistic efforts. Political correctness has invaded the Christian world. The "right" position on certain key political and social questions serves as a litmus test for fidelity to the cause. The cause aims to secure Christian values in the culture. The concern to introduce people to God is only secondary. The first order of business is to challenge their position or lifestyle, designating "them" as the enemy to be defeated. In previous eras, Christian leaders maintained that the best way to instill Christian values in the culture involved helping people begin and develop a relationship with Christ. For contemporary refuge thinkers, the most compelling concern is to get people to act right.

Two other prevalent forms of refuge ministry show up in American Christianity. The next may be described as *denial*. Denial leaders lead congregations and Christian organizations to practice a business-as-usual ministry approach. These enterprises typically withdraw from their communities. Congregations operating in this mode often withdraw from other congregations in their community and their denomination as well. These congregations focus on the past. Fearful of change, these churches create a safe, nostalgic haven for their members. They become sociologically cocooned from the culture. Thousands of church buildings sit in neighborhoods that members drive through to get to church and back. The community changed, the church did not. The members prefer to keep the real estate as a club for religious activity closed to the neighborhood.

A third form of refuge Christianity lies on the other end of the refuge spectrum from the sectarian mentality. This destination can be characterized as *cultural accommodation* or even capitulation. Christian leaders and churches who choose this response to culture practice a form of civil religion. They typically do not challenge people to enter a relationship tied to a radical faith in the person of Jesus Christ. They prosecute an agenda of providing some moral instruction to their followers. Their evangelism strategy is guided by the goal of maintaining a "presence" in the community, not realizing that mere presence in a religiously plural culture does not have the impact they suppose.

The leaders of refuge Christianity have made a choice. Some of them practice ministry as refuge because they have entered ministry as a personal refuge. They like the subculture of the church. It provides them a living and affords them escape from being around people and places that make them uncomfortable. Some have escaped to church ministry as a place to work out their own therapeutic needs. We will revisit this topic when we explore the heart-shaping category of call.

Evidence abounds that the choice for refuge is apparently compelling. This is the current state of much of North American Christianity.

The Mission Response to Culture

Instead of adopting a refuge mentality in relating to culture, other spiritual leaders view their mission to engage culture in order to transform it. The mentality supporting this approach stands in stark contrast to the refuge perspective. The theological and psychological presuppositions are entirely different. Rather than seeing the culture outside the faith as abandoned by God and operating outside his control, missional spiritual leaders see God actively at work in the world. They understand that he is on a mission himself, redeeming people to himself. They share a conviction that belonging to him involves partnering with him in his redemptive mission. Their hearts are captured by the heart of God for developing relationships with people made in his image.

Leaders who want to transform the culture seek to build as many bridges as possible to the world outside the faith. Christians in the constellation of these leaders attempt the transformation of culture through transformational living that engages people in heart-to-heart encounters. They deliver help and hope for people who search for significance and meaning. They place a high priority on evangelism as a means of introducing people to a loving God who cares for them. Their ministries reflect grace because their leaders lead with a heart of grace.

One new congregation has drawn in over two thousand people in less than five years. The leader's message of grace reflects his own sense of freedom, particularly because he turned his back on a legalistic religious background. His own heart transformation has helped him assess where he came from, share his own spiritual discovery with others, study the culture, and implement innovative ministry approaches to create a grace community.

Christian leaders who are intent on engaging the culture for the sake of the gospel find their model for ministry in Jesus. He chose mission over refuge. His heart, captured by the one who sent him, displayed a redemptive grace to all people created in the image of God. Jesus told his disciples that he did what he did because he saw the Father doing it. His invitation to his followers was to follow him, to do what he did.

Jesus struggled against the refuge mentality of his disciples. They had, after all, been steeped in the refuge religion of the Pharisees. Building on their fear of losing their faith, the Pharisees adopted an agenda that burned bridges to the culture they were supposed to influence. Their come-and-get-it evangelism, forcing people to change cultures before being considered for religious club membership, resulted directly from their view of the world as a hostile place. In an effort to avoid contamination, they became sociologically isolated. In place of personal relationship with God, they offered people the Sabbath plan for societal reform, believing they could bring in the kingdom of God by adopting the role of moral watch-dogs for the culture. Their thinking and actions trapped them in a vicious cycle of reading people's poor response to them as confirmation that they were the only righteous ones who enjoyed the favor of God. They began to fear and eventually to despise the very people they were commissioned to reach.

The book of Acts records the apostles' emergence from refuge think-ing. The book begins with the refuge-fueled question to Jesus by one of his followers as to when Jesus planned to restore the kingdom to Israel. By the time the book ends, Luke chronicles the expansion of Christianity into multiple cultures. Because the apostles and other early Christian lead-ers chose mission over refuge, the Christian movement survived and thrived. Thanks to their choice, and the choice of countless other thou-sands, you and I can ponder our own futures as part of their legacy.

Where Are You Going?

The stakes are high. How the spiritual leader responds to culture shapes the individual heart and the heart of the movement. The three-act drama of knowing where you come from, where you stand, and where you want to go is not just a private exercise. Those who surround the leader learn how to interpret their own lives through the leader's choices.

You have entered human history at a hinge point. Be assured that God is not caught off guard by the cultural upheavals that characterize this pe-riod of transition. Neither is he surprised by your intersection with the planet. It is not accidental that you live and lead at a time when the deci-sions you make, especially in regard to culture, will affect generations.

A few questions beg your consideration in light of this discussion:

- What cultural influences in your early years have shaped you most significantly?
- How have these influences fashioned your uniqueness?
- Are you a student of culture? Do you know what is going on in the world?
- Do you look for ways to connect with the culture or seek ways to escape from it?

- How comfortable or angry are you with those outside the faith?
- What is your track record of influencing people toward Jesus?

Your answers give you some important clues about your heart.

This discussion has intended to help you accomplish three heart tasks in relation to culture. The presentation has not progressed without a bias. The attempt has been made to persuade you to opt to be open to the world. By guiding you to take stock of where you have come from and what confronts you, it is hoped that you will gain the identity and security you need to confidently engage your world. This confidence also rests in the conviction that God beckons leaders to join him where he is working—in the world.

The decision of how you engage culture ultimately is yours. That decision will determine your legacy.

6

CALL

FIGURING OUT WHY WE ARE HERE

OUR CONVERSATION, BEGUN late in the evening, had lasted into the wee hours of the morning. The pastor rehearsed episode after episode of trial, both outer and inner. As we talked, I became increasingly convinced that the turmoil being experienced in his leadership assignment was symptomatic of the inner ambivalence and uncertainty of his heart. A few months prior, the pastor had accepted a new ministry post, thinking that a change of scenery would bring a new sense of direction. Unfortunately he now realized he had only swapped backdrops. The same scene was playing out in his new location. He felt he was headed for another disappointment in his developing life tragedy.

"Jim," I asked, "what do you feel called to do in this situation?"

"I don't have a clue," he said. "Nothing is working the way I thought it would."

"Well, then, let's explore this from a larger perspective. What do you feel called to do with your life?"

The question obviously agitated him. His response came slowly and painfully. "That's the point. I am not sure I have been called to pastor." With this admission, he seemed spent. So was I, for suddenly we had no foundational bedrock on which to construct a future for his pastoral ministry. Absent Jim's conviction of a divine commission, my advice would serve, at best, only as a coping strategy. Jim has continued in ministry, but it seems more a burden to discharge than a life quest.

Chad, on the other hand, celebrates his sense of call after over thirty years in ministry. Raised on a farm in the Midwest, he described himself as a shy, retiring boy. When he felt that God was calling him into ministry, the thought of preaching in front of people terrified him. In those days, he explains, answering the call meant becoming either a missionary or a pastor. Nonetheless the call seemed unmistakable. His inelegant, but honest, acceptance prayer was, "God, if I answer the call to do this, you'll have to supply the rest." God has, in ways that have followed the contours of Chad's personal awareness and development. Chad eventually realized that though his culture of origin was rural, he had become an urban person. After several pastoral experiences (all good), he now teaches in an administrative role in a theological school. He luxuriates in his current ministry, declaring it "more in line with my gifts." His calling had combined elements of certainty and flexibility. It has been a life journey toward fulfillment.

God shapes the heart of the leader through the call. This call is a divinely orchestrated setting apart of the leader for some special task. God's part of the call dynamic is to initiate, guide, position, and intervene. The leader's part of the call drama is to hear, respond, search, and order or reorder life.

The call is a mystery. It begins and ends with God, but it loops through a very human individual. It is personal, but bigger than the person. The call comes out of who we are as well as shaping who we are. It has both being and doing components. The call involves relationship at its core, not just function or task, though it carries clear task components.

Call recipients understand that God has a very special claim on their lives for special purposes. This awareness goes beyond a general sense of feeling purposeful or significant. Clearly God wants all people to experience this. Those who describe themselves as called mean that they have made a commitment of life into God's service, to be at his disposal, to be in his employ for the efforts of accomplishing his agenda.

The sense of being called to spiritual leadership is not to be confused with the more general sense of a *calling*. Many people, in all walks of life, describe their life's work or passion as a calling. An architect friend of mine uses this phrase. For him, it means he has found his life purpose and is living consonantly with his discovery. Christian theology maintains that all believers are called to serve others and to serve God. This kind of calling can be lived out in any life station.

Spiritual leaders, on the other hand, describe their whole lives in terms of the call. It involves much more than a vocational expression or function. It goes to the very core of one's being. It is the pivotal and life-defining decision. It may be sudden and dramatic, or more progressively revealed. The call may come early or late. It may find expression through traditional ministry venues, or it may show up in the marketplace. Recipients might be surprised or might feel they should have anticipated the call. The call may be crystal clear or initially ambiguous.

This volume focuses on the heart-shaping impact of the call on leaders' lives. Though the discussion will consider some call content, it is the impact of the leader's understanding of the call that is most important.

A leader with a clear sense of call represents a formidable force. The sense of destiny emboldens, energizes, and empowers the leader, as well as those who are a part of the leader's coterie of followers. Leaders convinced of their call do not easily succumb to disappointments and discouragements. Nor do they calculate odds in the same way as those who are not operating from a call basis. Leaders secure in their call will charge hell with a water pistol. A divine unction fuels their determination.

I recall a particularly memorable Sunday lunch in my childhood. My dad, a bivocational pastor of a small, rural church, came home late one Sunday morning. Mom gasped when Dad came through the door, blood splattered all over the front of his shirt. He was not injured. He had stepped in between two men determined to settle a family feud in the churchyard. In his recounting of the episode, he told about a threat one of the combatants had tossed at him as he left the scene. "Don't you come back up this road tonight, preacher. There'll be trouble." Mom asked, "Thomas, what are you going to do?" Without a nanosecond's hesitation, Dad said, "I'm going up that road tonight. I'm the pastor of that church." It never occurred to him to do anything else. His decision reflected neither foolhardiness nor a cavalier disregard for danger. His call simply preempted serious consideration of staying away. (Nothing happened.)

Following the call does not always require a dramatic response. Sometimes it shows up in a quiet persistence. Mary had turned down any number of inquiries through the years from larger ministries in larger cities. Her effective work in a county seat town had attracted notoriety in her denomination. Reflecting on her choices, she indicated her deep sense of call to serve Christ in that particular setting. "God has given me a passion for serving the people of this county," she said. "I feel that the twenty-five years in one location has helped me to influence a whole community." Mary's decisions could be considered just as heroic as Dad's.

Our discussion of the call experiences of Moses, David, Paul, and Jesus sets the stage for exploring its continuing importance as a heart-shaping dynamic for contemporary spiritual leaders. None of the biblical leaders can be understood apart from his call. Each of them ordered their lives around their conviction of God's assignment for them. Moses and Paul experienced dramatic calls; those of David and Jesus were more progressive. The call always carried some content, yet it was not always fulfilled immediately or even in the way the leader anticipated. The biblical leaders believed they had been set aside for special purposes. Even when they had little clue as to how God would achieve the assignment, even when others doubted, they held fast to the conviction of divine commissioning.

The call experiences of the four biblical heroes afford us different glimpses of the God whose call they heeded. Moses reveals God as deliverer and redeemer. David shows us God as shepherd and king. Paul's life experience captures a God on a mission as global grace giver. Jesus supremely demonstrates a personal God intent on establishing relationship with his people, taking the initiative to restore intimacy with his children, overpowering the enemies that threaten to keep us estranged from him and from one another. These studies teach us that leaders whose hearts are shaped by a call reveal something about God through their life message.

The rehearsal of these leaders' call pilgrimage opens the investigation of how God is shaping you through your own call dynamics. Several key issues in this arena claim the attention of every Christian leader. What constitutes a call or commission from God? Do you have a call from God? What did you answer the call to do? Have you seen the attendant gifts and talents come along? What has God anointed in you? How large is your audience? These questions will guide our discussion of how God might be shaping your heart through the call.

First Things First—Have You Been Called?

First things first. You need to know whether or not you have received a call from God, and you need to know what you have been called to do.

Discussions about the call have become fuzzied in recent decades by the emerging emphasis on the call of God to all Christians to minister in Christ's name. Although the church needs to hear this message, those delivering it have been left increasingly to wonder how their own call fits into this. If everyone is called, what's so special about the call? Considering the incredible significance of the call to spiritual leadership, we need to address some fundamentals of this issue.

As discussed here, the meaning of call goes beyond the general sense of this dynamic. Individual believers certainly should be helped to develop a personal sense of mission. The lack of this among Christians is one of the great tragedies of the modern church. A hopeful sign in more recent years is the recognition by churches of this general calling and the ensuing efforts to intentionally help believers identify their passion and personal servant profiles. Individual believers live out their personal sense of calling or mission in their jobs, their families, their churches, or in special ministry outlets. They play significant supporting and leadership roles in these various arenas.

However, this general sense of calling is not what this discussion targets. Many people are called to give spiritual leadership. Our focus is on those whose life identity centers on being spiritual leaders. It involves personal awareness of a special call to God's service. The ministry activity and leadership agendas that flow from it focus on the spiritual development of others. Spiritual leaders help others live out their callings in their families, their personal mission expressions, their church life. Those called to be spiritual leaders feel connected to the big picture of God's movement, his kingdom agenda. They feel personally responsible for partnering with God in his mission. They may work in very obscure places, but changing the world is their aim. This concern is not fitted in around the edges of life; it is the preoccupation of the called.

The call also is not a religious career or position. A career and a call are two very different things. Having a church job does not make one the recipient of a divine call. The call is not mediated through human appointment or election. Remember Jim in the opening story? He is convinced that he went into the family business (his father was a pastor) rather than answering a call from God. He has settled for a career rather than a call. His pride gets in the way of his convictions. He is determined to be successful. Leaving the ministry would be a failure in his eyes.

The collapse of the church culture means that many spiritual leaders will not serve out their call within the church culture nor be remunerated through payrolls of religious institutions. This trend has been emerging over the past decade or so. Some spiritual leaders are being called into ministry after years in the business world. This growing phenomenon represents a shift toward apostolic ministry (discussed later in this chapter). These leaders bring all the skills and talents of their marketplace to bear in kingdom enterprises.

The call we are discussing as a heart-shaping subplot in the leader's story is the specialized and specific setting aside by God to some special lifelong task in his kingdom. This kind of call orders life around it. Personal ambitions and goals become subservient to the call. The called live for a larger world than just themselves and their families.

The call may come privately, but it is validated publicly. The leader's call is usually recognized by the church even though it may not be expressed through the church. Others seem drawn to support the leader's call financially, with prayer, and with their physical energies. The call drama of the leader's life story is lived out on a stage designed and built specifically for it by God.

We have seen four wonderful examples of call dynamics in Moses, David, Jesus, and Paul. These biblical leaders were recruited by God and set aside for his special purposes. God's assignment involved these leaders' serving his people and expanding his influence on the earth. God himself placed these leaders where he could best leverage his efforts through them. He drew others into their life work who supported them in a variety of ways. In each case, the leader's personal goals and ambitions became inextricably linked to the realization of his call. Yet the call involved far more than their personal stories. They lived for more than themselves. They were caught up in something bigger than them.

The call was not their call. Nor yours. It is God's call. It is his decision. It involves a sovereign selection. Certainly you can run from the call and even refuse it. Some have! But you cannot drum it up. Nor should you try. The call is not invented; it is revealed. You may take years to solidify your call. Its expression can shift venues and applications. Nevertheless, life options and job opportunities are always evaluated and determined against the plumbline of the call. My call, for instance, has been to serve God by working for the renewal of the North American church. For twenty years, this involved local, congregational ministry. Currently I am pursuing my call by being a resource to Christian leaders through conferencing, writing, and consulting.

There may have been a day when a spiritual leader without a call could serve in call-like capacities or with call expectations. This will become increasingly difficult to pull off, especially with the demands placed on those who are being called into Christian leadership in the twenty-first century. The call will no longer automatically command the respect it once did in the church culture. It will involve more than service; it will exact a sacrifice. The call of God in the days ahead will not grant a person automatic privilege or power but rather potential persecution and certain pain. This has been true before; it will be true again. It is already the case in many parts of the world where Christians suffer for the faith. The leaders are the first to be imprisoned and tortured.

The point is this: it is tough enough to serve as a Christian leader *with* a call. Without it, the choice constitutes cruel and unusual self-punishment.

Every Christian leader needs to nail down his or her call. As we have said, the call may not arrive all in one piece, never to need refinement. David and Jesus show a progressive understanding of their call. Sometimes the call can shift in terms of its expression. Many spiritual leaders experience distinct chapters in their call lifetimes. Paul's initial ministry chapter was followed by hidden years of theological reconstruction and service in Tarsus before he burst onto the world scene. Sometimes the call seems delayed, as in Moses' case. In all cases, however, call recipients can affirm a divine intervention that establishes in them a profound sense of destiny, that God has his hand on them for very special purposes.

What Did You Answer the Call to Do?

Now we turn our attention to the content of the call. This may take years to fully define. (In fact, the content of the call lives on in the leader's legacy.) But the call always carries a content of relationship and task, of being and doing.

The question, "What did you answer the call to do?" gains importance at a time when many of the rules are changing. For instance, young people who are still immersed in the church culture may be contemplating a call to minister in a world that simply will not exist in only a few years. What then for them? This situation is not hypothetical. Thousands of church leaders in their late fifties experience this reality. They have been hit hardest by the tectonic shifts in the culture both inside and outside the church in the past fifteen years. The world in which they entered the ministry has passed away in many respects. Their ministry experience seems ill suited to take them to the future. The trip they prepared for has been canceled. Many of these leaders have the internal drive and determination to retool, but many more do not. Fearful and anxious, those in the latter category are trying to hang on until the pension can rescue them. Many are not finishing well.

God's call is always relevant to the times. He is not in the business of recruiting leaders to serve the past. He anticipates the need and then calls and equips leaders for each era. The growing spiritual leader keeps the call current, both in relationship and in leadership competency. It is useful to look at some significant developments in the calling pattern of the Almighty.

Past and Current Models of Christian Ministry

Throughout Christian history, several predominant ministry models have informed the content of the call for most Christian leaders. These models are all still operative. Some have been more formative during certain periods of history and within particular faith traditions.

The first model is that of *holy person-priest*. Every religious tradition has its holy people, who are trained and credentialed in the rites of the religious observances of the faith. Christian priests and ministers serve as representatives of God within the Christian community. The character of the call in this model is one of standing apart from the faithful, serving as intercessor and divine emissary. The content of the call includes knowledge about God as well as the acquisition of appropriate techniques and information for performing ecclesiastical functions.

A second model is that of *parish minister-chaplain*. This particular model found its highest expression in the Roman system, in which the priest served as the curator of souls for those in his particular geographical territory. The model of parish priest remains formative in many denominations and congregations. The biblical motif of shepherd heavily influences this model. The character of this call is one of pastoring or shepherding. The content of the call involves development of caring skills and in recent decades at least a minimum level of psychological insight and counseling skills.

A third model of Christian ministry can be described as the *wordsmith-educator*. This model emerged primarily as a product of the Reformation, the spiritual counterpart to the Renaissance. This period was fueled by the revival of the study of antiquities. In the church, this emphasis meant new attention to ancient manuscripts and texts. The Christian leader became the resident scholar of biblical and theological studies. The sermon replaced the mass as the central sacrament of the Protestant service. The grasp of Hebrew and Greek and other academic learning secured the preacher-teacher's stature in the Christian world. The character of this call focused on instruction of the faithful, the dissemination of the truth found in the biblical revelation. The content of the call involved the academic skills enabling one to grasp and communicate a body of knowledge that would inform Christians of God's truth for their faith and practice. This model heavily influenced the rise of theological schools and seminaries. These institutions were designed to train people for ministry largely by preparing them as scholars. This model still holds a lot of attraction for Christian leaders. An entire industry of theological education depends on its continuation.

A fourth major model of the Christian ministry has developed in this century. The rise of the business organization (a development that emerged in post–Civil War America) has produced a corresponding model of ministry in the church culture. It is the model of the Christian leader as *professional manager-CEO*. A minister's effectiveness is now measured by the ability to manage budgets, recruit and lead personnel, develop ministry programs, provide corporate vision, garner new customers, and communicate inspirational and instructional messages in daily living to church attendees. This model has reached its pinnacle of development with the rise of the megachurch. The character of this call is one of dynamic leadership. The content of this call is virtually identical to that of business executives who lead successful business ventures.

The "New" Apostolic Leadership Model

Until recently, when Christian leaders considered what they were called to do, the previous models provided the prevailing choices. As you read over the descriptions, you may have identified your own particular calling as being informed by one or more of these models. Congregations and Christian ministries have operational expectations that draw from these same categories. Over the past fifteen years, a new model of ministry has begun to emerge. It promises to be the predominant model for those wishing to connect with the pre-Christian world as we enter the new millennium.

This new and emerging model of Christian ministry can be designated as *apostolic leadership,* or leadership for a new apostolic era. The parallels between the first and the twenty-first centuries reveal conditions under which a return to first-century-style Christian leadership makes sense. These parallels include globalism, religious pluralism, spiritual awakening, the collapse of institutional religion, and a pre-Christian environment, to name the most obvious. Many of today's Christian leaders, faced with similar challenges to those of the first apostles, will draw on the leadership practices and principles of the initial leaders of the Christian movement.

God is calling out a new breed of Christian leader at this hinge point in history. Some answering this call are serving in leadership roles in the church culture already. They have grown increasingly convinced that ministry effectiveness depends on their adopting new leadership behaviors. Their "unlearning curve" is significant as they shift ministry models. Other new apostolic leaders are being called from outside the existing ministry cadre.

Several significant character traits typify this new tribe of Christian ministers. We expand on this model because of its relative newness and because many leaders will find that this description gives expression to a work that God has been doing in their hearts. They will sense a confirmation of ongoing heart-shaping in the arena of their call.

MISSIONAL. Apostolic leaders take seriously and personally the Great Commission as the marching orders for the church and for their ministries. Therefore, they are evangelistic and eager to share the gospel with those in a spiritually energized, but increasingly pre-Christian, culture. Their imagination runs toward ways they can build bridges to the culture in order to reach more people with the gospel of Jesus Christ. For example, one church rents out an amusement park one evening a year as an outreach event.

KINGDOM CONSCIOUS. The first-century followers of Jesus embraced his teaching and preaching on the kingdom of God. New apostolic leaders also find themselves captured by a similar vision. This vision does not imply political power, as some evangelicals have pursued in the past two decades. These leaders believe Jesus when he said his kingdom does not fit this world. They seek to discover where God is at work and to join him there. They discover that his designs do not limit them to one congregation or just to church–real estate programming. Thus, apostolic leaders tend to be more collegial than competitive, more community focused than merely focused on church culture agenda. These leaders are busy reconceptualizing and practicing a Christianity that is not dependent on the prevailing church culture for its expression. One cluster of pastors in a small southern town now plan joint events (marriage and family seminars, for example), whereas a few years ago these churches would have been competitors.

TEAM PLAYERS. The heroic leader scenario increasingly proves inadequate in a world where no one person knows enough or brings all the needed skills to the table. An information age populated by knowledge workers inspires networking, synergy, and ad hoc arrangements. Modern apostolic leaders create a team in order to accomplish their ministry objectives. This approach actually reflects more the initial leadership culture of the Christian movement. Jesus formed the Twelve. Within that group arose the senior group of three. In its early chapters, the book of Acts records the activities of Peter and John. Later it highlights Paul and Barnabas, Paul and Luke, Paul and Silas, Paul and Timothy, and so forth. Leaders for a new apostolic era desire and are comfortable with leadership plurality. They crave the accountability of a team to ensure their spiritual growth and personal integrity. Many congregations have several pastors who share pulpit responsibilities. Many more recruit lay leaders onto the ministry team.

ENTREPRENEURIAL. The accounts of the early leaders of the Christian faith reveal a creative genius that can be described as entrepreneurial. Do not hear this observation in a commercially crass way as meaning that they had something to sell. Rather, the point is that without the cultural props that many Christian leaders have come to rely on, they intentionally strategized ways to engage people who did not know them or their religion. They knew how to create a market for the gospel. The new apostolic leaders evidence this same creative spirit. Their ministries explode with all kinds of efforts designed to attract people to Christ. Coffee clubs, comedy clubs, concerts, Internet chat rooms, and business luncheons are just a few examples. Many of their efforts aim at engaging people on their own turf rather than waiting behind stained glass for people to show up. Spiritual leaders informed solely by the previous ministry models operate with a misassumption about evangelism and outreach. They believe that doing church stuff better will bring people in.

SCHOOLED BY THE BUSINESS CULTURE. Jesus recruited his initial band of disciples from the business community. This tactic revealed his determination to gather leaders around him who were in touch with the culture. People heard Jesus as being culturally relevant. The early apostles maintained the same connectivity. So do twenty-first-century apostolic leaders. Their approach does not represent an accommodationist strategy. They just want to gain a hearing for truth. Many of these leaders answer the call to ministry while pursuing a business career. Some leave that career in obedience to God's call, whereas others adopt a tent-making approach, helping finance their own ministry. One pastor I know left a six-figure income to begin pastoring. He does not bring seminary education to his role, but he does bring topflight leadership training provided by his former employer.

PEOPLE DEVELOPERS. The early apostles made a signally important decision early on. They decided to become ministry brokers rather than ministry managers. They empowered people to enter the ranks of significant leadership and ministry. Today's emerging leaders for a new apostolic era view their role as producers, not primary providers. They develop a ministry culture that frees the people of God to discover and develop their own ministry passions, gifts, and talents. They equip people with whatever skills they need for effective missional living. Developing people goes beyond merely training church workers. It involves the apostolic leader's passion to see people gain maturity in every area of life. They do not view people as resources to make their own ministry successful. Rather, they see themselves as resources for people's spiritual growth. A pastor in the Myrtle Beach area conducts monthly leadership development seminars for his ministry leadership. He personally mentors his ministry staff and lay team leaders.

VISIONARY. In recent years, business leaders have been challenged to provide visionary leadership. New apostolic leaders have brought this same emphasis into the church, believing that God calls out to his people from a preferable future. Their ministries and personal lives demonstrate an intentionality that attracts followers. They can articulate a compelling vision that translates the Great Commission into their ministry context.

Increasingly I am encountering men and women who have a vision for a particular city or region. One couple I know moved to Boston without a particular assignment but like Paul had a "Macedonian call" to that urban center.

SPIRITUAL. In one conflict episode recorded in the book of Acts, the detractors of the early apostles took note that Peter and John had "been with Jesus" (Acts 4:13). This association set early Christian leaders apart for their assignment. New apostolic leaders bear a striking resemblance to these early leaders of the movement. They possess a spiritual presence and energy that is unmistakably that of Jesus. They evidence a personal relationship with him that goes well beyond the capacity for rendering textual exposition about him. To borrow an apostle's phrase, they know him. They love Jesus and are sold on his agenda. Their enthusiasm for him invites others to make the same commitment. This relational emphasis rescues these leaders from being dry purveyors of doctrinal orthodoxy and turns them into vibrant conveyors of welcome and hope to spiritual searchers. A worship leader recently told me about his personal spiritual retreats, leaving me with little wonder why his ministry maintains such spiritual integrity.

The new apostolic leaders differ significantly from leaders who have adopted the other ministry models not only in terms of the character of their call. Their training and development also reveal a distinctiveness from that of prevailing and past ministry models. Practitioners in the previous models have been trained largely by the existing church culture, Bible colleges and seminaries, denominational conferencing, and support materials.

Leaders for a new apostolic era draw from different training resources. These include new tribe pastors, the pastors of entrepreneurial, new-paradigm congregations who have developed teaching churches. These churches and leaders conduct leadership conferences for thousands of people each year. A second training influence is the business culture. This source proves formative for two reasons. First, the business community understands the culture outside the church. Second, God is calling more and more leaders for the Christian movement straight out of business. These businessmen and women bring their business training and leadership skills right along with them into the church setting. God is upgrading the leadership of his movement by directly importing already-developed leaders. A third training source for new apostolic leaders is a number of parachurch organizations, particularly those that understand cultural trends.

A fourth development resource for new apostolic leaders is the growing number of consultants who offer a wide variety of customized assistance to churches and church leaders. Denominations that want to continue to be players will have to be as resourceful as these consultants and parachurch organizations.

A fifth element of leadership development for the new millennium leaders includes various emerging processes that offer a variety of mentoring approaches. This method recognizes the power of Jesus' initial training methodology. Learning clusters of peer mentors create venues where apostolic leaders can discuss their ministry experiences and what they see God as being up to in the world. (This discussion on apostolic ministry is treated more fully in the author's *Revolution in Leadership,* 1998).

By reflecting on what it is you answered the call to do, you are forced to take a backward look across your life and ministry. It also raises the issue of your call's future development. You may currently be experiencing a period of call transition. Previous ministry models may no longer adequately allow you to give expression to your call. Like Paul, you may be asking, "What do you want me to do, Lord?" It is a good question. Knowing the answer bestows you with intentionality. You have in place a decision matrix for determining how to budget time, energies, monies, and other resources in order to accomplish what you must do.

The reverse scenario creates a leadership dilemma. Not coming to a clear understanding of what you have been called to do leaves you vulnerable to competing agendas and imposing personalities in your ministry world. A lack of direction will eventually dissipate your leadership vitality.

Susan came to the conference exhausted and spiritually depleted. Just nine months earlier, she had gone to the congregation as youth minister with a lot of excitement. Now all of the thrill was gone. When she arrived, she found a youth committee unwilling to relinquish control of the planning. The senior pastor had an agenda that he wanted her to accomplish. And the parents seemed unwilling to assume any responsibility for the ministry to their own children.

One approach that Susan could have taken to deal with this dilemma would have been to get all warring factions together and try to reach consensus on the direction the youth ministry should take. This would not necessarily be the wrong thing to do, but it was not the best initial thing to do. The best first thing Susan needed to do was to nail down in her heart what she believed she had been called by God to do there. She then would be in a position to proactively engage the different constituencies to create a better ministry for the young people of that church. Susan's call was not uninformed by the situation, but it also needed to inform the situation. In other words, she had to arrive at a direction for the ministry that she could articulate to the various constituency groups. Merely trying to politick the situation and appease the pastor, the youth committee, and the youth was a dead-end street where there was no shared vision or values.

Susan had some clear notions about youth ministry. I encouraged her to develop these into a ministry program statement and action plan. She did. Not everyone was pleased. Some of the youth committee resigned, but other parents stepped up to the plate. At last check, even her pastor was coming around, especially since new life is stirring in the youth ministry.

One of the most challenging times in a leader's life can occur when the leader is transitioning the expression of the call in the ministry. Trying to live in two worlds can frustrate both the leader and those who are led. This is why it is important to have the support of a cadre of people who share the same vision as the leader.

John was convinced that the congregation he had served as pastor for eight years needed to become more evangelistic. He figured out that the transition would require that he shift some of his own behavior and time allocations. He knew he was going to have to spend more intentional time with people outside the church culture. He correctly realized that his personal modeling would be a strategic way to influence the congregation. Tactically, however, it meant that John was going to have to make some personal work adjustments. He deliberately led the elder board into an affirmation of what he wanted to do and why. They signed off on his plan. This support for John became critical when four families left the church because they disagreed with the new emphasis and how John was spending his time. John had done the important work of letting the leadership core become acquainted with his call so they could support it. The transition went remarkably well.

If the question of what the content and character of your call is perplexes you, take heart. You are not alone. The same question increasingly disturbs many other Christian leaders at this time. We know the old world is collapsing, but the contours of the new world are not yet entirely clear. Some of the call functions of the old models will survive. Many will not, at least not in their present form. It seems that the emerging apostolic leadership model will become more significant over the next decade, perhaps longer. Whichever model or combination of models you choose as a vehicle to express your call will influence the heart-shaping work of God in you. It will also shape the way God reveals himself through you to his people.

The next question pushes you to reflect over the history of your call experience in terms of its impact and effectiveness.

Have You Seen the Attendant Gifts and Talents Come Along?

One afternoon the phone rang in my office. On the other end was an anxious voice: "I need you to come up here and tell us how to get our church going." That was it. No greeting. No introduction. No name.

"Well, that part's easy," I chuckled, trying to transmit a grin over the phone. "Why don't we start with who this is and something about where you are."

A few minutes of conversation revealed the following facts. This pastor (I will call him Fred) was two years into his present pastorate. The church had gone from a congregation of eighty people to one of twenty-five. This was the third such experience for this fifty-seven-year-old man who had entered the ministry late in life. The two previous pastorates had ended after marked decline. It became apparent that Fred was the issue, not his congregation.

"What do you enjoy doing, Fred?" I asked in search of some strengths to use in constructing a strategy to improve his congregational leadership.

"I don't enjoy preaching much. I'm not much of a student."

I prodded. "You've told me what you don't enjoy doing. Tell me what you do find energy in doing."

"I like to be with people in the field," he replied. Further investigation revealed that this meant he liked to visit people in the hospital when they were sick.

After more listening, I finally took a deep breath, said a quick prayer, and ventured a cautious observation: "Fred, maybe you don't need to be a pastor. It seems that your efforts consistently fail to produce what you hope for, and your interests don't coincide with the skills you need in order to lead congregations." My heart was beating fast. This kind of entrance into someone's holy place is not something done lightly or often.

Several moments of silence passed. What seemed to be an eternity was finally broken by a sigh on the other end. Not a sigh of sadness. A sigh of relief. "That's what my wife has been saying too." Within a few minutes, we had sketched out a plan that would allow Fred to use his skills to minister to people without putting himself under the pressure to perform without a call. Guilt and fear had trapped this man for several years, injuring his own spiritual vitality. When he hung up the phone, he seemed thrilled to pick back up his basic life skills. I suspect his wife and congregation shared his joy.

Fred's admission that he was not much of a student and did not enjoy public speaking was verified by the foot patterns of parishioners—they were leaving. In three successive churches, Fred had created empty pews.

The problem was not in the pews. Fred knew it, because he gave in too easily at the suggestion that he had misread his call. Our brief phone interview invited him to look critically at his set of talents, gifts, and skills.

People who feel called should examine what they bring to the table. A refusal to engage in significant evaluation of competencies and gifts abdicates the stewardship of the call. Understanding our own mix of abilities is a very helpful way of coming to call clarification. Because God knew that he was going to initiate a call on your life, he has already placed some tools in you for him to work with. We saw this with Moses, David, Paul, and Jesus. Moses received instruction in early life in both law and leadership. David developed courage and self-reliance as a young shepherd. Paul's mind was first bent toward theological pursuits by Pharisees before his conversion and call. Jesus brought to his call a capacity to engage people that he learned through countless interactions with the townspeople of Nazareth who hired out his services. The same dynamic is at work with you. Your call enhances and enlarges work already begun.

Do the gifts, abilities, and passions you have match what you are trying to do? This sounds so simple but is so often violated that it needs reemphasis. I have witnessed people agonize over decisions for days, weeks, and even months that should not even challenge their decision-making energies. What they are considering may fall outside their gift range or heartbeat, but because of some notion that every open door should be explored, they needlessly wrestle over it. Even worse, I sometimes see leaders working where they are not impassioned or gifted to serve. The heartbreak that accompanies the oftentimes slow, sometimes sudden, realization of poor placement has caused many people to agonize over their call. Some mistakenly leave the call behind because of mismatched talent to opportunity. They misread the situation. Self-doubt wins in many cases in which practical wisdom could have prevented the tragedy's being set in motion. This is not meant to discourage leaders' attempting new ventures or trying out new skills. If this never happened, no new talents would ever be acquired. However, a certain aptitude should develop over time if the person is working in the area of his or her call.

Another way of asking this question is to reflect on how God is manifesting himself in your ministry efforts. Bill enjoyed his work as a youth ministry leader. The kids were great. He liked hanging out with them after school and on weekends. He had as much fun as they did at the special events he helped plan and coordinate.

At first, Bill did not notice. One of the youth workers first brought it to his attention after Bill had given a closing devotion at an after-game fellowship. "You know, Bill, when you talk, those kids really listen. Man, they were hanging on every word you said." Bill thanked him. On further reflection, he realized that more than anything else he just loved getting in front of those kids and helping them think through some of the issues they face. He was glad to know it connected. The evidence of Bill's effectiveness mounted. Whenever Bill spoke, kids responded. They opened up to him. More important, they opened up to God. Bill was anointed when he spoke to kids. He did not swell up with pride over this. He responded with humility, because he knew that something bigger than him was at work when he spoke. He gave God the credit. Bill did not take this anointing for granted. He worked hard preparing to teach and was always amazed at the results.

Bill's pastor began using him to preach on occasion. Bill loved to prepare for those messages, and the people really seemed helped. He discovered he could communicate important truths in ways that people easily grasped. Over time, Bill identified that his primary gift is that of teaching. Since those student ministry days, Bill has pastored effectively and now serves as a professor of theology. He did not ignore the obvious blessing of God in his teaching. In fact, he has ordered his life around this primary passion that God has affirmed in him.

You may identify with what Bill experienced because you have experienced the same dynamics yourself. Those times when you feel most alive. Those moments in ministry that you believe you have discovered why you have come to the planet. "This is what I want to do all my life," you say to yourself.

The concept of God's anointing is an old-fashioned idea. Chapter Two discussed David's sense of being anointed. You may never have called it this—maybe you use some other word or phrase to describe it. It is a mystery. But it is real. It is the sense you get that God has especially poured his Spirit and divine power over a certain activity that you engage in. Not just once, but consistently. You sense the power of the Spirit, a special energy, a strange aliveness. You know it to be a sovereign gift of God, not something self-generated.

Others notice it too. Your efforts bring results. People respond to you. You get through to them. You produce work that is helpful and touches people's hearts. Sometimes, like Bill, you may not have been consciously aware of the special anointing of God until affirmations from others began to come.

You may never have talked to anyone else about this phenomenon for fear of being misunderstood or even thought prideful. Just the opposite is true. The anointing humbles you, because you know you have done nothing to warrant it. God has sovereignly bestowed his power to do his work. You know that your effectiveness when anointed goes way past what you alone can produce. And you would be terrified to face the future without it.

So don't! Construct your life so that you are doing more of what God is anointing in your life. This is the heart of your call.

God does not limit his anointing to speaking arenas. Some people who sing are able to grab hold of audiences even though they may be less talented than some others. Some people find God's special anointing in dealing with the sick, or creating art that connects God's truth with life, or organizing ministry projects. The list goes on and on, limited only by the will of the Almighty, who chooses to anoint his chosen servants for the work he has called them to do.

We can come at this question another way. It could be treated as a separate question. However, it is closely tied to the issue of how God manifests himself in your life and ministry. What theological themes seem most operative or most often expressed in your ministry? Some reflection will probably surface around four or five of these. Perhaps grace occupies a prevalent place in your work (speaking, writing themes, openness to people, and so forth). Hope might characterize your counseling and preaching. A search for holiness might show up in the way you plan and lead worship experiences. You might combine evangelism with the doctrine of universal priesthood to fashion a strong missional theme to your ministry efforts.

A man once left the church where I pastored, complaining that I only had nine sermons (he had a few other issues too). That accusation caused me some pain, because I had pastored there for almost nine years at the time! However, I have now had the time to look over the corpus of my ten years of sermons. I think he was generous! The truth is, I only have four or five songs that I sing. Most folks cannot carry more tunes than that.

The identification of these themes is important not only for self-understanding but also for understanding what God is revealing about his own heart through you. God shapes the spiritual leader's heart in order to share his own heart with his people. Your life message reflects some significant truths about God. He has called you and positioned you for strategic purposes. The effective leader brings just what is needed to the situation.

Who Is Your Audience?

An old story recounts the dream of a preacher. To a packed house, the preacher pours out his heart. When he finishes—nothing. Then something. A lone figure way up in the balcony stands and begins to applaud. In his mind's eye, the camera zooms in on that solitary admirer, and he discovers it is Jesus! Suddenly it does not matter that all the others are not clapping their approval. As long as Jesus is pleased, it is OK.

The question, "Who is your audience?" concludes this investigation of the call as a heart-shaping process designed by God to develop you as a leader. The answer to this question is crucial, for we all play to an audience we hold in our minds. This is not a question about whom we are serving and how we are doing in our service to them. This question probes whose approval we are after.

A frustrated staff member in a large downtown church lamented to me that when his pastor describes the church, it is a different church than he sees. The pastor plays to the old guard, so his decisions always cater to them. This frustrates the staff member, who sees a more diverse congregation. The senior pastor's audience has a limiting effect on his vision of the future.

Some people put a parent in the audience, particularly if the parental blessing has been withheld. One leader in an organization I consulted was driving everyone crazy because of his hypercriticalness and his highly controlling personality. The benefit of his brilliance was more than being offset by the negative energy he was generating through his acting out. I eventually learned that he was desperately pursuing the blessing of his father, now dead and no longer able to give it. That man consciously and subconsciously placed his father in the audience. He mounted heroic efforts to win what could never be given to him. His choice of audience was killing him, and eventually did cut short his ministry with the organization he served.

Many church leaders place their ministry constituents in the audience. Spiritual leaders certainly cannot ignore their intended constituents. However, this becomes problematic when leaders serve them in order to win approval. This attempt to meet personal psychological needs through the call creates a very unhealthy relationship between leader and people. In this dysfunctional relationship, the call can become sublimated to meeting the needs of the one who is called to serve. When their sense of approval rests in the ministry constituents, some leaders allow their boundaries to be transgressed in order to gain acceptance. Some leaders fail to serve their ministry audience well by refusing to tell them the truth for fear of being rejected.

Other people can take their place in the leader's grandstand as well. These can be significant others in the ministry arena—perhaps mentors, professors, district superintendents, or fellow Christian leaders whose opinion matters. This can result from positive or negative dynamics. If leaders carry in their hearts a sure knowledge that others are cheering for them, the audience encourages them. But if leaders have something to prove to this crowd, they will become more interested in the admiration of the audience than in following their call.

Sometimes Christian leaders jeopardize the call's effectiveness by filling up their audience with faces of detractors or memories of past mistakes, embarrassments, or failures. These leaders run the race in their minds to the accompaniment of catcalls, boos, and hisses. They wilt under the glare of their enemies. When this happens, the call falls prisoner to those whom these leaders have disappointed or bruised. The unrelenting sense of failure haunts them and finally takes them out of the running. The call dies with the leader's resignation.

Every Christian leader at one time or another has populated the audience with representatives of each of these groups. If we are honest, we have all sought approval to some degree from those whose approval cannot ultimately satisfy.

There is an Audience of One that the Christian leader must cultivate. Only his approval assuages insignificance and loneliness and feelings of failure. Only he keeps perfect score. He is the One who has issued the call and convened the games. He is the one who will judge the efforts and award the medals. His is the only vote that counts, no matter how many seem lined up either for or against you. His "well done" will make every effort worth doing again.

Do you have an Audience of One? If not, the call is in jeopardy of being compromised, no matter how slightly or innocently your ticket sales for grandstand seats have been altered. Only One belongs in the audience.

Moses' One gave him a private burial. David's One secured his kingdom forever. Paul's One awarded him the victor's crown. Jesus' One sat him down again at his right hand.

Your One is your only hope of realizing the call that he has given to you. As you live out your life message through your call, you will help others discover their own ability to play to their own Audience.

What is going on in the call subplot of your life? Consider some important questions:

- What did you answer the call to do?
- Have you seen the attendant gifts, talents, and passion come along?
- What has God anointed? When do you feel most alive in ministry?
- How has your understanding of your call changed over time?
- How is the call being expressed in what you are doing right now?
- Who is your audience?

Someone is waiting to have these conversations with you. He is in your grandstand. And he is cheering for you.

7

COMMUNITY

CONNECTING WITH OTHERS' HEARTS

MANY LEADERSHIP IDEAS in American culture seem informed by the great American myth, the Western. In the story line, the bad guys hold the town hostage. They bully people to get what they want. They prey on the weakness of people who would like to stand up to them but do not have the guts to do so. Bad guys generally hang out in gangs.

Good guys come in singles. The Lone Ranger, the Rifleman, the Virginian, all help the townspeople realize that they can rise up and throw off the tyranny that oppresses them. Of course, the hero goes first. Usually alone.

Leaders do indeed show up as bad guys and good guys. Whenever bad guys get in positions of power, they exploit people. Leadership based on control is dark-side leadership. The people unfortunate to live under the influence of controllers whine and whimper but often lack the perceived clout to change the situation. Some gang (higher-ups in the organizational food chain) usually keeps the controller in power.

Good guys show up too. They empower people, tap into the motivations of those they lead, and energize them to work to accomplish their aspirations. People willingly follow without coercion. The good guys carry others on their own backs. This dynamic consternates the controllers; they do not understand how someone can get people to do what they are supposed to do without intimidation, bullying, and punitive measures.

In the Western saga, we usually do not know where the good guys come from. They abruptly appear on the scene from nowhere. They do not like to talk about their past. They are problem solvers, not community builders.

This part of the great Western myth needs to be debunked for its leadership implications. Leaders are not shaped in isolation. Leaders are shaped *in* community. And they are shaped *by* community. Leaders cannot be separated from the formative processes of community. Despite any claims to the contrary, leaders are not self-made people. There is no such person.

God deliberately and intentionally shapes the leader's heart through community. The subplot of community played itself out in each of our biblical leaders' lives. Nations and movements emerged and were nurtured as a result of the community dynamics at work in these four biblical heroes. Moses sought to establish a nation where he could finally be at home. David overcame the early views of his family of origin and others about his limited potential to create a community between the clans of Israel and forge them into a nation. Paul used community building (planting churches) as a primary strategy for spreading the faith. Jesus revealed to the world that community lies at the heart of the universe in the very nature of God himself.

The dynamic of community may be the least understood of all the subplots that constitute the spiritual leader's story. This chapter cannot address all the issues related to the lack of community in many, if not most, Christian ministries and congregations. It does take square aim at the leader's role in this problem by identifying some key ways in which God uses community to shape the leader's heart. If leadership is part of the problem, then it can also be part of the solution. Not until spiritual leaders are willing to move past the Lone Ranger, heroic-leader model of leadership will they foster genuine community and release its power for transforming lives.

No one suffers more from the lack of community than spiritual leaders themselves. A minister's wife sobbed, "We have no friends, no one close to us. I don't know who we would go to if we needed help. Our families are miles away." The Christian leader's wife expressed her frustration to a group of other ministers' wives. Her desperate cries for community, so long suppressed, exploded out of her in the quasi-community created at the weekend retreat.

A staff member confided to a friend: "My pastor tells me I can't have friends in the church because that will make me too vulnerable. So tell me, since I spend all my time with church people, what am I supposed to do for friends? We certainly don't do things together as a staff."

These two situations, unfortunately, are all too typical. The lack of understanding of community as a major tool in the hand of God for his heart-shaping work debilitates many spiritual leaders. As a result, the ministries they lead are impoverished at the same point.

It does not have to be this way.

Tom and Suzanne finally felt at home. They had begun their leadership as pastor and wife five years earlier. The five years had gone well, but they grew in their conviction that God wanted to grow people, not just a church. They knew they had to proactively create a transforming community. A key component of their strategy was to establish small groups as part of the church's discipling and ministry efforts. Tom and Suzanne each began a group of their own. In one year, the two groups became five. Within five years, the number of groups had reached almost thirty. Church members who were a part of a group enjoyed more care and personal support than they had ever received from church staff leaders who were paid to attend to them. Many people outside the church came to the recovery and support groups that sprang up as church members discovered the power of healing through community.

Tom and Suzanne also took care to develop a ministry team around them. The team spent time together praying and working but also having fun. The sense of belonging freed the team members to share their struggles with one another. Their successes were sweetened by the celebration that others would lend.

The experience of Tom and Suzanne needs to be more normative. Spiritual leaders need community. This discussion seeks to raise the leader's awareness of how God uses community as a heart-shaping dynamic. Some diagnostic questions will force some introspection. The chapter begins with a look at the leader's original community, the family of origin. Then it considers the impact that the leader's ministry community plays in the leader's heart development.

This investigation may make you feel uncomfortable. Try not to squirm out of God's scope. He has targeted your heart for greatness.

The Leader's Family of Origin

Richard knew that he needed to do something. He had never been so uncertain about himself before. During his ministry burnout, he had managed to pull through without losing his ministry post, largely due to the support of his wife and a group of friends who understood the pressures of leadership. But just now as he was emerging from that dark chapter of his own life, his emotional reserves became depleted from a moral crisis in one of his lifelong heroes, combined with a spate of tragedies in his church. Richard feared he might slip back into the wilderness of the soul.

Richard's response proved to be a defining moment for this young Christian leader. He determined to reengage his family of origin to hunt for clues as to why he was vulnerable at certain points. The journey for him involved traversing two thousand miles and visiting several generations of family.

Richard made some remarkable discoveries. He uncovered alcoholism in his family that had largely been ignored. Putting the pieces together, he figured out that his father had been the adult child of an alcoholic. The light bulbs went off inside Richard's head. He suddenly understood why his family of origin lacked genuine intimacy and was crippled when it came to making friends. The fear of risking emotional vulnerability had isolated the family. Work had been his father's drug of choice. Richard realized that he had adopted the same patterns. He used work, even church work, to cover him up so people could not get to him. Accomplishment meant everything, and his own drivenness was compounded by the fact that his father, so emotionally needy himself, had been unable to emotionally connect and bless his son.

Richard felt reborn with his new insights. They allowed him to take charge of the demons in his life, because he could now name them. The young leader also realized that some of the reasons for his ministry ineffectiveness had grown out of the deficits of his early community. God had used his family of origin to create a man very sensitive to the needs of others. Overplaying this strength had sent Richard into burnout, but it was still a strength. His enormous energy, stemming from his desire to achieve, had allowed him to enjoy great ministry accomplishment that had benefited a lot of people. But he could learn to rest now.

Richard will always be vulnerable at these points. He will always walk with a limp. Like Jacob after his encounter with the angel at Jabbock, Richard will have the limp as a trophy of his wrestling with God about who he, Richard, was going to become. He now realizes that God was shaping his heart in his early years, before he was even aware of it. Out of his struggles he has emerged a champion.

All leaders limp. Leaders become leaders, in part, because they are willing to wrestle with who they are, who they want to become, how they can overcome some deficit in their own lives. They often need to achieve, need to be admired, even loved, need to bring order to some chaos that is within them. And almost always, these vulnerabilities are established in the leader's family of origin, the early community that begins to shape the leader's heart before the young child can even speak.

The difference between healthy and unhealthy leaders often rests in the leader's willingness or unwillingness to explore these early heart lessons. Doing so yields insights that can free the leader through self-understanding. Failure to do so keeps the leader chained to the past and tormented by mysterious forces that are not understood. The damage is not confined to the leader alone. Those in the leader's constellation suffer from the unlocked and unlearned lessons of the leader's heart.

A significant investigation that the leader can conduct into the family of origin involves the search for hidden addictions and compulsions. These proclivities travel along family lines. Sex, food, money, power, pornography, work, adrenaline, and the need for approval join drugs and alcohol on the list of substance or process addictions. Addictions provide emotional anesthesia to mask or dull the pain in the heart. This is why they are so hard to break.

Certain addictions have become baptized in the Christian world. Work is one. Spiritual leaders are particularly susceptible to this one, because most leaders are given to hard work. However, work can be a convenient way of escaping from the family, or from one's self, or from unpleasant or unfamiliar territory, such as real emotional intimacy with a spouse. The ministry can become the mistress.

Adrenaline addiction can sometimes go hand in hand with a work addiction. Adrenaline can be an enticing elixir. It places the mind (and body) in a stage of preparedness. Stage fright awakens adrenal glands as much as any other fright. This chemical produces an emotional high, but the body goes through a withdrawal period on the other side. Some ministers, unable to tolerate the downside "blues" feeling, just keep it from coming. They introduce some other activity (more work) to keep themselves "up." They may not even consciously be aware of what they are doing.

Ross, a worship leader, told his small support group that before he understood adrenaline withdrawal, he often felt worse on his day off than on any other day of the week. He was grouchy, restless, and generally hard to get along with. On several occasions, his wife suggested that he go into the office. *She* needed relief. After he became acquainted with his need for down time, Ross learned to anticipate and appreciate his body and soul's need to repair. He learned to love the blues.

The overstimulation of adrenal glands over time can lead not only to the kinds of heart issues that we are concerned with (loss of genuine spiritual energy, family problems brought on by neglect) but also to real, physical heart problems. The overproduction of adrenaline has been linked to susceptibility to various cardiovascular ills.

The need for approval plagues some spiritual leaders. This compulsion becomes addictive because it actually earns the leader credit with others and thus results in a lot of stroking for the leader. Ministry constituents are astounded by the care and attention they receive from the leader. The overdoing of meeting others' needs is usually seen as benign by the recipients and heralded by them. This response feeds the leader's compulsion. If the need for approval drives the leader's activity, then the leader becomes too available, too responsive. In order to hear, "I don't know what we would do without you," the leader makes all sorts of irrational decisions, denying the needs for leisure, rest, and family and becoming hooked on the need to be needed. One form this addiction takes shows up in a ministry system that is too dependent on the leader for operation. Ironically, this is often accompanied by frequent complaining on the part of the leader. One of the warning signals of burnout is a growing resentment of the demands being placed on the leader.

Some Christian leaders also report an addiction to pornography. Pornography provides a pseudointimacy that usually reflects a lack of connectedness with others. Often this can be traced to a family of origin's failure to provide genuine nurture and intimacy. Usually the addicted person does not know how to achieve authentic intimacy with another.

Not all addictive or compulsive behaviors have family-of-origin roots. However, any investigation of these behaviors should probe the family of origin for potential physical, psychological, or emotional linkages. Some people have lived with behaviors all their lives that seem normal to them without ever realizing that these behaviors are problematic for them, their relationships, and their leadership. These usually include the need to rescue and the tendency to overfunction in the ministry system.

Harold declared to his cluster group that he had mowed the church lawn for the last time. Until then, he had thought that by setting the example of landscape care, others would follow his lead. Instead, the people of the congregation were willing to let him mow the lawn (and take people home and do office work). When he explored his growing resentment, Harold came to see that he kept other people out of ministry because of his overimplication of himself into every arena of church life. The issue was not the people's lack of serving. It was his difficulty setting reasonable boundaries.

This reflects another set of heart issues related to the leader's family of origin—the capacity of the leader to set and maintain appropriate boundaries. Boundaries tell us where we stop and the rest of the universe picks up. Boundaries are both physical and psychological. They are like fences. The problem comes when the fence is down or the gate has been left open.

The inability to say no, for instance, reflects a boundary issue. When leaders do not say no when they want to, they wind up doing things they do not want to do. They can grow to loathe themselves for this lack of assertion. Usually leaders who are struggling with this are afraid—afraid that people will abandon them if they do not yield to others' demands, or afraid that people will quit liking them.

Another boundary issue shows up when the leader responds to pressure by withdrawing and refusing to accept help. Another boundary problem can be the leader who fails to respect other people's boundaries and operates as a controller in the ministry community. Almost all leaders will deal with this issue whether or not it plagues them personally. Spiritual centers attract controllers. From Judeo-Christian theology, we learn that the origin of evil and suffering centers around issues of control. Jesus challenged the control mentality of the Pharisees. Their need for control was expressed in their obsessive-compulsive behaviors regarding ceremonial cleanliness and fasting as well as their legalistic theology.

Usually boundary problems can be traced back to certain habits and practices in the leader's family of origin. Having a boundary difficulty does not disqualify one from ministry. Many people struggle with these in some form. However, not knowing about or dealing with boundary issues can result in the leader's eventual self-disqualification. This is another reason why it is so important to reopen the family file and see what bags you are carrying on your life-leadership trip.

So far the discussion has focused on the potential negative aspects of the leader's family-of-origin community. A leader with true maturity, however, sees whatever was dealt by the family of origin as gifts promoting personal development. The finest leaders often are overcomers.

The family of origin also brings many manifestly good gifts. Many Christian leaders have emerged from homes where they were nurtured and blessed, their accomplishments celebrated, and their relationships securely anchored in health. This may be your experience. Certainly leaders with families want this to be the legacy of the family environment they provide for their children.

The people in such a leader's ministry constellation of influence are blessed. They are usually served, not manipulated. They are given permission to grow and to risk without punitive retribution for failure. They are privileged to earn credit for their work and are respected for their contribution. In addition, they enjoy a sense of community, because the leader's heart is aware of the benefits of community.

The self-integration that occurs throughout the leader's life will begin with a reckoning of the contributions of the first community of the leader's life. Whether good or bad, these factors and influences can be used by God to shape the leader's heart. Leaders who have made the effort to journey back home can see down the upcoming road farther and clearer.

The Leader's Current Family

God also shapes leaders' hearts through their current family situations. The home remains the chief laboratory and schoolhouse for human relationships and character development. This is why effective Christian leaders pay attention to home-and-hearth issues. The apostle Paul, outlining the qualifications for congregational leadership, granted disproportionate space to family relationships. Failure here, he implied, cannot be overcome by great talent and gifts.

No one has a perfect home. But a few standard checkpoints can diagnose heart problems, beginning with the spouse. God designed marriage to portray the close relationship that he desires with us. God works through the marriages of leaders to develop a heart more capable of experiencing genuine intimacy and community. The marriage relationship of effective leaders generally proves to be a key ingredient in their leadership capacity. A strong, vibrant marriage that evidences health and balance suggests that the leader maintains integrity when the lights go out and the public-stage curtain comes down. This assurance increases the leader's line of credit with his followers. On the flip side, a sick or conflicted marriage drains energy from the leader's emotional reserve and eventually limits the spiritual leader's ministry.

Marriage tending, then, for spiritual leaders is a priority. Paying attention to the spouse is not a second-mile responsibility; it is a first order of business. The spouse does not exist primarily as another resource for the work of the leader. The spouse is the gift of God, holding the promise of experiencing full life by enjoying another. Marriage is one course in the divine curriculum for learning how to lose life in order to discover it. When leaders devote themselves to a life partner, they reflect the heart of God in their desire for a growing, intimate relationship with his people.

Gerald was finishing up twelve years of pastoring a congregation. In the last week, he received a call from a person he had helped come to faith in Christ. The caller signed off by saying, "I don't remember a single sermon you preached (chuckle). But I remember that you took Sylvia (Gerald's wife) out on a date every week." Gerald received the comment as a high compliment. He realized in a fresh way that his core values had been showing and his modeling of them spoke volumes.

Enter children. Common wisdom maintains that children are given to parents so parents can instruct them. The truth is, God gives children to parents to teach the parents some things. Things like patience, and discipline, and self-sacrifice, and responsibility, and mercy, and hope. Also exquisite joy and celebration, and the meaning of legacy, and a glimpse of eternity. Mostly, children instruct us in the importance of the blessing. The fundamental need of our children is to receive our blessing. The blessing imparts love and acceptance and a sense of being believed in and a sense of covenant. It also implies community, because blessings are given in the context of covenant and community, by a significant other who has a relationship to us.

Leaders who themselves were blessed as children enjoy a head start in life. Those who were not sometimes leave behind a trail of blood. Until they find blessing, they rarely act as blessings to others. Instead, they compete, manipulate, intimidate, and use others to achieve their agendas. Forget grace-based relationships; to them, everyone is on a performance standard.

Children receive the blessing in concrete ways, through a sense of close relationship and the understanding of the parent for the child. This takes time, always a precious commodity for leaders. Without intentional planning for children's needs, the leader can become an absentee parent, even while living under the same roof and in daily contact with the kids.

A key factor for extending the blessing involves the availability of the leader-parent to the child, especially being emotionally present. A leader without any time or physical margin for the child rarely has the emotional margin for them either. The parent must enter the child's world in order to have the power to bless. And the parent must include the child in the parent's world in order to bless the child for his or her life journey. Time is not the only ingredient, of course. Many parents who spend lots of time with their kids use that time to no benefit in developing relationships. The key, again, is intentionality.

Michelle and Troy (a ministry couple) set aside Thursday nights as family night. The answering machine was on, and other caregivers were on call for their congregation. They felt their children needed a night to look forward to each week.

Luke, a pastor, admits that he looks forward to putting his preschool son to bed each evening. He always tells his son a Bible story with a twist. He scripts his son into the story somehow in a very positive way. That special time is not only cultivating the child's imagination and interest in the Bible. That boy is growing up as a blessed child.

The leader who learns to be a nurturer, an encourager, a blessing at home generally extends this character to the public ministry. Being a blessing becomes a way of life, not just a function occasionally done. This basic disposition of the leader toward the people in the ministry constellation demonstrates precisely the heart of God—to bless his people. It is a lesson learned most profoundly at home.

In a culture desperately needing a reemphasis on basic human relationship skills, spiritual leaders can hardly make a greater investment than in their own home. The community of the family in the leader's world becomes a powerful way to influence the culture and live out the calling of ministry.

Watch Your Love Life

This admonition is not aimed at the leader's romantic life. This charge really serves as a warning in one sense. Many spiritual leaders have lost their love for people. They probably did not start out that way. More probably, they began ministry out of a compassion for others, with a desire to help others. However, a variety of factors over time can conspire to diminish leaders' love for people. A series of questions can help leaders think through their love capacity.

What's Love Got to Do with It?

This question confronts every spiritual leader. For an answer, journey to the Upper Room for that special time of community that the disciples shared with Jesus the night his Passion began. As the disciples gathered for the celebration, Jesus commandeered towel and basin to wash the disciples' feet. Because the disciples were too proud themselves to do the menial acts of hospitality, Jesus shouldered the servant's role much as he would shoulder their cross just hours hence. His actions were designed to shape the character of the band that would soon become the leaders of the movement. Just in case they missed the lesson, Jesus revisited the point after supper. "Love each other *as I have loved you*" (John 15:12, emphasis added), he said. He called this a new commandment. Its newness lay in its character of reflecting the love that Jesus had demonstrated. His kind of loving—sacrificial and servantlike—raised a new standard for the quality of the disciples' love for one another, then and now. He went on to say that this kind of love would be the trademark of the true community of believers in Christ.

The apostle John made the point in his gospel that Jesus loved his disciples to the end. This was not a casual observation. It punctuated the quality of Jesus' love. Surely the Lord had the temptation to give up on these fellows. Even this far in, at the Last Supper, they still did not get it. They were still too proud to serve one another, still concerned about the pecking order, still jockeying for the good jobs coming when the kingdom was established. (John's own mother had recently lobbied for her sons to receive important cabinet positions.) Within a few hours, Jesus' own inner circle would fall asleep on him in the Garden of Gethsemane. He already knew they would deny him and desert him. Yet he loved them.

God calls spiritual leaders to do the very same thing—love people who do not get it, who are too proud to admit they need us or one another, people who are fickle, who love us when the crowds show up and desert us when the going gets tough. Spiritual leaders reveal God's heart to his people, including his love for them. Maintaining an uncomfortable presence in the company of those who reject or despise us teaches us that God will not depart from his people even though they misbehave. Staying by those who disappoint us reflects the heart of Jesus, for all of us have disappointed him at some point in our lives.

This high standard means two things in terms of heart-shaping. First, following Jesus' lead, the Christian leader cannot make the giving of love contingent on the actions and attitudes of others. If we reflect the fickleness of others, we have not called them to a higher standard. If our love does not have the character to wash the feet of proud people, then we have heart work ahead. Second, we cannot generate such a love on our own. After all, we are sharing Jesus' love. This means we must discover Jesus' love for ourselves and for others. We will not exhaust the reservoir of Jesus' love for people; ours can run dry pretty quickly.

Cheryl made this releasing discovery on a spiritual retreat. She realized that she had become emotionally and spiritually exhausted. Her spiritual director helped her see that she needed to release herself from the need to minister and begin to intentionally act as a conduit of Jesus' love. She began to pray for Jesus to love people with his love through her. She began to experience joy and energy as she ministered with a new sense of abiding in him.

Too many Christian leaders wind up losing their love for people. Telltale signs of this loss include joylessness, cynicism, and bitterness. This heart failure is serious. According to Jesus, if we do not get this one right, we blow the mission!

What Is Your Own History of Being Encouraged?

In the arena of love, it is tough to lead others where you have not been. The capacity to love, in huge part, depends on your having been loved. People who know they are loved, who have been nurtured, find it less challenging to extend love to others than those who are running a nurturing deficit.

You may want to do an inventory here. Does your life experience include your having received much encouragement? Beginning with your family of origin, have you had people who have cheered you on, who have believed in you? If you can answer these questions affirmatively, you are fortunate. Not everyone has this advantage. You may be working from a lack of being encouraged. Perhaps you got a good boost in early life, but your memories of being encouraged are distant ones. Do your life experiences increase or decrease your ability to express love for others? One way of determining your own penchant for loving others could be to examine your own practice. How many people have you intentionally encouraged over the past month? Two months?

What Formative Experiences Have Shaped Your Capacity to Risk Loving Others?

This question relates to the last one. Love requires risk. All of us, in varying degrees, have experienced times when the risk ended in pain. The hurt may even have been traumatic. Sometimes, not wanting to risk this kind of pain again, leaders become unwilling to risk love. When this happens, they begin to insulate themselves from others, or guard themselves, letting only a few "safe" people into their lives with access to their heart. In worse-case scenarios, leaders isolate themselves from everyone, becoming recluses from love or the chance of being loved.

This was what happened to Bill. He was called as pastor to follow a well-loved leader who had died suddenly from a heart attack. Compared with the former, now sainted, pastor, Bill could do no right. His own personality, however, proved his ultimate undoing. If love covers a multitude of sins, the lack of love leaves one defenseless. Bill was a recluse, preferring books to people. On top of this, his lack of trust in people soon became apparent in the way he did business. His exaggerated close-to-the-vest style signaled to others a genuine lack of care for them. The sad fact was that he had a huge nurturing deficit that he had carried from childhood. Unable to love himself, he was unable to love others. He became the "Teflon" pastor when it came to relationships. No one stuck to him. Eventually no one stuck with him.

What Circumstances Make It Difficult for You to Express Your Love?

This question takes into account that external factors do contribute to the leader's internal love landscape. Certain settings, situations, or personality types make it easier or more difficult for all of us to express our love. Some leaders, feeling incapable of demonstrating their heart for people in one situation, are set free in another to form a fabulous community. Unless leaders know this about themselves, they can inadvertently script themselves into a situation that is self-inhibiting or even self-damaging. A part of heart-shaping for leaders includes engaging in adequate reflection and self-examination to determine under what circumstances they are best able to love others with Jesus' love.

Karin came to realize that the staff on which she served acted like poison to her spirit. The competition and lack of mutual trust kept her from being able to experience the support she needed. In a new situation, the corporate culture affirmed her and practiced healthy relationships. She blossomed and developed significant friendships as well as a support team of ministry partners.

Do You Choose to Forgive?

Because love involves risk, it involves pain. Because it involves pain, it involves the need for practicing forgiveness. Practicing forgiveness is an essential part of learning to love. Practicing forgiveness is the willful act that allows leaders to grow beyond their pain rather than being its victim. The choice not to forgive is a self-imposed jail sentence in terms of heart development. The leader who decides against forgiveness arrests love's development and expression. The leader's heart never moves beyond its disappointment or unmet expectations. Love withers. Life diminishes.

Steve and Wanda had served faithfully for twenty-five years in one place. They were suddenly, and without warning, let go, the victims of sub-Christian behavior on the part of other ministry leaders. The financial devastation meant that they had to sell their home, move, and postpone much-anticipated retirement. Wanda never got over it. She harbored bitterness. She chose to live in a prison of bad memories and shattered expectations. Wanda's death left Steve grieving, not only for her loss but also for the life they had lost before she died.

Steve, on the other hand, refused to let the uncharitable deeds of others keep him from growing. He chose to bless those who cursed him, and acted out for his family the sacrifice of forgiveness. As a result, his ministry actually expanded, and his capacity to love increased. He is a greater blessing to others now despite and even because of his pain. The power of God was released into Steve's life through forgiveness.

Love wins. On the other hand, spiritual leaders who quit loving quit leading. The spirit of Jesus no longer anoints their efforts. Their hearts grow diseased. A leader can become a cardiac cripple spiritually and emotionally.

Friends

God sculpts our souls through friends in our lives. Friends afford us the chance to hear the voice of God's encouragement, feel the warmth of God's embrace, experience the intensity of his listening, understand the wonder of his life by receiving the love of people who, though they know us, love us anyway. In theological terms, friends incarnate God's love to the spiritual leader. This love is at once supportive and challenging, forgiving and expectant. Friendships provide real-life opportunities to practice love and grace, to receive and to give. These are the practice drills for heart development.

Many Christian leaders report a lack of significant friendships in their own lives. In addition to the feelings of insignificance that occasion such loneliness, the lack of significant friendships signals a deficit of heart-shaping activity. Many aspects of spiritual leadership militate against the development of friendships. Long hours and multiple demands combine with the emotionally draining aspects of helping other people. The lack of time and emotional margin generally means that relationships get squeezed. Many leaders apportion their existing relationship resources into family life. In the end, the time margin left for developing friendships is fairly diminished.

Emotional health, however, consistently tracks with the number of meaningful relationships in life. Christian leaders do well to intentionally pursue friendships that can be nurturing. The development of friends can reduce some of the pressure placed on spousal relationships in clergy marriages. Often the minister (especially men) will report that his wife is his best and sometimes only friend. The burden this places on the wife does not promote her emotional or spiritual health. Much of her own emotional energy becomes used up in sustaining her husband's needs. Often this isolates her as well from having friendships and contributes to her own sense of loneliness.

One Christian leader I know suggests that his own adulterous behavior would not have happened had he taken time to develop men friends. His wife could not meet all his emotional needs. He turned outside the marriage to another woman for emotional nurture.

When I encounter spiritual leaders who maintain friendships, I detect more joy, more balance, more vitality. Joel tells of his friend who listens to his bellyaching, absolves him of guilt, then tells him to get over it (or whatever he needs to hear).

Sometimes those in Christian leadership find it easier to bond with an audience or a ministry constituency than with a peer in a heart-to-heart relationship. A checklist of interpersonal concerns or qualities can help leaders determine whether or not they are capable of sustaining friend relationships. Six qualities are essential for establishing friendships. Each of these is a benchmark of heart development. Paying attention to these heart dynamics becomes a way the spiritual leader cooperates with God's heart-shaping designs.

Integrity is a character quality that permeates every arena of a person's life, including the capacity for friendship. Having integrity means that friends' confidences are kept. It means that promises are backed up. It means that telling someone, "I'll call you next week" is followed by a phone call next week. Integrity does not keep people waiting or take advantage of them. It reflects genuineness and results from a one-to-one correspondence between public and private life in terms of truth and the treatment of people.

Friendships do not develop without some risk. A certain amount of *vulnerability* must be demonstrated in order for people to connect at the heart level. Sometimes vulnerability is forced. This happens in forced accountability or is artificially created by a shared crisis during which people bond through common pain. The vulnerability associated with friendship is voluntary, offered from one heart to another. Christian leaders often have difficulty with this because the culture in which they serve does not always reward vulnerability. The result is devastating. Without some arena in which the leader can be real, great soul damage occurs. The leader becomes adept at denial. This leads to other problems.

The third quality is *humility*. Some leaders cannot have friends because they are in competition with everyone else. The spirit of competition sometimes gets translated into sarcastic humor that subtly (and not so subtly) puts others down. Camaraderie is only a thinly veiled attempt at trying to top another's last line or joke. Humility, on the other hand, allows a leader to accept being less talented than others in some areas. Healthy people can admit this. The capacity for humility begins with a coming to peace with oneself. Feelings of inferiority and insignificance do not foster genuine humility. Humility is the opposite of self-centeredness. Humility can give another soul some attention without demanding reciprocity. Humility sets others free to express their ambitions, their desires, their victories, and their pains without judgment.

Fourth is a *willingness to listen*. Leaders are used to being heard. Great leaders know how to listen. Listening gives a great gift to a friend. People know when others are listening or whether they are merely taking time to formulate their next thoughts or opinions. Friendship requires listening, and this requires time. It takes time to really hear what is being revealed about someone's heart, not just what is being said with someone's lips. Active listening requires a commitment of emotional, spiritual, and physical energy. But this is the activity that provides most of the stimulation for growth in the relationship. Listening uncovers the friend's interests, the topics for exploration, the sharpening of iron on iron that characterizes leadership friendships. Sometimes friendships are born when a leader discovers another person who is willing to genuinely listen. Over time this has to become a two-way street or the friendship suffers.

The fifth quality of friendship is *reasonable expectations*. Many friendships fail to mature because of unrealistic expectations on the part of one or both parties. Friends will at some point fail friends. Can the leader forgive this? Can others' shortcomings be overlooked for the potential of friendship? Is there any room for others to grow? Can we accept them if they remain where they are? Can we admit that we have blind spots? The leaders who have a landscape littered with broken relationships probably suffer from unrealistic expectations of others. Unrealistic expectations and a critical spirit often go hand in hand. They are deadly to relationships.

Sensitivity and responsiveness are in combination the final quality for establishing friendships. Being sensitive and responsive to friends' needs secures the friendship. So many demands are placed on the leader that this essential component of friendship can get squeezed. The capacity to actually give, not just receive, is a losing of one's life that helps the leader find it.

Don emerged from a period of burnout with the recognition that he was vulnerable to some family-of-origin–related compulsions. One of his chief enemies, he discovered, was loneliness. His marriage was fine, but his wife was not capable of supplying all of his emotional needs. In short, he needed friends.

When he came to this realization, Don had another learning in store for him. He discovered that he was a lousy friend. He viewed relationships as functional and utilitarian. He rarely initiated any contacts. He responded only to those that he considered beneficial for him in some way. He would generally get to know someone, begin to spend some time together, take out of the relationship what he wanted, and then back off when the relationship began to develop to the point that friendship expectations began to arise.

Don became distressed when he saw himself in this light. Publicly he espoused the importance of relationships to those in his ministry constituency. Privately he had no friends. With the aid of his wife, Don began a program of relationship rehabilitation. He determined to grow into authenticity through the development of genuine friendships. He began to make a habit of lunching once a week with a friend. Couples who were potential friends were invited over for dinner. One night a week was set aside for this activity. Each friend or friend couple was scheduled into the calendar at least once a month.

Though Don is no longer living where he was when he made these life-changing decisions, he and his wife enjoy several meaningful relationships that have survived the distance and time barriers. Phone calls and joint vacation times keep the friendships alive.

Don (and his thoughtful wife) made a life-enriching decision that God has used to more fully develop the heart of this leader. By creating community in his own life, Don has paved the way for God to speak to him through the advice, counsel, nurture, and admonition of good friends. Don is a more balanced person and a more effective leader as a result.

Intentional Learning in Community

Tony finished his seminary education with a doctorate. Throughout his college and seminary days, he had served churches in various staff positions. At the conclusion of his academic training, he assumed the pastorate of a brand-new church-planting effort. Suddenly he faced an entirely different set of questions than those he had been trained to deal with in school. Within months, he was running out of answers, treading water, and hoping not to blow the tremendous opportunity he had before him.

That is when the idea hit him. Tony dialed up a few of his school buddies that had wound up in similar ministry situations to his. He found that they were all struggling just like him. Tony asked four of them to join him at a conference that he knew was coming to his city. For two days, the five young leaders sat together at the conference, ate lunch together with the conference leader, and began to discuss during the breaks and over dinner the implications and applications of the information they were being presented.

A *learning cluster* was born. Once a month for several months thereafter, the group got together to think out loud, hammer out new ministry approaches, and run ideas by one another, before they released them to their congregations for consideration. Everyone was equal in the group. Biases and assumptions were challenged through this *peer-mentoring* process.

Something else happened. As the learning cluster became a community, a personal dimension began to develop between the group's members. Eventually the support system included the wives. Some of the ministry couples even vacationed together. Some still do.

Tony and his colleagues (now good friends) did not know they were pioneering a new methodology of leadership development. They did not refer to their group as an *intentional learning community;* yet that is precisely what it was.

A critical intellectual capacity for twenty-first-century leadership success will be the ability to build knowledge together with other colleagues. The rate of information growth, coupled with the collapse of the Christendom paradigm, makes it no longer possible to prepare for ministry challenge through traditional preparation processes. Academic, conferential, and self-guided learning must be supplemented through a peer-mentoring process for debriefing life and ministry experiences.

This process of an intentional learning community is exactly what Jesus established with the first apostles. The leaders of the movement were trained to share and discuss what they had encountered together. Jesus performed the role of learning coach during the early days. The Spirit took up this role in the book of Acts.

Peter, for instance, participated in all three Pentecosts. After the Samaritan and Gentile Pentecosts, he returned to Jerusalem to confer with the other apostles. This was not so that he could stand trial and defend his activities (the usual spin put on these accounts). Peter had to get back to his learning community to make sense of what he had experienced. Was there anything he had missed? What could he have done differently? What were the implications for the movement? The critical Acts 15 conference was informed by these earlier discussions.

Chapter Six identified a new model of spiritual leader that is emerging for a new apostolic era. A different training methodology is also emerging for this new tribe of apostolic leaders. Variously called a mentoring group or a learning cluster, it captures the dynamic of an intentional learning community. Learning communities are developing in all kinds of settings, from cities to countryside, from colleges to mission posts.

Todd serves as a facilitator of a learning cluster in his denomination. He has recruited three other pastors, who meet with him six to eight times a year for two to three hours, usually involving lunch or dinner. The four of them enjoy fellowship and prayer time together. However, the driving force of their cluster is learning. At each meeting, they have a learning agenda that they have agreed on beforehand. Sometimes they read a book and study it together. At other times, they bring case studies out of their own ministries. Occasionally they use a learning guide produced by their denomination. Todd is covenanted together with these other learners. Together they are coaching one another to greater ministry effectiveness. (See author's *Revolution in Leadership,* 1998, for details on the architecture for learning communities.)

Larry has been feeling a burden for his town in the rural South. An Anglo pastor, he feels the need for spiritual renewal for his community. Larry believes this renewal involves the search for racial unity. He also believes that racial reconciliation is a concern that crosses denominational lines. He has pulled together a learning cluster of three other pastors, all of whom are of a different denomination from his and two of whom are African American. This cluster is taking the lead in promoting understanding and even putting on joint events aimed at breaking down the walls of separation and building up the kingdom of God.

The leader prepared for the challenge of the new century will be a learner. However, this learning will develop differently than in traditional methods that are linear, didactic, privatized, and parochial. Learning in community is nonlinear, layered, and experiential. It is also just in time. The process of learning community will reshape those academic institutions that choose to remain a viable part of the credentialing process for leaders in ministry.

Join the Team

Throughout most of church history, spiritual leaders have used sacred texts and worship rituals to create community. Worship remains the most powerful community-building activity on the planet. In true worship, we recognize the truth that every human being bears the image of God. This is the point of connectivity that transcends any division. The book of the Revelation provides us glimpses of this reality when it reveals that the worship services in heaven involve every nation, every race, every tongue.

In recent decades, programming has been added to increase social interactions as another community-building tactic. Real estate acquisition has also encouraged physical gatherings of believers for church activities. Although these strategies for creating and sustaining community still work (particularly with the churched culture), the most promising efforts in building community now center around creating a missional vision and practicing values that support it. Different ministries express the vision differently, but one component generally characterizes the ministries that evidence healthy community and experience the transforming power of God released in community. These ministries have spiritual leaders who practice community dynamics in their leadership style. In short, these leaders are team players.

In Part One we noted the significance of the team approach to ministry in each of our four biblical leaders. Moses led the Exodus along with Aaron and Miriam. David relied on a host of players to rule his kingdom. Jesus recruited a team to help him establish the Christian movement. The book of Acts details the efforts of Paul's ministry entourage; the apostles' letters signal his relationship with and reliance upon local leadership. Though each of these men carried enormous leadership burdens, they did not carry them alone.

Team approaches to ministry help satisfy the hunger for community. Because team ministry captures the power of community, it carries some significant benefits. Teams encourage and support the risks needed to bring about behavioral change. Teams create synergy both in formulating vision and in turning it into reality. The relational component of doing ministry through team creates the value-added dimension of fun to the challenging task of spiritual leadership.

Sam and his team share pastoral and preaching responsibilities. Though he is the "senior" pastor, he has formed a great group joined at the heart. They are on the same page in terms of ministry vision and values. They affirm and build on one another's strengths. The team approach renders their individual weaknesses irrelevant to the functioning of the congregation. They model what they expect in every ministry area of their church. Each ministry is led by a team of people who have a shared passion. Through this approach, Sam and his cohort have put community into the DNA of their church.

Unfortunately, spiritual leaders often resist developing team around them. This malpractice results in heart blockages and heart damage. Their failure to develop community contributes to the heart diseases of loneliness, feelings of insignificance, and spiritual and emotional debilitation that accompany isolation.

The reasons that spiritual leaders are reluctant team players reflect the spiritual and heart issues that exist in the community of faith. Five issues retard the development of team ministry. The first of these, affecting all the others, is the *prevailing church culture.* The clergy-laity distinction has cultivated for centuries a qualitative separation that militates against broad-based ministry. Ministry empowerment has been reserved to a few. The Reformation will be completed when the clergy-laity distinction (in terms of ministry empowerment) finally yields to the biblical doctrine of the universal priesthood of all believers. The work of God will finally return to the whole people of God.

This movement is already under way. Thousands of church leaders intentionally help those they serve identify and develop their own intentional ministries. These leaders understand that community develops when people assume responsibility for the mission and legacy of the world they are creating.

The reluctance to challenge the church culture reflects a second resistance factor to the development of team ministry—*fear.* Many spiritual leaders live in fear. They know the right things to do. However, they are afraid to challenge the prevailing culture of their congregations. Many conflict-allergic spiritual leaders hesitate to introduce anything that adds to the conflict level of their ministries. Fear also results from financial concerns. This represents one of the emasculating dynamics of the stipendiary ministry model. Fear arrests the leader's heart. Vision atrophies. The spirit weakens. Growth stops. The leader dies in place.

Another resistance factor militating against the development of team ministry by spiritual leaders is a crucial heart-shaping issue—*control*. Some spiritual leaders are reluctant to release control of ministry. Several factors can contribute to this, including fear that ministry quality might suffer or fear that the leader will lose some leverage in the system. Accountability is spiritually positive; control is demonic. God grants freedom; the devil enslaves. Whenever control types gain places of spiritual leadership, a negative energy begins to thwart creativity and synergy. A dysfunction develops that can become institutionalized. Power becomes inappropriately wielded for personal agendas. The Kingdom ultimately suffers no matter what gains appear to be taking place. If control needs are a part of a leader's personality or ministry style, they must be ruthlessly exposed and dealt with. Power must be given away in order to foster team and the community that develops as a result.

A fourth contributing resistance to team ministry development is the *risk of failure*. This too is a corollary of a church culture that holds leaders inappropriately responsible for the performance of all ministry. Such a view feeds the fear that lurks in many leaders' hearts. What if an idea or approach does not work? What if people fail? How will the failure be viewed by the ministry supporters? Will they judge the leader as a result and withdraw support? Will the leader lose the needed credit line for launching other new ventures? How the faith community perceives failure reflects the teaching and modeling of its leadership's response to failure. People ultimately will make judgments of the leader's failures based on the honesty of the leadership and the competency brought to other endeavors.

A cluster of heart issues is involved here. Can the leader tolerate others' ineptness? Does the leader's own self-image depend too much on public image? How driven is the leader to succeed? How does the leader personally handle failure? What is the leader passionate enough about to be willing to risk failure for? Can the leader share credit? Can the leader learn from mistakes, admit weaknesses, risk vulnerability? Does the leader always have to be right? These are the significant heart-shaping issues that God targets in the challenge for the leader to develop community in God's people.

A final resistance factor that impedes the development of community in ministry efforts is a competency issue for the leader. *Can the leader coach others?* Coaching abilities differ from performing abilities. Most church leaders have been taught to perform. Few leaders have had training in coaching. Coaching is both a set of skills and an art. The skills involved include the capacity to assess problems (not just symptoms), the ability to offer remedial strategies and regimens, the insight to recruit wisely and make appropriate placements, the know-how to create and to manage momentum, and the desire to motivate. These skills, combined with experience and intuition, develop into an art of coaching that reflects the personality and core values of the coach. A spiritual leader determined to develop a team will go to school to learn how to be a coach.

A leader intent on creating greater community will do several key things. First, the leader will speak a different language. "We" will replace "I" and "our" will replace "my." The talk will not be about my vision, but our vision. Vocabulary reflects an important shift that cannot be overstated in terms of its significance.

Leaders who create team figure out how to empower others, literally giving power away. These community-minded leaders listen more than tell. Team builders shape the corporate culture through living out the values they espouse. They go first in trusting, in risking, in being vulnerable, in yielding, and in supporting. Their actions signal a different attitude that is required of all team spirits—humility.

Each of the four biblical leaders in Part One modeled this kind of leadership. Moses relied on Aaron's leadership with the Hebrew elders. David depended on his military commanders in his military conquests. Paul formed leadership teams of elders in the churches he established and dispatched ministry colleagues on mission assignments to the various congregations he started. Jesus sent his disciples out in early ministry ventures to prepare them for their later assignment. His ascension left the movement in the hands of those close, few followers.

Hope on the Horizon

Anyone in touch with generational characteristics is well aware of the significance of relationships for Generation Xers. The cry for community reaches a fever pitch in this group of Americans. Often born into or having experienced a broken home as part of their family of origin, they are determined to establish some nurturing connectedness that gives them a sense of belonging. As a group, they rebel against the materialism of the baby boomers and are willing to devote time and energy to relationships.

Most often, these relationships are in multiples, not exclusively one-on-one. A Generation Xer will typically develop a few very deep, very tight relationships.

Spiritual leaders that emerge out of this generation will have their own set of challenges unique to their time and culture. However, one corrective they are bringing to spiritual leadership is the focus on community. They share leadership more willingly. Church planters of this generation are often interested in beginning with a partner (the apostolic model).

The current institutional expression of Christianity will not satisfy this community-hungry generation. They will either transform or abandon the current forms that lack relational depth. Most builder-generation (born between 1925 and 1945) and baby boomer–generation church leaders do not get this and go on planning ministries that will not survive them. The church for Generation X and for the millennials (transgenerational postmodernists) will recapture the heart of the Christian movement—the heart of God expressed in community.

Taking this arena seriously will help leaders uncover a rich story that has been developing throughout their entire lifetime. The family of origin, then friends, mentors, key players in the ministry, peers, all of these combine to become a significant community of influence on a leader's heart. Leaders cannot be fully comprehended apart from this intriguing but often under-understood subplot in their life drama.

Consider some tough questions as you consider the community component of your own leadership:

- What gifts have you brought forward from your family of origin? What have you claimed responsibility for?

- What level of intimacy have you been able to achieve with your current family? Why or why not?

- Who will attend your funeral? What will they say about your relationship with them?

- What kind of community are you building through your ministry? With your coworkers? Among your leadership constituency?

- Who would be a good person or group to talk to about your answers to the above questions?

The medieval mystics and contemplatives believed that simplicity lay at the heart of the universe. In this, they were right. They sought the One. In this, they were not completely on the right track. The search is for Three. For community.

8

COMMUNION

REHEARSING FOR ETERNITY

COME IN.

Shut the door behind you. It does not want to close all the way. Usually you will have to lean up hard against it. Pressure from the outside threatens to blow it open—and will, unless you get it secured.

Have a seat. Or stand. Or lean against something. You can even lie down. You may go to work on whatever. Or you can choose not to. This is your room. Yours . . . and Another's.

The One who gave you life comes here too. The One who thought you up and imagined your leadership and knew you would be reading this page right now comes to this place also. This is where you let God work on your soul.

Sometimes the room fills with music. Fresh fragrances heighten the senses, sometimes. Light bathes the experience in a warm glow that gives rise to contentment. You want to stay forever. Sometimes.

Yet again you are sometimes startled in here. The entrance of the Other stuns you out of speaking, as if the wind is knocked out of you. What you expected is not what you receive. The agenda is not always yours. You both welcome and fear the intense interest the Other has in you.

Sometimes it stinks in here. The stench can be suffocating. Rotting, filthy, putrefying stuff gets dragged out from underneath hell. Stuff stuffed in closets you thought you would never have to open. Stuff that nobody but you and the Other know about. You recoil from the horror of it. You are repulsed. You want to get out of here. But the Other does not turn away. He wades into the mess. He is not put off by having to deal with this. Only His unflinching presence gives you the capacity to stay in, to overcome shame, to face down the unseemliness.

Then, sometimes, nothing happens. Or so it seems. He and you. Like a quiet night spent by the fire absorbed in a book, or like a long drive with a loved one shared without spoken words. Just there. Nothing much said. No big agenda. Comfortable.

For too many leaders, the room is musty. Shut for too long. Memory cobwebs go undisturbed by fresh air, the stir of encounter. The thrill of a rendezvous here with the Other is gone. Maybe the previous meetings were too intense. Maybe what goes on here is too unpredictable and untidy. Unsettling. Not controllable. For many, the lure of this place cannot seem to compete with the sights and sounds of the "real" world outside. Trouble is, living life exclusively out in that real world keeps the leader from becoming really real.

Leaders often neglect communion more than any other heart-shaping arena. Many spiritual leaders seem oblivious to the battle that actually targets them. Perhaps they see the arsenal of weapons arrayed at them as benign. The leader often appropriates them, accommodating their deployment in self-destruction.

Fax machines, e-mail, telephones, beepers, an overcommitted schedule, the press of people's needs, program concerns, ministry agenda—these are the tools of mass destruction for spiritual leaders. Their development and deployment proceed often without inspection. They threaten to shut down the spiritual leader's communion with God. Once that happens, the leader's effectiveness is destroyed. The leader becomes a casualty of a struggle that is as old as humanity—the drowning out of eternity by the screams of temporal concerns.

A small neglect of God occasioned by an unanticipated spate of unusually consuming problems signals the beginning of a skirmish. God-time yields to "more pressing" concerns. The leader's communication line with the commander begins to register static. In response, the leader sometimes does exactly the wrong thing. Instead of repairing communication by altering the busy schedule to make time for God, the leader compensates for the lack of divine guidance by increasing chat time with the established network. The only approval that satisfies, the "well-done" of the Commander-in-Chief, is set aside to curry favor from ministry constituents. Ministry efforts increase. So does the static. Episodic interruptions in the communication lines to God give way to a routine neglect. The leader goes off-line with headquarters.

Out of touch with command, the leader begins to operate from the memory of previous orders and directives. As time goes on, these seem in-

creasingly unrelated to more immediate issues. Activity replaces pro-
ductivity. Genuine missional enthusiasm and purpose give way to main-
tenance and routine, with an accompanying loss of joy and a rise in
self-doubt.

Leaders who continue to act in this way become cut off from genuine divine intervention on their behalf. They begin to rely on their own dimin-
ishing reserves of spiritual firepower. Their activity becomes sustained either
by adrenaline or perfunctory performance rather than the Spirit. They bank
on their talents, their smarts, their relationship skills, and their position
to cover their basic failure at the critical core function of their call. That
function is to reflect God's heart to God's people. This cannot be done
apart from a leader's firsthand knowledge of God's heart. This knowledge
does not derive from historical encounters in a leader's past; it springs
from a vibrant, up-to-date walk with the Almighty.

Devoid of a growing, personal, dynamic relationship with God, spiritual leaders become casualties. Some are removed from battle, too
wounded to go on. Some remain engaged but are missing in action. Others desert, going AWOL on God and his people. Perhaps the worst scenario is the tragic figure of a spiritual corpse going through ministry
rituals like the zombies of science fiction horror movies. However, this is
real, painfully real. No amount of promise or talent or intelligence can ultimately shield the spiritual leader from some variation of this fate if communion with God is neglected.

Communion lies at the center of heart-shaping. Through communion,
the leader learns the lessons of God's activity in the other subplots. The
examining and distilling of life experience occurs here. Through communion, the leader secures the relationship with the Heart Maker and Heart
Shaper. In communion, the leader strengthens the spiritual foundation that
will support total leadership effectiveness.

Lack of attention to this essential aspect of heart-shaping explains many
spiritual leadership heart ailments. Anemic communion creates shallow
leadership, the kind of leadership informed only by methods and style
without substance. "Pop leadership" practices knee-jerk reactions, adopts
the latest fads, uses "with it" vocabulary. However, without a real center
this leadership is hollow at the core. It implodes, collapsing in on the
leader, who frantically and frenetically tries to stave it off by paying too
much attention to the props and not enough attention to the story itself.

"Faux leadership" can be explained, in part, by a lack of communion.
Fake leadership comes in several distinct styles. In American culture, leadership often parades as charisma. It often manipulates and exploits to
maintain its power. Spiritual leaders who mimic this kind of leadership

do so because they fail to submit their leadership to the surgical knife of intimate communion with God. With false leadership, it is all about the leader and not those served. The leader's agenda. The leader's vision. The leader's passions. The leader's goals. People play a role in helping the leader get to where the leader wants to go. People are not served. They are used.

These statements may seem too harsh. Unfortunately, I have seen too many wasted lives, too much pretension, and too much lost opportunity to pull punches. On the other hand, I have witnessed powerful spiritual leaders who attend to communion with God. They have a sense of presence that comes from only One source.

The noncommuning leader can hardly be a servant. Voluntary servanthood requires an intact self at the center. This self has to be developed in communion with its Creator. The power and mystery of Incarnation lies in its willful act of self-emptying. As we have seen, Jesus could stay on task with this constant servanthood only through vibrant communion with the Father.

A spiritual leader practicing communion leads from a solid, integrative sense of purpose. The vision of God's preferred future both for the leader and for those in the leadership constellation gives direction and meaning. This vision for the future grows out of time spent with the One who has already been there.

We need to investigate some critical aspects of the spiritual leader's communion with God. Those who expect a guide to "quiet time" activities will be disappointed in what follows. We often drain the Spirit from encounters with the Almighty by focusing on activities, on techniques, on more doing. A lot of busyness (a prevalent soul cancer that strikes leaders) gets imported into quiet times. We fill out workbooks, do memory work, study over texts (all good activities) rather than having genuine conversation with God. Much of what is written about spending time with God seems more like manuals for mechanics or tapes for aerobics enthusiasts than hints about how friends or lovers should spend time together. The discussion of communion in this chapter is free of mechanical how-tos.

Besides, the arena of communion encompasses a much broader notion than mere consideration of a slice of time given over to a religious activity. We are talking about developing a life of genuine communion with God. A life that is really real because it is lived out of a sense of eternity, not just urgency.

Telling leaders they should spend time with God hardly accomplishes the desired results. Approaching communion from a sense of guilt or shoulds has the same lasting motivation as being told to clean up your room. Our marriages usually succeed because we develop a satisfying relationship, not because the wedding vows are posted on the refrigerator door. Communion is about relationship, not about fulfilling obligations.

Communion enables the leader to explore. It offers discovery about one's self. Remember, self-knowledge is the single most important piece of information a leader needs. Without it, there is no leadership center.

Communion also offers an opportunity to discover God. The One who made us intends us for himself. Our understanding of him will never be exhausted. Each new insight whets our appetite to know more. The more we know him, the more we want to know him.

In short, communion helps the leader make sense of it all. Here is where the lessons are learned and the insights gained that will help the leader leave a legacy of people who are better off because that leader's life touched theirs.

Moses' tent meetings provided him not only instruction from Yahweh but also some sanctuary from the press of needs associated with leading the emancipated Hebrew slaves. David forged his friendship with God in solitude while shepherding. Paul retreated to the desert to rethink his theology. Jesus withdrew often, not to escape people but to be available to the Father for instruction and nurture. The High Priestly prayer of John 17 reveals how these times of communion prepared him for his assignments.

To entice you to the place of communion, this chapter reexamines an ancient notion now lost on postmoderns—the place of Sabbath in our lives. To draw you to the Person of communion, the chapter inquires into the purpose God has for you in it.

Practicing Sabbath

Old Testament Hebrew thought introduced the idea of Sabbath into human spiritual practice. Its basis grows out of the creation story of Genesis 1. After six days of creative frenzy, God rested. He "sabbathed."

To this day, any mention of the word *Sabbath* will bring the word *rest* to the discussion. This word association poses a difficulty. For God to rest means something very different than it does for humans. An all-powerful God presumably does not tire, at least physically. His need for rest would not be for refreshing. His rest really means a change of activity. He shifted gears from creation to reflection. Work gave way to evaluation. The pause signaled a shift for God from writing the score to rehearsing the piece. God's Sabbath, then, did not mean a cessation of activity, but a different activity.

Humans have gotten it only partially right. Sabbath has been translated into setting aside a day of rest. This has meant time off from the job or a hiatus from work-related activity, not less activity. Those who live for the weekend try to cram life into the gaps between work schedules. Days off often require several subsequent working days to get over. Something is not quite right with this picture.

The picture does not get righted by the typical Christian congregation. Christian Sundays are often chock-full of religious activity. Church calendars wear out adherents to the faith. It takes enormous stamina to be a church member.

The elevation of one's participation in church activity to being a litmus test for true Christian piety might be the most ingenious ploy of the enemy ever. Rather than tempt Christians and their spiritual leaders with works of wickedness, he encourages more and more good efforts. The effect in terms of spiritual vitality is remarkably the same. Tired Christians do not evangelize. They lose judgment and choose expediency over values-based decisions and living. Very few make the connection, because each new challenge from the church and pulpit adds another layer of activity to their already-overcrowded lives.

In many circles, the notion of Sabbath has thus been translated into a day spent working hard to please God. Wasn't this what Jesus scolded the Pharisees for? He admonished them for their obsession with keeping Sabbath by reminding them that the Sabbath was a gift to humans by God for their benefit ("the Sabbath was made for man"), not as another religious obligation ("not man for the Sabbath"; Mark 2:27).

Spiritual leaders need to recover the ancient meaning of Sabbath, its original purpose as envisioned by God. Then they need to practice Sabbath personally and lead those in their influence to do the same.

God created humans for eternity. But he knew that left to our own ordering, we would live out our lives for the moment. We tend to lose eternity as the conscious backdrop against which we develop our life stories. Without his intervention, he knew our thoughts and energies would be dominated by temporal concerns.

Enter Sabbath. It is not a day off to pursue whatever fancy is attainable and affordable. Rather, it is a day to restore eternity to our souls. God established Sabbath to accomplish a re-creation of eternity, a reminder of what is really real. This re-creation of eternity has two major activities—the worship of God and reflection on the work of our hands (translated—what is going on in our lives).

Worship is preparation for eternity. Genuine worship anticipates the full manifestation of the kingdom of God. Worship is what all believers will be doing a million years from now. Worship gets us back in touch with an eternal God. In worship, God reminds us of his purposes for us and for all people. Worship also heals the fractures in our souls. The walls that divide us from ourselves and from our God are broken down in the presence of God. This work of God in worship anticipates a time when we are completely whole. True worship, then, restores the soul because it rehearses eternity. This is one function of Sabbath.

Sabbath was also intended to provide people a rhythm by which to reflect on their lives. The establishment of a routine day to evaluate progress provides the chance for the plumbline of divine perspective to be dropped into human efforts. Sabbath allows people to reflect on the promises they have made to God, to other people, and to themselves. It provides continual opportunity to measure one's spiritual advancement by assessing life's experiences in between Sabbaths. It affords a chance to look back across the landscape of life endeavors to search for kingdom outcroppings.

In ancient times, God gave explicit instructions to the Hebrews for observing Sabbath. The commands preserved both elements of Sabbath—worship and reflection. The family began Sabbath with worship. Preparations were made ahead of time so that normal routine would not consume valuable moments of reflection on God and eternity and what is most precious in life.

This ancient practice has all but been forgotten in Christian circles. Only a semblance of the original remains. Worship is now routinely removed from the center of home and family. The activities on the Temple grounds (the church) squeeze out reflection for most. Sunday has its own special hustle and bustle.

Putting off Sabbath means putting off life. Without Sabbath, our souls lose touch with our true destiny. Life becomes too common and profane. Transcendence is lost. The tyranny of the urgent rules our lives. We forget what is really real. We neglect the kingdom. We fail to rehearse for eternity.

The recovery of Sabbath would lead to the renewal of spiritual leaders by restoring communion practices where heart-shaping could occur. Leaders who long for the renewal of the church should not let this connection escape them. If God's people are to be once again captured by his heart for them, they are going to have to be in communion with him to hear his voice. Until church leaders come to their senses, they will continue to pass out methodological pabulum to their followers as a drug to dull their pain and to anesthetize their spiritual yearnings for more vibrancy than they currently experience. We will not have renewed congregations and ministries until we have renewed leaders. The restoration of Sabbath can provide a key to personal spiritual renewal by enhancing communion between the spiritual leader and God.

Two Images

What does Sabbath look like?

Perhaps a better question would be, What are some contemporary images that might give leaders some clues about practicing Sabbath in their lives?

Two images come to mind. Each has a different appeal, so one may not work for you. However, most of us can imagine both of them even if they are not a part of our own personal experience. These images speak to the dynamics and content of Sabbath, not to a methodological prescription for how it is done.

The first image is that of a married couple who continues to date after the wedding. This has been a practice that Cathy (my wife) and I have considered a key to continued marriage vitality. Every week, we have some sort of date that we look forward to as much as we did before we were married.

Some of our dates are very romantic and intimate. On some, we take our calendars to check signals. We look at the whos, wheres, and whens of our lives and those of our kids. Some of our times together are agenda driven, like special occasions or the need to discuss a specific issue. Many are fairly routine—nothing profound occurs, no life-changing decisions are made. Nevertheless, we feel that even these routine dates significantly contribute to our relationship and to the health of our marriage. Because of our dating practice, we have never forgotten what attracted us to each other and why we like each other still.

Spending time investing in our relationship as a married couple has paid enormous benefits. In fact, there is no substitute for this kind of time together. Quality would never make up for quantity. We know what the other likes, dislikes, feels, and yearns for, because our hearts have been consistently and frequently united. Genuinely becoming one flesh requires this kind of intentionality. It does not just happen because of a ceremony or a few great times together.

God gave us marriage for more reasons than as a procreation strategy. He could have designed other ways for that to happen. In marriage, we find the picture of God's designs for a relationship with us. He desires the intimacy and oneness with us that we experience with our married partner. In fact, he created us for this very reason. He gave us his image so he could recognize himself in us, thus making relationship possible. In addition, being created in his image means that we possess the Godlike capacity to choose. We can choose to love or to reject him. We can even choose estrangement over intimacy. The joy that well-marrieds experience arises from the realization that they have been chosen by the object of their own affection. This is God's heart for us. When we respond in love to love, he is thrilled. We are made complete.

Sabbath is the date life of our marriage with God. Sometimes it is characterized by wonderful intimacy (we usually call this praise). In those times, we cannot tell God adequately how much we love him and want to be near him and desire to live with him forever. On occasion, Sabbath time with God might include checking calendars. Going over time commitments and rehearsing the schedule of our lives vitally interest him. Like a life partner, he can caution our overcommitments and remind us of the importance of balance. He also wants to be a part of the big events of our lives and wants to discuss how that is made more possible. He can help us see things about how we are spending life.

Some special times with God might focus on issues that clamor for attention. You may need to pour your heart out in disappointment, or consider some major decision. He hears patiently and promises not to chide you for needing his counsel. He delights in granting you his wisdom. In the exchange, you can trust he has your best interest at heart.

Many Sabbath experiences might seem routine. No particular agenda claims your attention. Just time with your Beloved, the One who made you and then gave himself up for you. Yet even in these nondescript, non-mountaintop experiences, you get to know him better. You know what he likes and dislikes, what you do that pleases him and what causes him grief. You learn to anticipate his thoughts and insights. Just as with your marriage partner, there is always more to learn. The relationship is never exhausted. But you become more and more like him. In the process, you are becoming one.

Try another image for Sabbath. In this analogy, God serves as divine Coach.

Several high school football coaches attended the church I pastored in Texas. During football season, I knew what those guys did on Saturday morning. Win or lose, they watched film. Films of the game recorded from high up in the stadium would show them all the plays of the Friday night contest. They could rewind the film a dozen times to look at the same thing or at different things. By watching film, they could gain more understanding of why the game went the way it did. From their viewing and reviewing, they developed their coaching strategy for the following week. Armed with film, the coach could show a player what worked and what didn't.

God keeps film. As the divine Coach, he can help us learn how to play our life game better. Learning to practice Sabbath can give him the opportunity to review with us the film of our lives.

I remember the discovery of this insight during one Sabbath meeting with Coach. He played back an encounter I had had the previous week with our younger daughter. It had been a brief episode. She had done something that upset me. I scolded her for her actions and then moved on. I had forgotten about the incident until Coach brought out the film. What I said in the exchange was not appropriate. I wounded her spirit. It showed up in the film. Not until he played it slowly for me did I see the look in her face. I had missed it at the time. Because Coach replayed the scene, I could go back to her and get it right. Plus, I learned a valuable lesson for future plays where she was involved.

The Coach also delights in showing great plays. He celebrates good performance if we let him. These viewings can boost our confidence and help us get better at what we are good at. This is what great athletes do. They build on strengths, the talents they have discovered, to improve their play.

Unfortunately, many spiritual leaders do not know what their strengths are. Or if they do, they ignore these to continue to work on their weaknesses. The return on investment is much higher when leaders, like athletes, spend their energies on what they do well. Much of life conspires to tell us what we are not good at. Most spiritual leaders can tick off the list of what they need to improve much more easily than they can identify their strengths and detail how they are practicing and getting better at them. Most people attempt self-improvement through remediation of weaknesses. Leaders who do this tie their growth to their least talent. They employ a pathology model of fighting sickness rather than a wellness model of promoting health. Their ministry often reflects this approach, targeting people who are led to believe they are a problem for God to fix.

Giving God a chance as Sabbath Coach would be a strategic move for helping you move to a strengths-based approach. He made you. He designed the wonderful gifts and talents you have. He can show you things about yourself that can set your leadership soaring. You can trust him. People will line up to tell leaders what they need to work on. Usually it will benefit them if you heed their advice. With God, you can always trust that his interest is in making you as successful as possible. He only wants to make you into a champion.

Think of it! You have a chance to spend time with the One who understands the game better than anyone else. He designed the game, after all. And . . . he has played the game. This is the wonderful truth of Incarnation. Jesus understands what it is like on the playing field.

You might employ other images in imagining what Sabbath time could look like. Perhaps God is the trusted Parent, or the Wise Counselor, or the

Expert Consultant. Develop whatever image works for you. Give your-self a positive reason to spend time with the Almighty in reflection over your life.

This approach stands in sharp contrast to the many challenges issued to spiritual leaders about their time with God. Guilt and shame are poor substitutes for being drawn into the presence of the lover of our souls. To hear some experts exhort spiritual leaders in this area, one would suspect they had been schooled by the Pharisees. Their exhortations feel like added weights to leaders' lives. The joy of Sabbath as a time to be spent with God becomes replaced by its demands. Contemporary Pharisees talk of communion with God as something owed to him. They devise things for leaders to do to spend the time with God, to be busy in his presence.

Remember, Sabbath is a gift to us from God. Accept his invitation. You can relax in his presence because he is safe to share your life with. More than anything else, he just wants the time to be with you. Unfettered and unbusy time to enjoy you, to show you his love. Time to make you a champion at living.

Special Challenges to the Practice of Sabbath

A few challenges face any leader who wants to practice Sabbath.

The first challenge is a theological and psychological one. It has to do with how the leader views God. For leaders who see God as a hard taskmaster who can never be pleased, the notion of spending extended times with him conjures up anything but pleasant anticipation. For lead-ers who believe that God wants to spend time with them just so he can beat them up, Sabbath will be resisted. For leaders who believe that the primary path to spiritual improvement lies in remediation, Sabbath can become a way to practice more self-atonement. This would result in less joy, not more. This perspective can also turn time spent with God into a source of increased pride and legalism. Such a development would obvi-ously militate against increased grace and tolerance in leaders. False views of God like these are fed by faulty theology and unhealthy psychoses. On the other hand, a biblical and emotionally healthy view of God will fos-ter the desire to spend time with him.

A second challenge for practicing Sabbath involves the need for devel-oping the discipline of *listening prayer*. Leaders typically spend a good deal of time talking as part of their leadership role. Many leaders have trouble listening. This weakness extends to the spiritual sphere. Many leaders can fill up time with God with much speaking. Listening to God is a different ball game.

Several issues relate to this challenge. First of all, listening takes time, more time not speaking than many leaders are comfortable with. In addition, once leaders begin to listen, they realize that a lot of voices clamor for their attention. Distinguishing God's voice from the others involves a learning curve. Finally, learning to listen to God is presumed a private activity and therefore difficult to learn from example, one of the favorite ways many leaders learn.

Learning to listen to God is a developmental discipline. The beginner will make some mistakes. If the listener is a novice, announcing multi-million dollar building programs on the basis of a prayer vigil may prove ill conceived and ill fated. The best approach usually involves discussing the content of the leader's conversations with God with others whom the leader trusts. It is best to test out what one hears from God with others who are also listening to him and who know the leader well. It also helps if they know the circumstances facing the leader.

Developing the art of listening prayer takes some trial and error. However, with perseverance, the leader will begin to recognize a voice that is distinguishable from the chatter on other self-talk channels. The leader will probably come to the realization that a lot of what has been viewed as prayer in the past has literally only been self-talk. Prayer must be dialogical if it is to change people and move heaven and earth.

Some Practical Suggestions

Think of the images of dating and coaching. These both contain elements of review and reflection, planning and preparing, courtship and love-making. Sabbath must work for you, and will work differently depending on temperament, wiring, interests, and circumstance. Some will enjoy stimulating their conversation with God through print media. This has long been a way that God has spoken to people. Scripture works best, but other books can help. Some enjoy music to establish the mood and drown out some noises of the outside world, so that their spirit can listen for God. Outdoor walks to admire God's handiwork can serve as discussion starters. Some leaders keep journals of their thoughts and find it easier to hear God through writing their impressions.

The strategy to develop listening prayer addresses the inevitable question that arises when leaders entertain the prospects of beginning a Sabbath practice: What do you do? This query clinches the argument that Sabbath is desperately needed. A culture requiring frenetic activity as an initiation rite does not yield up its subjects readily.

The issues of time and calendar always pose the most formidable challenges to the establishment of Sabbath. The best approach involves building on some kind of rhythm whenever possible. When life and work admit no rhythm, then it has to be artificially imposed. The original set of Sabbath instructions involved twenty-four hours every seven days. That will prove too ambitious for many leaders, and it should not even be a goal or standard. For many, one half day a week provides enough reflection time. Some leaders cannot set time aside on a weekly basis for any number of reasons. In this case, a Sabbath time every two weeks might be the answer. Again, any number of configurations will work, depending on the rhythm of the leader's life. Waiting for the time to present itself will postpone action. The practice of Sabbath requires a proactive determination on the part of the leader.

Many leaders prefer a daytime Sabbath, joining the family in the evening. Some prefer the mornings, some the afternoon. Usually Sabbath is personal, yet many spiritual leaders have found time spent with the family or spouse in God's presence to be very powerful. Many Christian leaders have found the addition of occasional prayer retreats into their schedule to afford them times of wonderful refreshing and increased pleasure in their relationship with the Lord. An increasing number of leaders are submitting to the coaching of a spiritual director. Different leaders want different settings for Sabbath, from indoor sanctuaries to outdoor natural cathedrals. Some prefer familiar places; others find themselves drawn to explore God in a new place.

The communion of the leader with God certainly involves more than "sabbathing." However, Sabbath (or the lack of it) establishes the tone of the leader's relationship with God. That is why it deserves so much attention.

Be All That You Can Be

Communion defies containment to any one observance or practice. The spiritual connection between leader and God involves the entire spectrum of their interaction and relationship, its content as well as process. Transparency, immediacy, honesty, all characterize mature communion. *Prayer, posture* (of heart, not just body), *presence, penitence, petition, perseverance.* These words describe other aspects of communion.

Communion involves the conscious awareness and cultivation of the person of God in the leader's life. "Life" here means life in its broadest sense, involving individual, family, and community dimensions, as well as ministry enterprise. Through communion, God shapes the leader's heart toward displaying the character of Christ in all life pursuits, thoughts, and transactions. Through communion, God pursues the leader relentlessly, searching for entrance into every area of the leader's heart—ambitions, emotions, passions, fears, loves, prejudices, assumptions, character, behaviors.

The self doggedly holds on to these territories. God's advances into these areas will be resisted. Forays into these areas raise the ongoing issue of "Who is God?" Made in his image, we can choose to act the part of God. This is why we yield so stubbornly. Yet when we realize that God is God, and we are not, we experience peace and release. In our submission and obedience, we discover freedom. Only as a servant can we realize our full divine inheritance. Moses forged his leadership legacy by serving Hebrew slaves for forty years. Jesus' Messianic mission expressed an unanticipated suffering servant motif. Both leaders proved that great leadership is leadership that serves followers.

Great spiritual leaders are great spiritual leaders because they enjoy exceptional communion with God. The failure to establish intimacy with the Almighty imposes a limit on genuine spiritual leadership. No amount of giftedness or skill will make unnecessary the development of this arena. This does not mean that leaders cannot accomplish great things on their own prowess and steam. They can. However, full leadership potential can be reached only with the communion subplot well developed. Only God knows what insights he alone grants to the leader who pursues his heart.

The leader is not the only one counting on the leader's having a healthy communion with God. All those in the leadership constellation have a vested interest in the leader's spiritual development. Those in the leader's world of influence need to know that their leader has been with God, like Moses of old. They are encouraged and comforted when they detect the glow of the leader's face-to-face encounters with God. Their confidence for the journey ahead is directly informed by the knowledge and conviction that the leader has spent significant time with God pleading for his presence to go with them.

Contemporary leaders who, like David, can rehearse a full range of emotions with God in private can lead with greater equanimity in public. Leaders maintaining vibrant communion establish a peaceful kingdom. The followers can relax. The borders are secure. The sovereignty of God over the heart of the king (the leader) extends the blessings of God to his people. Conversely, a leader unruled by God creates insecurity for followers.

Like Paul, today's apostolic leaders need strengthening for their work through communion. When they are nurtured by times with the Resurrected Lord, the quality of their leadership is transforming. Because God is always at work revealing himself to them, well-communed leaders maintain a spiritual dynamic that allows followers to participate in the fresh movements of God in the world.

Jesus came to understand his person and his mission through his communion with the Father. A leader similarly enrolled in the school of divine instruction will lead from healthy self-awareness. Followers need to know what expedition they are signing up for. The leader's vibrant communion alone will establish appropriate sureness of the mission.

Becoming God's Friend

Communion represents such a powerful heart-shaping dynamic because it opens up the possibility of becoming God's friend. The biblical witness confirms that God desires this friendship. God created us in order to enjoy us (Gen. 3:8; Rev. 4:11). God called Abraham his friend (2 Chron. 20:7). Jesus told his disciples he considered them his friends (John 15:15). Of course, God will not force the friendship. The choice is ours.

If we choose to be God's friend, we can cultivate some attitudes and actions that facilitate the development of the friendship. We have already talked about the key ingredient of spending time with him.

We need to get to know God firsthand and not rely on what others tell us about him. Many human friendships never get off the ground because of preconceptions that one party has about the other. Often the preconception has been informed by another party or another experience. If people can get by the assumptions and get to know the other personally, a new appreciation for the person usually emerges.

The same dynamics hold true in our relationship with God. Many leaders have absorbed consciously and unconsciously ideas and notions about God from a number of sources—parents, spiritual authorities, popular culture, friends. God has gone to great lengths to give us firsthand knowledge about himself, including a signature creation, a planetary visit by his Son, and direct access to his Spirit. He wants us to get to know him. If we do, we will love him.

We can also find out what God likes and does not like. This kind of information improves human friendship. It will also work with God. For instance, God likes humility but detests pride. He likes paying attention to the plight of the poor and needy; he does not care for the willful ignoring of others' needs. He likes parties; he abhors religion that sucks the life out of people. The list can go on and on. Once we know what God likes and what he doesn't, we have an obvious choice. If we want to be better friends, we will choose to do more of what he enjoys and less of what drives us apart. The scriptures call this obedience.

We can also improve our relationship with God by becoming interested in what he is doing. Part of friendship with God includes our taking an active part in his mission. He will let us stay in our tiny, self-absorbed corners of life. However, he is up to so much more and would like to cut us in on some of it. A sure sign that we have been captured by God's heart is that we begin to see him more and more at work. We see him at church but also in the city commons. We see him in believers; we see him in the world outside Christ. We see him mostly in people's lives, drawing them to him and working in them. Because our interest is what interests him, we find ourselves also drawn to others.

Good friends celebrate one another's achievements. God has done good work. Learning to exult in his creative genius involves praise. It also includes researching his wonders in order to appreciate his creativity even more. Celebrating God's work thrusts us into the lives of people in whom he is working, helping them discover his abundance. Celebrating God's achievements extends to growing in appreciation for yourself. You are a work in progress, a work of God's heart, a masterpiece of divine heart-sculpting efforts. The more you grow to celebrate God's work in you, the more freed up your relationship will be.

Let God in on your own celebrations. Make him a part of your family good times, your vacations, your fun. Do not just get in touch with him when you need something. Include God in the wonderful joys and abundant moments.

The last chapter included a discussion about our need for friends. It detailed some qualities, or a checklist of personal characteristics, that we need to cultivate if we want to develop friendships. The same list could be rehearsed here. Vulnerability, intentional listening, integrity, and the rest all play an important role in our attitude in communion.

If we view our communion with God as something functional and mechanical, we will be consumed with figuring out how to pray, how to study the Bible, how to . . . whatever. These issues are not unimportant, but they are not the goal of communion. The goal of communion is the becoming one of two hearts—yours and God's.

Communion ultimately exposes leaders for who they are. Over time, those who crave God's heart-shaping work in this arena also become more transparent, more available to others, and more open displays of the heart of God.

One could argue that developing and maintaining quality communion with God is the hardest work of the spiritual leader's life. If it is hard, it is also crucial in establishing leadership potential. Shallow communion equals imploding leadership. Deep communion equals a positive leadership legacy.

So, how is your communion going?

- Do you have regular dates or coaching sessions with God?
- What other images invite you to spend quality time with him?
- When God thinks about you, what expression comes over his face? Does he smile or frown? Why? (By the way, you are always on his mind.)
- What can you do to improve your communion?
- What do others know about the conversations you have with God?
- How do you keep God on your heart throughout the day?
- How are you cultivating God's friendship?
- What is the last thing you have learned about God in your times together?

Leaders in touch with heaven can move earth. As spiritual leaders come to know the heart of God in communion, their own hearts begin to beat with his. Like resonating tuning bars, their hearts become conformed to the perfect pitch of the One who woos them in the quiet places of their hearts.

Go on in.

CONFLICT

LEARNING TO DIE SO WE CAN LIVE

SHAWN AND GLENDA met me at a restaurant that is an hour's drive from the town where they lived and pastored. They poured out buckets of pain as they recounted a recent incident that had caught them completely off guard. After their best year in five, with the congregation reaching new people and all vital signs looking good, a new church board had just had its first meeting. Shawn discovered at that meeting that half of the board declared an agenda of getting rid of him as pastor. Completely disheartened and bewildered, Shawn resigned on the spot, securing only thirty days of severance. He and Glenda had no place to go and no prospects for financial support. On top of this, it was the first of December, with Christmas around the corner. They did know they wanted out. They were defeated and did not want to tackle another ministry assignment.

Mark and Christy have endured two years of an incredible smear campaign and even legal battles. A person who previously belonged to the congregation had moved back and rejoined the church. The man had served as a church officer under a previous pastor and was almost immediately reassigned his old responsibility. However, the church had changed significantly in the man's five-year absence. He wanted to return to old ways of administration. He crossed swords with Mark over several decisions and concluded that Mark "wasn't good for the church." He set about building a coalition of long-tenured members who did not really know all the issues but saw this as a chance to regain the church they had "lost" due to growth and new operational procedures. The church board, supportive of the pastor, relieved the officer of his duties. He had become a terrorist in the congregation, never missing a chance to create havoc and controversy, seeking to destroy Mark and Christy's ministry by challenging the pastor's leadership. Throughout the ordeal, the ministry couple has kept their composure, deepened their spiritual lives, and operated with a smile in spite of the pain.

A member of the board of a Christian organization, who sees the unethical personnel and financial dealings of a new leader, becomes disillusioned. She has chosen to stay and fight for a ministry she has spent twenty years helping build. She is a person of prayer and integrity and stays in the fray despite enormous personal attack.

A leader in a large denomination has mounted a multiyear campaign to take back his denomination from "forces of liberalism," as he puts it. He has been successful but has lost himself in the struggle. Years of political maneuvering have made him almost unrecognizable as a person of genuine spiritual leadership. He operates more like a political party leader.

These four vignettes from my file of acquaintances represent hundreds more. The decision to serve as a spiritual leader signs one up for conflict. This fact comes as a shock to many Christian leaders. The conflict they encounter blindsides them. Suddenly the people they are trying to serve refuse their leadership, question their motives, and even conspire against them.

God uses conflict to shape the leader's heart. The conflicts in the lives of the four biblical heroes significantly fashioned their leadership legacy. It still does. Unfortunately, many spiritual leaders prove to be conflict allergic. Their heightened sensitivities, so often a strength for them, render them especially vulnerable to deal with the pain associated with conflict situations. The tenderness and personal connectedness that make them effective also leave them personally exposed. Unless they develop a strategy for dealing with conflict, they may withdraw from the battle. If they do, their hearts remain stunted relative to what they could have been.

Our rehearsals of the lives of Moses, David, Paul, and Jesus introduce our discussion of the conflict subplot in spiritual leaders' lives. These men have become known to us in part because of their conflicts. Moses' battle with the mightiest king on earth landed him in the history books. David fought his way to the throne and fought to extend Israel's borders during his reign. Paul's ongoing struggle with the Judaizers took place in city after city, ultimately propelling him to Rome in order to defend his faith. The demons shrieked as Jesus invaded their territory; the simmering feud between Jesus and the Pharisees erupted into his blistering indictment of them right before his arrest; and the Passion pitted him against the ultimate enemies of sin, death, and hell.

We learn from these four that leaders cannot escape conflict. No amount of leadership skill can enable one to avoid it entirely. The presence of conflict does not necessarily signal the displeasure of God with the leader. Sometimes leaders encounter conflict precisely because they are doing the right thing.

How is it that conflict strengthens some and collapses others? Isn't it paradoxical that some who "win" really lose, whereas others who take huge hits turn out better for the battle?

We need to examine some key strategies, both attitudinal and behavioral, that will put you in the winners' category. Your goal should not be just to merely survive conflict but to wind up more than a conqueror, a genuine champion whose life has been enriched by conflict rather than impaired by it. Spiritual leaders must welcome conflict as a heart-shaping tool of God.

Strategy Number One: Get Over It

The first strategy for dealing with conflict is an attitudinal one. Many spiritual leaders seem caught off guard by the fact that they encounter conflict. One of the best strategies for letting conflict work for you involves coming out of denial and coming to grips with the reality that challenges go with the territory of leadership.

Frequently spiritual leaders suffer from an idealism in this regard. They believe that they will escape conflict because they are pursuing a wonderful mission. They think that as long as they are not in it for themselves, they should get a pass. Others will surely see their altruism, they reason, and exempt them from unfair (or fair) criticism. They underestimate the powerful, intensely personal emotions that spiritual issues engender. Differences over vision and values do not remain merely cerebral. They set up contests over direction of life and ministry. In short, spiritual matters matter a lot to people. They will fight for them and about them.

The experiences of Moses, David, Jesus, and Paul ought to be convincing evidence that no matter how noble the leader is or how lofty the dreams and agenda, the leader is going to get shot at. And sometimes hit. Moses did not have to come out of retirement to lead a slave revolt. David rid the land of Philistine incursions. Jesus' mission accomplished world redemption, and Paul just wanted to invite people to the party that Jesus got going. All gave themselves to undeniably noble endeavors. Yet each leader was questioned for motives and methods by friends and enemies alike.

Get over it. If you are a spiritual leader, you will be embroiled in conflict occasionally or frequently precisely because you are leading. Leadership that is not encountering difficulty probably is not trying to accomplish much. Leadership in the hinges of history (which is where we are now) is no game for cowards.

Not all conflicts result from attempting great things. Some conflicts arise from poor judgment on the leader's part, or from arrogance, or from stupidity. Some of the other strategies in this chapter are aimed at minimizing conflict on these accounts.

Expect conflict. You are no better than your fathers (to borrow a phrase from another Old Testament prophet involved in a conflict of his own). Moses knew it would be no picnic against Pharaoh, and his experience should have told him his own people were going to be a challenge as well. David suffered no illusions about becoming king without having to fight for it, even though it was promised him by God. Paul knew he was a marked man before he regained his sight. Jesus died before the world was created (the Lamb was slain before the foundation of the world, the scriptures say).

If you want to emerge better through conflict, go ahead and die. Die to expectations that everyone will love you. Die to getting a pass on being mistreated and persecuted. Then get over it with resurrection power, and live a truly free and powerful life, having already counted yourself as dead. Be surprised by affirmations and commendations. Do not count on them. Count on being frequently challenged and sometimes resisted. This perspective will set you free from having to lead from popularity or approval ratings. You can lead from a true moral and spiritual center.

Strategy Number Two: Choose Your Pain

A ministry leader complained to me over a two-year period about the criticism he endured. As I studied his leadership, I realized he had failed to establish a ministry direction. The result was 360-degree criticism. Trying to please everyone was not working. It never does. I told him to choose his pain.

The leader who is going nowhere will take hits from all sides. The leader who sets a direction will at least know what direction the arrows will be coming from. A leader can more likely survive pain that results from vision. Purposeless pain is much harder to cope with.

Spiritual leaders who operate from a sense of God's call and mission in their lives can deal more intentionally with conflict. Without a confirmed call, leaders face the challenges that confront them without an overall game plan for handling them. Leaders must have some internal vision and value grid for decision making that govern response to the conflict. This internal decision-making apparatus is informed first and foremost by the mission of their lives.

Moses knew that a showdown with Pharaoh was inevitable in securing the Hebrews' release. David, on the other hand, chose never to confront Saul in order to secure the throne. Both decisions were informed by their respective missions. Paul knew when to get out of Dodge (Lystra, Derbe, and so forth) and when to appeal to Caesar to extend his incarceration and get to Rome. The mission made the call. Jesus would not go to the cross for the wrong reasons (political revolt) or at the wrong time (the disciples needed time to mature and Jesus wanted to capitalize on the theological symbolism of Passover and Pentecost).

The spiritual leader without a clear sense of mission or call might interpret conflict as signs of God's displeasure or as reason to doubt the leadership direction that has been chosen. If the advent of conflict automatically spelled divine disapproval, then Moses would have quit after the first plague did not spring the captives free. However, a conviction secured in the heart as to why the leader is on the planet will not be overturned easily by travails.

A clear sense of mission will also keep leaders from suffering for stupid reasons. Some leaders, not knowing exactly what their objective is, choose to go to the mat over every issue. They waste valuable leadership collateral and dissipate their energies through this operational approach. They sometimes claim to operate from "spiritual authority" when in fact they are operating out of a deep sense of insecurity and lack of an overarching life mission. Winning contests is not a sufficient motive for entering the spiritual leadership arena.

Strategy Number Three: Examine Your Critics

When criticism or conflict breaks out, the leader does well to take stock of the opposition. Jesus talked of this in the stories about counting the cost. Smart generals size up the enemy, and prudent builders establish sufficient credit lines to be able to finish the projects they start. Wise leaders take their opposition seriously. Custer did not appreciate the formidable leadership of Sitting Bull; the rest is history. Several significant tactical moves contribute to this overall strategy.

Weigh Them, Don't Count Them

When criticism comes, the smart leader knows how to weigh it. Is the criticism coming from the leadership core? If so, it weighs more than comments from the fringe. In this case, the one source of conflict in the leadership pool might be enough to warrant significant attention. On the other hand, consistent criticisms from fringe elements may be better to simply ignore.

Sometimes a leader will realize that the opponent is a tribal chief in the ministry organization. In other words, the person challenging the leader may represent a number of others who have similar positions or who owe fealty to the person for family, financial, or other reasons. This one voice has to be heard at its true decibel level.

Leaders will often hear a complaint accompanied by the statement, "A lot of people feel this way," or something similar. These threats can only be evaluated by a grasp of who is delivering the information. Those who oppose leaders typically will inflate the size of their support. The leader who knows only how to count will be backed into a corner by these blusterings. There may or may not be reason to fold or to change course.

One congregation I worked with had entered a worship war between various factions of the membership. The staff, particularly the worship leader, heard each week the threat that large numbers of people were dissatisfied and "about to leave the church" if the decision to introduce contemporary worship was not rescinded. For several weeks, I conducted an assessment and then called the staff together. I told them to call the bluff of the next threat. The leadership core of the church was solidly behind the move to more contemporary worship options, and the direction supported the congregation's mission. Armed with new information provided by the assessment, the staff took heart and faithfully pushed ahead. From that day, they were compassionate but not ambivalent in their attitude. They knew how to assign the criticism its appropriate weight.

Numerical strength is not always the only advantage a leader needs. Typically spiritual leaders operate in family systems. Most congregations behave this way, particularly when conflict surfaces. Congregations and boards are not Congress. A 51 percent vote does not constitute a mandate. Some leaders fail to realize this. Superior numbers do not always deliver victory. At the Battle of the Little Bighorn, Custer thought his superior number of troops would carry the fight. Perhaps they would have if the playing field had been level. But it wasn't. It rarely is.

Many spiritual leaders, thinking they have the votes, are devastated by the quick erosion of advantage when the fighting actually begins. For instance, congregation members are often more concerned with preserving long-term community relationships than in persisting in a fight to the finish. A leader becomes expendable quickly in these situations. Blinded by the "right" of the cause, the embroiled leader sometimes fails to appreciate the tenuousness of the situation in the face of relationship dynamics. The ice may not support the weight of the leader's efforts.

Listen Behind the Criticism

Effective spiritual leaders understand that the presenting issue is not always the real issue. A criticism about how something is done often camouflages the real concern of the leader's detractor. Perhaps (and often) the struggle is over control. However, because most people in spiritual contexts prefer not to present their concerns as control based, the issue rarely gets tagged this way early on. The leader is sometimes bewildered that once an objection to a decision or policy is met, the "issue" suddenly becomes something else. This can serve as a tip-off that the real issue is indeed control.

Rachel learned this lesson quickly. In her first ministry assignment, she had a group confront her with a list of "concerns." Believing these were all fixable, she went to work on addressing the specific issues. Before long, she discerned that no matter what she did, a new list of "concerns" would be forthcoming. She sized up the issue as one of control. She shared her perspective with her supervisor, who filled her in on the group's history. She had pegged their motive. The group had once been more influential in the church. They preyed on new staff members. Rachel did not play along. She confronted the group, who folded when their cover was blown.

Control is not always the issue. The leader must discern the genuine source of concern. Some people who oppose change fear the loss of things other than control. Perhaps they fear the loss of security or relationships. Demonizing people for their having normal reactions to loss constitutes poor leadership. Unfortunately, this is done all the time by those who see every issue as about them and whether or not people will support and follow them. Mature leadership that understands transition dynamics works to allay fears and to provide emotional support for those struggling with the implications of change.

Charles knew that the relocation issue had claimed the leadership lives of many well-meaning people. In his study of transition, he had learned the value of broadening the planning involvement, selling the problem, communicating vision, listening well, and providing emotional support. His enlistment strategy of bringing key people on board, plus his listening sessions and patience, resulted in a 100 percent secret ballot vote affirming the relocation proposal. Charles's obvious commitment to helping his people make the transition demonstrated his heart for them and for God.

Sometimes situations arise that threaten mission. A competing value system may vie for control of the ministry. In these cases, a leader who appeases will yield valuable ground. In fact, the leader who cannot take a stand when the issue is the mission will fail to serve as a champion for those who believe in the mission. The failure to do this will cause a loss of heart in followers. Many leaders, afraid of conflict or lacking sufficient sense of mission, exile the very people who could have helped them create a better future. These are people who want to follow someone they can count on to keep the faith and fight the good fight.

Trevor offered his resignation to the group of assembled senior leadership of the church. A coup attempt led by a staff member had come to light. "I will get out of the way to spare the congregation," he said. "And just what will that accomplish?" fired the personnel committee chairperson. "We will be left here to deal with this mess." Trevor quickly decided that he dare not demoralize the people who had the ministry mission at heart. He hung in for a rough ride, but one he ultimately survived, and helped solidify the congregation's support of the ministry.

Evaluate Critics' Motives

Leaders also need to be good at discerning the motives of their challengers. This works both positively and negatively. Some leaders, insecure and spiritually immature, cannot countenance any criticism. Like would-be emperors, they banish people from their presence (and from leadership in the ministry organization) who dare to criticize or even question them. David's greatness showed up in his keeping Nathan around even when the prophet failed to approve of the king's behavior or decisions.

The leader has to know the motive of the critics. If the motive is for the good of the leader or for the well-being of the faith community, then they must be listened to and evaluated from that perspective. Perhaps the information the leader needs most is information that will prove troubling or fail to confirm the leader's plans. Too many times, leaders switch advisers until they hear what they want to hear. This results in leaders unprepared for battle.

If, however, leaders fail to discern malevolent motives, they are in just as great a danger. If the motive is to sabotage the mission or introduce a leadership virus into the system, then action sooner rather than later is advised. David's failure to deal with Absalom sooner almost cost him his kingdom. The loss would not have been a failure of God to deliver on his promise to preserve David's kingdom. It would have resulted from David's dysfunctionality as a father. A leader simply must be savvy about the ultimate objectives of those who are giving criticism or instigating conflict.

A final word of warning should help many spiritual leaders avoid heartache and lessen the combative nature of some conflict: do not demonize the opposition. Sometimes criticism or unexpected differences arise from those whose motives do not include challenging the leader's leadership. These people do not need to suddenly find themselves dubbed and treated as the opposition. Leaders who establish compliance from followers as a litmus test for remaining in favor disqualify themselves as spiritual leaders. Spirituality does not flourish without accountability. Accountability cannot develop without freedom of expression.

Leaders who routinely demonize critics establish unhealthiness in the system. Issues get lost in personal vendettas and invective. The leader eventually becomes the issue, and the leader's agenda is placed in serious jeopardy. Over time, spiritual leadership cannot be about the leader. If the leader does not keep the debate at the mission-issue level, then a systemwide conflict can precipitate a leadership crisis that could result in the leader's demise.

Derrick responded very differently from his predecessor. He had assumed leadership of the ministry less than a month before encountering resistance to a decision he had made. He refused to attack his attackers as evil. Instead, he kept the discussion centered on the issues. This maturity created enormous credit for him with the other ministry constituencies.

Strategy Number Four: Look in the Mirror

While examining critics or opponents, the leader must also initiate a thorough self-examination. This is not easy and can even be painfully revealing. Nevertheless, it must be done. Leaders who do not exercise discipline over themselves, asking themselves the tough questions, do not finish well. This does not mean that the leader must never act, paralyzed by endless self-analysis trying to ferret out every impure motive. It does mean that the leader is secure enough to revisit decisions and give appropriate consideration to judgment calls in responding to conflicted situations.

A few key questions will open up the leader's heart (both to the leader and to God).

Do the Critics and Opponents Have a Point (or Two)?

Leaders should ask themselves if they understand the viewpoint of the challengers. I want to preserve the reflective dynamic of the leader's own self-examination. This obviously does not require agreeing with their observations or criticisms. However, the capacity for negotiating the conflict is heightened considerably if the leader is able to articulate, and even understand, the opponent's position.

By beginning here, the leader keeps from automatically assuming that criticism is personal. This point has been raised several times in this volume because spiritual leaders are very susceptible to problems associated with the inability to practice self-differentiation, thereby becoming so connected to the ministry that any criticism from any part of the organization (ranging from policy to program to personnel) is taken as a personal challenge or criticism.

This difficulty can be further aggravated and complicated when the leader has unresolved psychological boundary issues. Many spiritual leaders tend to be compliants, meaning that they have a hard time not acceding to others' demands on them, even to the point of their own detriment. Often compliants will say yes to a new demand when inside they hear themselves saying no. Their fear of not being liked (whether because they did not measure up to expectations or they might have hurt other people's feelings) keeps them inappropriately exposed to others' claims on them. Afraid of being abandoned (or exiled), they try to keep everyone happy. They have great difficulties handling situations in which people get upset with them. Internally they place their self-worth on the block even though the external discussion may never approach this subject.

Awareness of this boundary issue can sometimes be enough to help the leader guard against this unhealthy response mechanism. In some cases, some professional counseling can help leaders discover why they permit others to violate their boundaries consistently. The insights into this vulnerability frequently lie in the family of origin. Fear of abandonment, brought about by the failure to establish secure emotional bonding with significant others early in life, can contribute to this problem. Self-surgery in this area can be very bloody, as well as unproductive or counterproductive. These issues need sorting through with a trusted counselor who has good insight in these particular dynamics.

To return to the main point, leaders need to practice sufficient self-differentiation. This allows them to evaluate criticisms or objections to their leadership without their first reaction being that of feeling personally assaulted. Lowering the internal-background emotional noise gives leaders a wonderful advantage in dealing with the conflict. This advantage results from leaders' capacity to frame the debate. Usually whoever can frame the issues will win the discussion. This is particularly true in public arenas like ministry organizations. This is why leaders need, as much as possible, to keep the contest as not about them.

The leader should ask, "Does the criticism or objection have merit?" Sometimes leaders deserve criticism. All of us make mistakes and exercise poor judgment occasionally. The key is to get in front of critics by owning mistakes quickly, thus removing clubs from the hands of those who might want to use the opportunity to beat on the leader. The capacity of the leader to do this, or the unwillingness of the leader to do this, reflects on the leader's character either positively or negatively. One of the heart-shaping outcomes God wants to accomplish through the conflict subplots in the leader's life involves character development.

Early in ministry, Craig responded to criticism punitively. He took all criticism as proof that people were not being supportive. He blocked the critic's ability to gain significant ministry opportunity. He withdrew from the "negative" people and made sure others in his personal constellation did the same. While attending a conflict management seminar, he became aware of his negative tendencies. He shared his insight with some friends who could hold him accountable for the changes he wanted to make. His heart grew through his increased self-awareness and subsequent behavior modification.

Of course, critics and their criticism can be entirely off-base. Some famous advice to Christian leaders through the years goes something like this: "Behind every criticism, there lies a nugget of truth." That is bad advice. Living with that fiction has sent many spiritual leaders on internal psychological and spiritual excursions where they wind up chasing their emotional tail. The truth is, some criticism has no merit. Furthermore, some critics are jerks, pure and simple. Even worse, they may be malevolent figures intent on destroying the ministry of the leader. In those cases, it would be ridiculous for leaders to consume enormous personal energies beating themselves up looking for the "what is God trying to teach me?" insight that does not exist. God may not be trying to teach them anything except to discount the criticism, meet the objection, and move on. Sometimes the delay caused by this misbegotten search can create more problems and increase the level of conflict.

The first question, then, in the leader's internal discussion focuses on examining and evaluating the merits of the challenge at hand. Another question has to be dealt with at the same time.

Is This Criticism Pushing Hot Buttons?

Often the leader feels an internal temperature rise during conflict. The normal survival instinct automatically kicks the adrenaline in as it rouses the fight-or-flight response. This becomes a problem when virtually any challenge results in an overheated emotional state. When this occurs, another level of self-evaluation has to take place. The leader needs to figure out what hot buttons are being pushed.

We all have hot buttons. Leaders should know what theirs are. If they do not know what triggers emotional responses, they cannot respond to deep-seated tapes in the psyche. They may not even be aware that they are overreacting or misperceiving a situation as more threatening than it actually is. When hot buttons go unrecognized or unguarded, leaders often make wrong assumptions about the degree of danger they are in, or they impute the wrong intentions to others' actions and statements. Acting from hot buttons can precipitate a conflict unnecessarily or aggravate an existing one, making it more difficult to resolve.

Hot buttons get implanted in one or both of two shops—family of origin and formative negative leadership experiences. Family-of-origin issues can be many and varied. For instance, perhaps the leader's family of origin considered anger to be an inappropriate emotion. Because emotions cannot be denied and we all get angry, the leader was taught to stuff anger. This created a psychological subterranean lava bed of hostility. Leaders who have not reckoned with this part of the past may vent molten anger through the most minor fissures in the emotional terrain. They will respond to challenges with an immediate rise of anger, accompanied by punitive attitudes and countermoves. Leaders who have never learned how to deal constructively with anger may mishandle it and damage their leadership credibility.

Another example of a family-of-origin issue could involve the leader's internalized performance standard as the basis for approval. This often leads to insecurity because the leader's standard of self-worth is measured against others. The comparative nature of this dynamic will often create a very competitive theme in the leader's life, manifested in an exaggerated need to win. Every exchange, every relationship, every issue provides an arena for competition. The result, of course, is a leader always poised for battle, a one-upmanship persona style that exacerbates life and ministry.

Early negative leadership experiences can also implant hot buttons in the leader's psyche. One minister was ousted at his first church by the elder board. He went out and planted a church with no provision for a ruling board. He determined never to be subject to the decisions of others. This negative lesson showed up not only in the polity of his new congregation but also in the minister's style of handling conflict. Any time he was challenged, he had a severe adverse reaction, as if a virulent emotional virus had been released in his spirit.

The list of these kinds of situations can run as long as every leader's own experience. Almost every leader has had some kind of early conflict. These have shaped the leader either positively or negatively. If the leader does not exercise emotional rehabilitation, the scars will show. The leader needs to avoid institutionalizing negative emotional and psychological reactions to the past. Otherwise, the leader becomes vulnerable to emotional triggers that spark inappropriate behaviors and attitudes.

Hot buttons need to be identified and guarded against. Smart leaders who struggle with these give permission to trusted colleagues to warn them when they see evidence of a hot button at work. This move to accountability demonstrates that the leader has done sufficient introspection to identify the emotional trouble areas and has enough self-security to trust others.

Lyle finally decided to deal with his anger and hostility. He realized that a certain person evoked in him a fright surge that manifested itself in internal rage. Lyle quit blaming the other person for his anger, took responsibility for his emotions, and faced the fear that the adversary evoked. He confided this to a prayer partner, who agreed to check on his progress.

The capacity to learn from experience is a hallmark of good leadership. Sometimes this exercise is an internal journey into one's own soul, in which you look for markers from the past that help you understand where you are today and why you are reacting the way you are. Another leg of this trip involves the sheer courage to look into one's inner being. The situations most challenging in this regard are those times when the leader does not feel strong emotionally or spiritually. Conflict zones typically challenge the leader to the core, making it especially difficult to risk adding pain to that already being inflicted by the struggle. Yet this is potentially the time of greatest insight breakthroughs. Great leaders have run the risk of opening themselves up to themselves for a close and hard look.

Strategy Number Five: Get Good Advice

Counselors are especially helpful during conflict. When difficult situations or seasons arise, all previous efforts of the leader at developing a support network can really pay off. The leader, while sizing up the opposition and taking internal stock of resources and potential pitfalls, frequently will need to think out loud with some confidants. Three sources will be most helpful.

Godly People

People never complain of having too many godly people in their lives. Usually the opposite is true. Godly people tell the truth in love. Both parts of that statement are important. Leaders need the truth. They may be blinded to their own attitudes and actions that are contributing to the conflict. A godly person will tell them so. But they will deliver the message with love, especially if it is painful. Nathan provided David with this kind of truth telling after the Bathsheba episode.

Cultivating godly people as confidants and advisers helps a leader prepare to endure hardships. This priority does not emerge in the lives of those who choose not to risk friendship and accountability. It does not develop in the proud or ambitious heart that seeks only to use or manipulate followers. A mark of emotional and spiritual maturity shows up in the extent to which a leader has developed relationships with godly people.

Carolyn had spent years discipling women in small groups. During an intense time of personal trauma, she called on some of these women for support. These friends stayed with her throughout the ordeal. At first, they commiserated with her by listening to her pain. Eventually, as Carolyn progressed through her grief, they challenged her to forgive her oppressors. They provided what Carolyn needed at every stage. They monitored her heart.

In order to benefit from their wisdom, leaders must grant these godly people permission to challenge them, to tell them the truth. Receiving encouragement and affirmation from those who are empowered to tell us the truth provides genuine nurture. The leader can genuinely take to heart the support freely given. Leaders who permit people to tell them only what they want to hear cheat themselves. Cultivated and manipulated affirmation shrinks to sycophancy. It is insipid. It fails to provide encouragement that the leader can take to heart.

The leader who is mired in a battle will need the courage to stand. This boldness can be encouraged by godly spirits who help the leader see more clearly, who hear out doubts and fears, who ask good questions, who hold the leader up while others seek to tear the leader down.

Scripture

During times of conflict, the Word of God will provide wonderful tonic to the soul. The Davidic psalms prove especially helpful. David knew court intrigue, betrayal, political maneuverings, and crafty opponents. He knew his own pride and sinful heart. In his communion with God, he held nothing back. This is why the psalms prove such good friends to the leader in conflict. When David was angry, it showed. He asked God to mutilate his enemies (sometimes leaders need to vent). David pouted. Sometimes leaders do that. David whined (as did Moses and Paul). Leaders will do that too. In the psalms, the leader can exercise all the emotions—from anger, to loneliness, to fear, to trust, to resignation, to resolve.

Other biblical texts are also engaging and instructive to the leader during conflict times. As already discussed, Moses' forty years as the leader of the Hebrews of Exodus is a powerful lesson in long-term perseverance.

The gospels are full of Jesus' battles. The book of Acts records Paul's hardships. Texts touching on other leaders' lives also abound in scripture. The diary of Nehemiah has long been a favorite place for leaders to camp out when doing archaeological digs into compelling conflicts of the past. Genesis offers the story of Joseph, whose conflicts became rungs on the ladder to greatness.

Prayer

The leader will never feel closer to Jesus than in times of persecution or conflict. Jesus identifies with the leader's heart. Remember, he is a man of sorrows acquainted with grief.

Some of the pain of conflict is sometimes too deep for words. God can understand the unspeakable. Sometimes the leader still has to make difficult decisions even while receiving conflicting input from wise and godly people. God gives wisdom. In the midst of the worst of storms, the leader will sometimes face enormous self-doubt. God will not turn his back on the spiritual leader. The ambivalence in the leader's heart does not trouble him. The Father has had a son in the leader's shoes. He understands.

Will came to see me. When I asked how he was doing, he shoved a piece of paper toward me. "I wrote this yesterday. It pretty well says it all."

> Dear Lord,
>
> I'm so tired. My strength is completely gone and so is my desire to continue on. My resources are spent and all that remains is an empty, dry, shriveled shell of a man. I'm exhausted. I'm tired.
>
> I'm tired of giving to people who are never satisfied. I'm tired of pouring the best that I have to offer into people's lives only to have them demand more and become angry when it's not provided. I'm tired of demanding, thankless people.
>
> I'm tired of being abused. I'm tired of being talked about behind my back by people who are supposed to be my brothers and sisters.
>
> I'm tired of being ignored. I'm tired of comforting grieving people while my grief is ignored. I'm tired of bearing the burdens of others while I bear my burdens alone. I'm tired of binding the wounds of others while I'm bleeding to death. I'm tired of drying the tears of others while my tears go unnoticed. I'm tired of soothing hurting hearts while my own heart is breaking. I'm tired of feeding people when I'm starving to death.

I'm tired of busybodies. I'm tired of people who never open their Bibles assuming that they know what God wants me to do. I'm tired of unspiritual people giving me advice. I'm tired of unappreciative people imposing on my time with my family.

I'm tired of expectations. I'm tired of being asked for advice. I'm tired of representing God. I'm tired of living on a pedestal. I'm tired of performing for the crowd. I want to be human again. I'm tired of being nice to people that I don't like and who don't like me.

I'm tired of hospitals and nursing homes and funeral homes. I'm tired of early morning hours in waiting rooms. I'm tired of graveside services and cemeteries. I'm tired of sickness and death.

I'm tired of the loneliness. I'm tired of being invited to share the tragedies, hurts, tears of people's lives while being held at arms length when things are going well.

I'm tired of serving and giving and feeding and comforting and teaching and encouraging and ministering.

Lord, I'm so, so tired. I don't have anything left to give. I've got to rest. I can't go on. Lord, please let me quit.

Will's healing began with the prayer. He was gut-level honest about his feelings. He did not sanitize his thoughts for fear of running God off. He determined to pursue some health by getting some pastoral counseling, taking some time off, and beginning to cultivate friendships.

In times of conflict, the leader who turns out to be more than conqueror turns to God, not away from God. He is the Soul Surgeon whose cuts are clean and whose hands perform healing operations. He has anticipated every struggle that the leader faces and has already determined how this situation can shape the leader's heart for even greater effectiveness.

Strategy Number Six: Be Kind and Honest

Leaders need to be kind to and honest with two factions during conflicts—themselves and their enemies. Both are important.

Treating Oneself Appropriately

First, leaders need to be kind to themselves. Some leaders seem intent on beating themselves up. They go to inordinate lengths to castigate themselves for their leadership failures, real or imagined. Many spiritual leaders feel that the presence of conflict signals some leadership failure. This arises from two sources—psychological and theological. The conflict-allergic nature of some leaders makes them view all conflict as negative. This is the psychological part.

Poor theology has also contributed its share to the problem. Some have advocated that if leaders pray hard enough and wait on the Lord, then the body of believers will come to agreement. Disagreement or distress in the body is thus seen as a sign of poor spiritual leadership. Some have suggested that these situations automatically signal that leaders have placed their own ambition and will ahead of the Spirit. Conflict, they assert, is symptomatic of a leader's lack of obedience. Although this may be the case, it is not necessarily the case.

This theological position rests on two major misassumptions—that the leader is dealing with regenerate people only (a huge stretch) and that every believer in the congregation or organization is being led by the Spirit. Added to these misassumptions is a poor recollection of history. The biblical leaders constantly faced conflict. It was not all of their making. Not even Jesus could keep all the disciples in line. Judas's disaffection was not a judgment on Jesus' leadership ability.

Does some conflict result from leadership failures? Sure. Sometimes leaders strike at people to cut their heads off and only catch their ear. Sometimes they get the whole head. Sometimes they lash out because the circumstances are exacerbating. Sometimes the leader is indeed a jerk. But does all conflict result from leadership failures? Absolutely not. If so, the rebellion of Satan and his angels signals a leadership problem on the part of God.

Leaders can afford to be kind to themselves if they have the grace to be honest with themselves also. Leaders who are honest with themselves about foibles and fears as well as about strengths and gifts can make appropriate determinations of personal responsibility for the conflicts they face. Kindness to oneself, the capacity to cut oneself some slack, flows from honest self-appraisal.

Treating Enemies Appropriately

The same approach needs to be taken with enemies. The leader can always afford to be kind, and must deal in honesty. Both elements are essential to the leader's emerging from conflict strengthened in the heart by the experience.

Rarely does the leader gain much from being unkind or exceedingly harsh with opponents. What feels so good to say in the moment will leave a pretty bad aftertaste the next day. In addition, followers are genuinely heartened by a leader's composure. An outburst to get things off one's chest may gain vapid applause. However, a leader's continued composure inspires a more enduring confidence in followers. If exchanges get really ugly on both sides, the leader loses some credibility with some followers. Above all, maintaining self-disciplined control over emotions increases the power of spiritual witness and influence.

Andrew demonstrated enormous poise. For over two hours, the business meeting centered mostly on attacks on him from a small minority of vocal people who had created difficulty in the church for some time. Andrew's gentle but firm spirit refused to feed the fire in his opponents. His spirit showed up in marked relief to theirs. This inspired confidence in him from the other members who supported him.

Having said this, the leader does not need to equate being kind to enemies with being untruthful or adopting a doormat position. Using honesty in the conflict keeps the level of accountability high. This is particularly important in family systems. Honesty provides some restraint. It allows the Spirit his most freedom. The truth really does set people free.

Being honest with critics means first of all telling the truth. People in America are sick of spin doctors. They need spiritual leaders whose word and integrity are unimpeachable. Second, being honest keeps the discussion on issues whenever possible. If the discussion has centered on personality, honesty will reveal this as a dysfunction. Third, honesty lets an enemy have a way out. They can, upon changing their minds, more easily reestablish relationships than if the struggle has been a knock-down-drag-out fight over personal ideas and loyalties. Fourth, honesty keeps responsibility where it belongs and recognizes the power of choice. Telling the truth in love is the operating principle of the leader. Once this is done, any false sense of responsibility on the leader's part can be released. This avoids situations driven by the leader's need to win, or even to be agreed with. Using honesty as the currency in dialogue keeps the leader's boundaries intact and places responsibility for response on the opponents.

Honesty must be motivated by love. Brutal honesty can ignite an inflammatory situation. Honesty without love is harder to receive. In fact, it feels like something other than honesty. It can feel like manipulation or campaigning or browbeating or demonizing. Honesty supported by love creates the possibility for forgiveness and redemption to take place.

Strategy Number Seven: Forgive!

Greg took his pastor out for coffee. They had just come from yet another brutal meeting occasioned by the rebellious activity of several in the congregation. The most bruising part of the episode was the discovery that a staff member had betrayed the pastor. As the pastor vented his anger, the deacon loved him enough to tell him the truth: "Pastor, don't let this get the best of you. You will eventually have to forgive him." It was good advice from a man who knew what he was talking about. Just the year before, his company had survived a hostile takeover attempt supported by a rogue corporate officer. The deacon had suffered a good deal of mental anguish but had emerged with his heart stronger. His scars gave his advice credibility.

Some leaders get through initial conflict fine. They analyze the situation well, do not overreact, size up their opponents, create support for their position or negotiate a settlement, demonstrate self-control and integrity in the battle—and then blow it! They choose at the point of victory to script ultimate defeat for themselves. They decide never to get beyond the conflict. They choose to peg their emotional focus to the past. In short, they fail to forgive.

The power to forgive is a Godlike quality that blesses others by releasing them from the power of a poor past. Conversely, the failure to forgive sets up a dynamic that perpetually binds people to pain and hurt. The failure to forgive is the sure recipe for stunted personal growth. Put another way, it creates a terminal heart disease. The blood of the Spirit's nourishment is prevented from flowing freely to the leader's heart. Failure to forgive blocks the blessings of God. The heart begins to die.

Many leaders are defined by the great conflicts of their lives. Some react positively, like the four biblical leaders examined in this volume. Some defining moments prove negative, as in the countless numbers of cases in which leaders choose to send themselves to jail for spiritual violation.

Those who withhold forgiveness do so in the belief that in some way they are inflicting damage or hurt on the object of their unforgivingness. The trouble is, while the unforgiving deals with excess stomach acid and sleepless nights, the unforgiven sleeps like a baby. An unforgiving spirit is a cancer of the soul.

The leaders who emerge from conflict as winners do not withhold forgiveness. Whether or not reconciliation may be possible does not deter them from exercising forgiveness. They absolve their offenders for hurts they have inflicted. In so doing, they can extend grace to their offenders and choose not to let the pain they have felt be the book on their leadership.

The leaders who do not forgive wind up with bitter spirits, persons of negative energy. They wonder where their spiritual energy and power went. Their negative spirit pushes people away from them. They live in the past, their conflict scar tissues making it difficult for them to move forward. They see the world and life experiences through victim eyes. They walk by sight and not by faith. What they see is a self-fulfilling scenario of rejection, spiritual entropy, and discouragement. If this sounds too harsh, it actually only begins to describe the real damages. This matter of the failure to forgive is serious business. Jesus took time out from dying to do it.

One of the truest evidences of God's heart-shaping activity shows up in the leader during conflict. It is the presence of a forgiving spirit. The leader who forgives has allowed God to do the radical surgery, radiation therapy, or whatever approach was necessary to rid the heart of its cancer pockets of unforgivingness. On the cross, Jesus forgave those who were killing him. Moses pleaded for Miriam's and Aaron's lives when they rebelled against him. Paul forgave John Mark for letting the apostle down in his expectations. Even David passed along the gift of forgiveness that he had received, the most notable case being his attitude toward Absalom during his son's challenge to the throne.

The leader can always afford to forgive. The leader cannot afford not to forgive.

Strategy Number Eight: Make a Decision

The leader who profits through conflict has done one thing that forms the foundation on which all other strategies rest. The leader who grows through leadership challenges has not done so accidentally. This leader has made a decision to grow.

Some leaders develop an attitude that automatically deflects any criticism as having been offered by idiots and inspired by the devil. They hide emotionally and spiritually from the people they lead. They cannot afford to let people get close to them, to see them for the hard-hearted persons they have become. Shriveled hearts neither inspire long-term followings nor leave a positive legacy. Even their supporters wind up feeling a little used and misused.

Some leaders choose to become cynical. A cold, uncaring heart beats at the center of the dysfunction it creates. People abandon the leader's constellation for lack of nurture, because they cannot tolerate the deficit of help and hope.

Leaders who grow through the conflict arena make a conscious decision to give God access to their hearts. The decision may come early in their experience, perhaps even before they encounter serious conflict. Or the decision may be made at some critical juncture or at the eleventh hour of some potentially catastrophic leadership challenge. No matter when it is made, the decision itself is the same: the leader chooses to look for God at work in every situation.

The heart-shaping work of God in the arena of conflict is, in the heat of it, the hardest and most painful of all the operations of God on the soul of the leader. The work is done without benefit of anesthesia. The leader has to be wide awake through these proceedings.

No other heart-shaping arena is as public as this one. The leader typically draws more scrutiny and attention during conflict episodes than at any other time. Leaders tend to play out the subplot of conflict to a sold-out house. How they handle conflict will often be the way they are remembered.

The conflict of a leader can reveal God's heart to the leader's followers. The suffering servant leader plays out the Passion for those in the leadership constellation. This is another way that Jesus is incarnated among his people.

Some significant questions can help you consider God's heart-shaping work through conflict in your leadership:

- What family-of-origin issues influence how you deal with conflict?

- What are your memories of early leadership conflicts?

- What happened during your most recent conflict experience? What, if anything, would you do differently now?

- Which of the strategies outlined in this chapter for dealing with conflict do you find the most difficult to embrace?

- Which one(s) of the strategies are you going to begin working on?

- How has conflict shaped your own leadership legacy?

Hearts destined for greatness usually get hammered on now to be rewarded later. Those who are not afraid to enroll in the graduate school of heart development afforded by conflict are preparing to win the championship trophy. They are determined to be more than conquerors.

COMMONPLACE

DISCOVERING THAT THE ORDINARY
IS EXTRA-ORDINARY

ANDY WANTED TO strike back. His leadership had been called into question, and now the future, so bright earlier, looked foreboding and uncertain. The three board members on a rogue mission had made their demands. A summit meeting had been called. As the conference approached, Andy felt certain that he should take a different tack than he had initially planned. When the meeting began, he brought in a basin of water and a towel. The trio of adversaries could not refuse Andy's request that he be permitted to wash their feet. The simple, yet profound and risky, act of servanthood paid off. The oppressors' hearts melted. Andy, the one willing to serve, regained his spiritual leadership and preserved the organization. Andy's response came out of a heart that had long been accustomed to practicing obedience to the Spirit's promptings. For him, this was not a departure, but a common reaction when he felt the Lord directed him. Years of serving God in the commonplace prepared him for a significant spiritual challenge.

Caroline and her husband manage a very vibrant Christian ministry. On top of a heavy travel schedule and huge financial demands, the couple maintain a magnificent obsession with bringing people into personal relationship with Jesus Christ. Accordingly, Caroline opens her home one night a week to a group of neighbors. She cultivates a relationship with them in order to share Christ with them. Caroline's young children even share in the effort through prayer. Caroline practices what she preaches through her Christian ministry. No one would notice if she did not host her neighbors to extend Christ's love to them. Yet Caroline's consistency backs up her teaching and gives her enormous leadership credibility with those she touches through her ministry. Caroline would never see herself as a heroine of the faith. Yet through the commonplace choices of her life, the choices she has made when no one was looking, she has allowed God to shape her heart.

Sam and Rachel coauthored a book that took off in religious circles, selling more copies than anyone had expected. Quietly, they give away half of their revenues to a ministry organization they both love dearly. Their sense of stewardship did not develop overnight. They give out of a sense of gratitude cultivated over a long time. The couple gave sacrificially for years when they lived paycheck to paycheck. Whereas most people have income goals, Sam and Rachel have established giving goals. A commonplace decision for most people, how to spend money, has become another way God continues to shape Sam and Rachel's hearts. They want to share their blessings in significant ways.

Each of us knows leaders who do common things profoundly. One leader takes a lunch hour each week to read to school kids. Another leader prioritizes his daughter's ball games and his son's piano concerts. One successful Christian businesswoman works with underprivileged kids in an inner city. Common things. Not heroic things, except for the effort and time involved.

A closer look at the lives of these leaders would reveal that these expressions of their heart do not constitute an aberration, a patch on the fabric of their lives that is different from the whole. No, these leaders have been shaped through thousands of common decisions and interactions. They have developed kind, caring, generous, servant hearts through the commonplace of life and their response to it.

When we think of leadership making and breaking, we usually think in terms of the huge moments, the climaxes and catastrophes, the public and the prominent episodes. Our tendency, looking back at the lives of great leaders, is to believe that greatness showed up in the big moment, just in the nick of time. It did. But it did not show up without foundation work being done. Through the commonplace, everyday experiences and how the leader responds to them, the piers of spiritual character are sunk and poured. This foundation determines the kind of ministry superstructure that the leader can build.

The leader's choices and behavior in the commonplace can open up doors of ministry opportunity. I can personally illustrate this truth through a decision that Cathy and I made just last year. When we decided to build a new house, we settled on a builder who, five years earlier, had performed a random act of kindness to us. Late one afternoon, he had offered to help my wife carry groceries up three flights of stairs in the apartment complex where we lived at the time. He did not remember us when we approached him about being our contractor, but we remembered him. We believed that the character exhibited in the small episode transferred into his life work. Conversely, we would have remembered rudeness. One wonders how often leaders close doors of ministry opportunity without ever knowing it.

Leaders work on their life story every day. Sometimes the day turns out to be momentous. Big decisions have to be made. Destinies hang in the balance. Directions must be determined and courage summoned. Every leader has these days. They can be exhilarating or frightening or anywhere in between.

Between these days, and even between the big moments of these days, are moments of the commonplace. The commonplace is the stuff of routine life. The moments when no one is looking. The commonplace experiences fill in the backdrop to the leader's life drama. They are like the unstaged, spontaneous photographs that complement the staged pictures in the wedding photo album. Over time, the candid shots often prove to be more intriguing. They capture life in the making.

That is what the commonplace is. It is life in the making. Stuff that nobody pays much attention to or may not even be aware of. Nevertheless, it is the stuff that big moments draw upon. Actions and attitudes that in and of themselves do not necessarily change the course of history. It is what is left over when the spotlight fades.

God uses the commonplace to shape the leader's heart. We saw glimpses of his handiwork in this arena in the lives of the four biblical leaders. Moses memorized the Sinai desert through countless shepherding experiences. His knowledge kept the Hebrews alive in the wilderness. David's target practice with wild animals served him and God's people well in felling a giant oppressor. Paul's cultivation of a joyful heart showed up in a midnight song service in the Philippian jail before it surfaced as a topic in the Philippian correspondence. The gospel writers note that Jesus routinely attended synagogue, though not every occasion turned into a healing service. In each of these cases, the commonplace served as the workshop where God prepared these leaders for greatness.

The significance of the commonplace as a heart-shaping dynamic shows up in the choice of the Father in how the Son would experience earthly life. Much has been made of the common elements surrounding Jesus' birth. But his entire earthly life of preparation as a carpenter's son exposed him to common human experiences of hard work, painful splinters, dead-line pressures, weather delays, and budget restraints. He knew long days, bruised thumbs, and difficult people. His response to all these experiences and forces helped to form his character. It showed up in patience as well as decisiveness, graciousness for common people, as well as intolerance for those who made common people's burdens heavier.

The discussion of the commonplace as a heart-shaping dynamic for spiritual leaders now focuses on you. The goal of this treatment is to raise your awareness of the sacredness of the ordinary. The hoped-for result is a fresh offering of yourself on the altar of the commonplace. This is not a one-time offering, of course. It involves a decision that God can have everything of ours, even the stuff we think matters little to him. And he can have it all the time. Submitting to God's work in the commonplace of life recognizes that heart-shaping does not go on and off the clock. God remains attentive to our hearts, to what we are becoming, even if we our-selves are not (nor can we always be).

The altar of the commonplace can be either exhausting and threaten-ing or comforting and liberating for the spiritual leader. It is threatening for leaders who always feel that they are striving, never offstage, driven to achieve. It can be especially exhausting for leaders who have to work hard to present a public persona at odds with their heart. This would be true especially for those who have character flaws or lead secret lives. If God is always paying attention, there is no room to hide. Those who seg-ment life sometimes do so to avoid dealing with the sacredness of the commonplace. They want some jurisdictions to be off-limits to the de-mands of spiritual leadership.

On the other hand, the awareness that God is always at work on the leader can be a comforting, even liberating thought. This is particularly true during those dry seasons of spirituality when God seems inexplica-bly or explicably absent. Knowledge of the importance of the common-place in leader making can also ameliorate the feelings of insignificance that threaten the well-being of many leaders. A media-hyped, superstar-studded culture has affected even the Christian world. Those who do not show up in the panoply of big names or do not know any who do can be tempted to feel less important. To realize that the commonplace, routine, pedestrian arena is also a place of God's heart-shaping activity can restore a sense of intentionality to most any leader.

This subplot of the commonplace has been reserved for the last because it links all the other plots together. It provides grist for the mill of the other heart-shaping activities of God. The leader's response to the ordi-nary, the common, limits as well as unlocks the possibilities of story line development in the other subplots of the leader's life drama. The leader can adopt some important habits that will make the commonplace a heart-shaping friendly place.

Habit Number One: Look for God

Leaders whose hearts are shaped through the commonplace have trained themselves to look for God . . . everywhere. God uses circumstances to train our hearts. We tend to disregard circumstances, particularly challenging ones, as nuisances to overcome or to avoid. This attitude will keep us in the dark as to much of what God is trying to teach us through the circumstances of our lives.

Consider pain for instance. Pain focuses our attention. C. S. Lewis gave us that fabulous insight that God whispers to us in our pleasure, but shouts to us in our pain. Everyone suffers some form of pain, physical or psychological. The leader who accepts pain as the work of God in the commonplace grows from it rather than being diminished by it.

When our oldest daughter was eight years old, she had an accident while playing a game. She fell and split open her bottom lip. The pain and the sight of blood had her physically trembling with anxiety by the time I connected with her and her mother at the doctor's office. My wife had done the hard work of driving a terrified child to the physician's emergency room.

Now it was my turn to help. The doctor indicated that allowing the lip to heal by itself would almost certainly result in disfigurement to Jessica's mouth. Sewing her up, however, was going to require a precision that could be jeopardized if she moved around during the procedure. My job, he explained, was to hold her still while the doctor did his repair work.

"Jessica," I began, "you are going to have to lie real still while the doctor sews up your lip."

"Is it going to hurt, daddy?" she asked through quivering, bloody lips.

"Yes, at first, until the doctor gets it numbed. Then you will feel some touching and tugging while he works on you."

"Do we have to do this, daddy?"

"Yes, darling. You are going to have to be real still. I am going to help you. I will put my hands on your shoulders and look straight into your eyes and talk to you the whole time the doctor does his work. You just look at me and keep talking to me, and the doctor will be able to fix you up just fine."

So we started. Many of you have gone through far worse than this, but it was my first time to watch stitches being put in my child's lip. Lips are so tender. I tried not to wince with each new stick. I certainly was not thrilled with the doctor's shots and needles. Yet I held Jessica down so she could be repaired through these instruments. She came through fine with no scarring.

Reflecting on that experience, I realized that God had instructed me through the ordeal. God takes no pleasure in our pain. But he does delight in our wholeness. You may feel pinned down by God right now. You might be in a difficult place, some place you would rather not be. Perhaps you are busted up and bleeding. You have prayed for deliverance, but everything feels like more shots and surgery. Knowing that God is not happy about your hurt, the key is to keep looking into his face and talking with him while the soul surgery takes place. Wriggling out of the situation prematurely may allow you to escape immediate discomfort. But you might wear the scar of emotional and spiritual disfigurement as a result.

Pain has been a master teacher for all effective spiritual leaders. Rather than running from it, the spiritual giants have embraced it to learn from it. They believe that God has purposes in pain that he does not always share with us. But they want to be whole. The cross reminds us that in this world there is no wholeness without some pain.

Great spiritual leaders in my acquaintance have all confided something similar to me about their struggle with pain, disappointment, or failure. They have all asked God for relief, but they have also asked God not to take them off the operating table until they learn all he wants to teach them. This reveals the heart of the spiritual champion. These spiritual Olympians would rather walk with a limp to possess life wisdom and a closer relationship with God than to escape the trauma of the match. They learn, like David, to take their pain to God. Like Paul, they come to exult in their thorns.

Joys and triumphs also form a common part of human experience. This part of the emotional spectrum also provides opportunities for heart-shaping. God exults in our accomplishments. He wants us to enjoy them as well. Emotionally healthy leaders know how to savor the moment and truly rejoice. When the leader does celebrate some milestone or achievement, it affords a marvelous opportunity to see the work of God in the leader's life. To be amazed at the wonders he has wrought through the synergy of his Spirit and the leader's spirit redounds to God's glory. It excavates in the leader a larger heart chamber that can be filled with gratitude and wonder.

The leader who walks with joy has made a decision to look for God. Joy rests on the awareness of God's presence. Joy does not depend on circumstances. It grows out of a relationship with one's God. It is a habit supported by hundreds or thousands of decisions when the leader chooses to look for God. When joy is chosen, it always gives rise to hope. Hope always leads one to God. Leaders who consistently choose joy keep delivering their hearts to God for his work.

Where the leader finds joy often depends on life situations. Some routinely rehearse joy in family relationships. Others find joy in the company of friends. Other leaders are given to joy at seeing the transforming work of God in people. Still others look for God in the faces and lives of strangers. They see every evidence of goodwill as a common expression of the divine. They engage needy people and draw joy from having lightened someone's load. They receive each act of kindness as coming straight from the hand of God.

Learn to look for God. A naval chaplain once told me of his experience of helping victims, victims' families, and hospital staff involved in an airline disaster when a jetliner crashed. For several days, he dealt with the tragedy, attending to the grief of hospital workers and victims' families. He also had responsibility for coordinating and speaking at a large memorial service. As he prepared his remarks, he knew the question on everyone's mind would be, "Why would God let this happen?" He eventually decided that he would not use the occasion to defend God. He wanted to give hope. He chose as his text the magnificent Psalm 46, a psalm for times of trouble that reminds us that God shows up in the middle of calamity. The chaplain admitted the question on everyone's mind, the uncertainty over why things happen (pilot error, in this case). But the certainty was that God was there. He recounted the dozens of ways he had seen God in the horrific circumstances—the skilled care by the hospital staff, the support of family and friends, the response of people all over the world. The message of hope he delivered pointed to the God of the commonplace, who invades each moment and human experience, whether good or bad.

I am writing this chapter while on a trip away from home. The last twenty-four hours have been uneventful, yet I have seen God, especially as I have reflected back over time. A son squealed with delight when his dad jumped in the hotel pool to play with him (heaven means that pain passes, but laughter is eternal). Two lovers hugged as they walked together on a scenic path, lost to everything but each other for the moment (God is love). A group of friends enjoyed dinner together in a restaurant celebrating the birth of a new baby (relationships lie at the center of the universe). A tiny bird snatched a morsel of food left behind as garbage on the parking lot (his eye is on the sparrow). Dinner was good (I thanked God for making turkeys). "I miss you, Dad," my daughter said over the phone

(one day we will not have to leave to go home). From my mountain view, I could see the lights of the city come up as the sun went down (there is a city whose builder and maker is God). A friend gave me a new insight (I am not finished yet). Cathy and I firmed up details for some private time together soon (the greatest of these is love).

God is present in the beauty we are often too busy to see and hear and taste and smell, in the joy of being with people we love, in the enjoyment of doing small tasks exceptionally well, in the pleasant serendipity of everyday life. Our hearts would be enlarged and enlivened by being more attuned to the graces we are often too busy to enjoy. Creating more space for the commonplace would be a wise leadership strategy for improved heart-shaping.

One leader reported a moment of heart-shaping involving a family member. He had been scheduled to go overseas on a mission trip. At the last minute, his plans changed. The next day, his daughter came home from school and asked him to help her with her bug collection for a science project. He was not usually home at this time of the day, but he had cleared his schedule to be gone, anticipating his now canceled overseas trip. He went out with her in search of insects. During the outing, his seventh-grade daughter said simply, "Thanks, Dad, for helping me. You're the best." They walked hand in hand through the woods back to their house. The leader felt that the one-hour excursion had been worth staying home for. The episode reminded him that being there for his kid was also a part of his mission on the planet. God did a bit of sculpting in those joyful moments.

Habit Number Two: Keep Learning

A second habit serves as a corollary to the first. Cultivating the commonplace through learning can provide powerful spiritual and personal renewal. Learning expands the capacity for God to affect the leader's heart. All of the learning does not have to pertain to theological or ministry-related subjects. In fact, mental recreation is critical to leadership stamina.

One highly effective, task-oriented, hard-charging leader I know has one passion besides his ministry and his family—fly fishing. He contends that standing in mountain streams fishing for trout feeds his soul. He will also be quick to tell you that fly fishing is something you learn. His learning quest keeps him connected to creation and to God in a much different way than poring over sermons, which he also likes to do. The skill of tying the flies, competing with himself in the cast, the art of enticing the fish to take the lure, and the thrill of the catch are the simple joys he experiences. God strengthens his heart through the workout. For this leader, fly fishing is spiritual cardiac rehabilitation.

Another spiritual leader works in his garden. Another builds model ships; another studies art and writes novels. The range of interests is as broad as life, and life is generally as broad as the interests the leader develops and maintains. This is not an argument for frenetic dabbling. It is a plea for learning something besides work. Not only will this likely make you more interesting, but it also will remind you of a profound truth: God did not create you and put you on the planet only to get a job done. You are destined for an eternal relationship with him far beyond the several decades of your life on earth. He wants to make you into a person.

The sheer thrill of learning itself opens the leader up to more amazing things about God's work in the world. For instance, the study of field theory, or microbiology, or quantum physics might seem a purely scientific inquiry. However, God's fingerprint of creation energy is all over these rapidly growing sciences. As scientists push deeper into the material universe, below the surface of atomic and molecular physics, the universe seems far more relational than mechanical. The physical affinities between bits of matter in energy fields at the subatomic levels reveal a literal fabric in the universe of space between them. Perhaps the Colossians 1 language referencing Jesus' holding all things together is more than figurative language! I am just fascinated that chaos theory (popularly expressed in *Jurassic Park*: "Love will find a way") promotes the notion that while chaos presents itself as random, over time or with enough distance, a pattern emerges. Weather patterns are another example. "Strange attractors" is a technical term in this field that identifies what seem to be invisible forces that establish the parameters of the system or phenomenon. In theology we call this providence.

Spiritual leaders involved in learning about and engaging the world we all commonly share sharpen their minds and enlarge their exposure to God. The seemingly commonplace habit of learning holds enormous heart-shaping potential. A fertile heart responds to God's creative designs.

Habit Number Three: Say Yes to God

A habit of obedience will allow God to shape the leader's heart. This dynamic is often associated with obedience in decisive moments, like answering the call to devote a life to kingdom ministry. But it is also an important dynamic in more commonplace experiences. The leader who makes a habit of saying yes to God will keep a heart tender toward God. Those who do not live in an attitude of yes will miss his instructions, his insights, his presence.

God whispers in the commonplace. Saying yes to God as a habit of life keeps the leader in touch with him. The leader's yes may involve some heroic action at some international incident. More usually it shows up in commonplace expressions like being kind, being patient with others, being gentle. It shows up in a pleasant countenance and a word of encouragement or affirmation. Saying yes to commonplace heart-shaping might mean sacrificing a little time in order to write a note or make a call to someone who needs a touch from someone.

One leader tells of an incident in a restaurant that demonstrates this habit at work. She had taken her two daughters out for supper. While they were eating, the girls pointed out a schoolteacher they both had. The teacher had come in and sat down at a nearby table with her husband. The mom instantly recognized the teacher's name as being that of one of her daughters' favorite teachers. As she and her daughters stood to leave, she felt an urge to go over and thank the teacher for the contribution she had made to her children's lives. She tried to shake off the urge as she headed out of the restaurant. All the way to the exit the urge continued. As she reached the door, the mom turned around and went back to the teacher's table, introduced herself, and delivered her sentence or two of gratitude. The teacher almost burst into tears: "I was just telling my husband that I don't know if I can teach any longer. I've had the worst day I've had in twenty years of teaching."

The mom's words came at just the right time. Coincidence? Only to those who do not know the power of hearing and obeying God's voice in the commonplace. That leader's heart, through saying yes, became even more convinced that the Spirit would play an active role in her life if she would pay attention.

Saying yes is not always fun or as thrilling as making someone else's day. It also means replying with soft words to the rude store clerk. It may mean returning to the store later to apologize if you did not. Either way, a gentle spirit can open up a chance to share God's heart with another. This habit of the heart may mean nominating others for awards. It may mean letting others go first. It could even influence driving habits. It might prevent you from pointing out others' every mistake or using sarcasm as a weapon or criticizing others who "deserve" it.

Saying yes to God can keep you honest on your expense account as well as help you tithe before taxes. It may mean that you offer fewer excuses for not getting things done, or tell the truth about when things can get done rather than overpromising. It could mean that gossip stops with you, no matter how harmless it seems.

Saying yes to God means seeing each exchange with another human being as fraught with God potential. Creatures made in the image of God can bless or curse one another in their conversations and attitudes. A heart being shaped by the commonplace is inclined more and more to be a blessing. There are no small obediences. Every yes further ingrains the heart with the character of Jesus.

This dynamic holds for circumstances as well as for human interactions. For instance, saying yes means accepting that the wilderness is as grand an assignment as headquarters. Viewing the wilderness experience as a mere detour to greater things will ensure a failing grade in the leadership school of the commonplace.

Every commonplace circumstance provides a heart-shaping opportunity. Being caught in the express lane that is as slow as molasses presents the leader a chance to work on patience. If this seems absurd, then consider the alternative. Churning up stomach acid, elevating one's blood pressure, then being rude to the slow checker seems pretty un-Christlike on reflection. The first response does not waste a common opportunity to grow. The second does not miss the chance to diminish the heart.

Living in obedience is a courageous way to live. It requires gutsy faith to believe that God is at work in everything, especially the commonplace of routine. Saying yes to God means that the leader can have hundreds of victories every day. Many, if not most, of them will be private victories celebrated only by the leader and God. But when it comes to pleasing someone, God ain't a bad choice.

Habit Number Four: Stay Grateful

A fourth habit of the heart opens up the leader to God's work in the commonplace things of life. It is easy to say but tough to do: stay grateful. Maintaining an attitude of gratitude undergirds all the other heart habits that have been discussed. Gratitude provides the basis for contentment with the commonplace and the leader's commitment to discover God in the common areas of human experience.

The leader can easily move out of gratitude. The call to change the world in a sense stirs up a certain discontent with the way things are. Leaders will often throw themselves into the gap between what is and what should be. Battles have to be fought. Obstacles overcome. The work is exhausting. Things often do not go as expected. All of this can challenge the leader's thankfulness for the assignment. Every leader at some point has wanted to give the job back to God.

Adopting a sense of gratitude as an emotional, psychological, and spiritual lifestyle serves as a powerful antidote to discouragement and a sense of failure. It militates against the feelings of insignificance that plague many leaders. Whenever the leader struggles with unmet expectations, gratitude can cut off the leader's entry to the pity party. Being thankful for the privilege to suffer with Jesus sheds a whole new light on a difficult situation.

Gratitude focuses leaders on what they have rather than on what is missing. Gratitude taps into the eternal. The leader who practices gratitude gets a head start on heaven, because gratitude gives birth to praise, and giving praise is what we ultimately are designed to do. A grateful leader has a heart of joy that is practically unassailable by bad circumstances. This kind of leader proves particularly powerful. Not drawing on this world for strength, the leader's gaze is fixed on the horizon of hope.

Look for God. Keep learning. Say yes to him. Stay grateful. These are habits of the heart that will help you stay offered to God on the altar of the commonplace.

A list of questions to ponder could be as long as the commonplace moments of your week:

- Where have you seen God lately?

- What joys can you recite?

- How have others blessed you today? How have you been a blessing?

- What beauty surrounds you?

- What pain drives you to God?

- What kindness have you received recently? Who have you befriended in the last few days?

- What small or large obediences to God can you celebrate?

- Is your heart song one of gratitude?

The commonplace subplot turns out to be a bit more comprehensive than one might suspect. It is not easy to see God's work in the times when we are not receiving immediate and public feedback. It is hard to measure progress in the routine. It is difficult to accept that God's greatest work in your life might currently be under way in venues that seem too commonplace to be so determinative. Yet they often are the most important activities under way in your heart.

CONCLUSION:
COLLABORATING WITH GOD'S
HEART-SHAPING PROJECT

SPIRITUAL LEADERSHIP IS a work of heart. Spiritual issues are ultimately heart issues. Values, attitudes, convictions, motivations, beliefs, vision, hopes, dreams, ambitions. These are the things people live and die for. These are the things that give meaning to life. These are the building blocks of legacy. They are far more enduring than wealth or fame. Heart decisions affect generations because they change lives.

This is why spiritual leadership is at once so complicated and so simple. Spiritual leadership is so critical because what is at stake are human beings made in the image of God and the world they leave behind for others to inhabit. Spiritual leadership has as its focus nothing less than the kingdom of God. This kingdom is the only one that endures. All earthly kingdoms will pass away. This reality raises the ante.

Spiritual leadership needs to be competent. Spiritual leaders must develop their microskills to the fullest capacity. They must understand leadership dynamics and organizational dynamics and family systems dynamics. They must be good at resourcing their work, understanding how to obtain for their ideas the broad range of support that they need to become reality. They must know what needs doing. Bringing the best skills and energy to bear on something that is not worth doing is a waste of time, of people, and of leadership.

Yet a spiritual leader with the right answers and the right skills still falls short of providing the kind of leadership that will expand the kingdom of God. Added to these competencies must be a grasp of the knowledge that is indispensable for spiritual leaders. They must be experts in matters of the heart. They must be more than just counselors with clinical skills and psychological insight. Spiritual leaders must possess an integrating understanding of God, and people, and how God and people interface in life and death. These are the heart issues that spiritual leaders grapple with every day with those they serve.

The leader's school for these heart issues is his or her own life. The curriculum includes experience, observation, and participation. Ultimately all of the leader's insights and ideas get tested in a set of comprehensive exams. The comprehensives occur in the leader's own heart. Unless the leader does well with these tests, he or she is severely limited in effectiveness or even eventually disqualified. The ultimate test of spiritual leadership, then, centers on its own heart matters.

In this volume, I have suggested that this heart-shaping activity is being carried on in six major subplots in the leader's life. The story of what is going on in the leader's heart is informed by the forces of culture, call, community, communion, conflict, and the commonplace. I have also observed that these heart-shaping dynamics do not operate in the leader arbitrarily or haphazardly. Nor does the leader get to designate which ones will be engaged. I have argued that God is the producer of the leader heart-shaping drama. He has chosen the plot and the subplot elements of the story. He has marshaled the scenarios that challenge the leader in each and all of these arenas.

I offer a concluding observation. Heart-shaping is an interactive process. Heart-shaping hinges on choices. How the leader responds to God's initiatives codetermines how the story plays out. The leader is not responsible for devising the categories. Nor can the leader solely dictate the content of what elements constitute each subplot. God introduces the story line. But the leader's responses do influence the development of the drama.

These responses are the choices that the leader makes. Hundreds and thousands of choices. Some daily and routine. Others precipitous and unrehearsed.

Identifying all of the choices that present themselves to spiritual leaders cannot be done. However, a compendium of major choice options in each category can be generated from the investigation put forth in this book.

Culture

God decides into which culture(s) the leader will enter the world scene and focus leadership efforts. In this volume, culture has been considered in a very broad sense, including the historical period of the leader as well as the sociopolitical and environmental forces influencing the leader's assignment. Out of this discussion, several key questions emerge for the leader to ponder:

- How has your culture shaped your view of God's agenda in the world?

- What forces, positive and negative, have contributed the most to your worldview?

- How do you see your leadership role vis-à-vis culture?

- How do leaders best influence culture for the kingdom of God?

- How have you been uniquely prepared for your ministry role through cultural forces?

- How have you transcended your culture?

- What culture(s) are you most effective in as a leader?

- What are you revealing to your culture about God, his work, and his attitude toward people in your culture?

Call

The subplot of call as a heart-shaping dynamic brings the leader to discover why he or she is on the planet. Several key questions will force choices on the leader's part:

- How would you describe your life mission?

- What vision do you have for the current and the next chapter of your life's ministry?

- What hoped-for results of your leadership efforts are you willing to be accountable for?

- What strengths do you have to build on? How are you using them right now?

- What weaknesses must you manage in order to be more effective? What is your plan?

- What have you learned and what are you learning about the effectiveness of your leadership?

- What are you telling people about God's mission in the world?

- How are you helping people in your leadership constellation partner with God's mission themselves?

Community

Spiritual leaders have been shaped by the powerful dynamics of community throughout their lives. Several major issues arise from the consideration of the impact of this formative subplot:

- What family-of-origin issues contribute positively and negatively to your leadership?
- How have ministry communities contributed to your heart development?
- How are you practicing community in your own life? In your family?
- What kind of community are you developing in your ministry assignment?
- What obstacles to developing community in your own life must be addressed?
- What challenges to community threaten your ministry community, and what are you doing about it?
- What are you revealing to those in your leadership constellation about God's work through community?

Communion

The leader's heart that beats with God's heart has been tuned to the divine frequency by listening to God's voice and regularly meeting with him. These questions characterize the major issues in this critical arena:

- Do you spend time with God?
- What kind of time do you spend with God?
- What do you and God talk about?
- What images of God guide and inform your communion?
- What are you learning about God because of your own time with him?
- How do others and what do others know about your time with God?
- How does your communion with God challenge and change your assumptions, biases, and prejudices?
- How do you encourage others in their own communion with God?
- How do you and those in your ministry constellation practice communion with God?

Conflict

The reality of conflict forces its way into the life of every spiritual leader. For some, it comes more often and more intensely than for others. Leadership challenges and struggles provide extraordinarily fertile ground for heart-shaping. The discussion on conflict has raised some questions the leader should consider:

- Are you conflict-allergic, or do you love a good fight, or is the truth about you somewhere in between?
- What has shaped your view of conflict?
- What early experiences in conflict do you remember?
- How do you respond to those who challenge your leadership?
- What have you learned about yourself through conflict?
- In what ways are you contributing to the amount or nature of the conflict you experience?
- How have you taught your ministry constellation to deal with conflict?
- What have you learned about God in times when your leadership has been threatened?

Commonplace

The routine circumstances and ordinary stuff of life provide a constantly active arena for God's intervention in the life of the leader. The effective and growing spiritual leader has learned to see God's heart-shaping activity in what deceptively appears as a minor subplot but really turns out to be a major theme in the leader's development. Some important questions need the leader's attention:

- Do you look for God?
- Do you celebrate well?
- How do your responses and actions differ when no one is looking?
- Do you view circumstances as interruptions or learning opportunities?
- What joys keep you going?
- How do you incorporate beauty into your life?
- How do you help those in your leadership constellation develop heart habits to encounter God in their own common places?

These questions all force choices. They beg for intentionality on the part of the leader. Intentional reflection, intentional analysis, and intentional decisions about courses of action toward a desired outcome—all these are a part of a strategy designed to raise the leader's IQ about God's heart-shaping activities.

Leaders choose to grow or not to grow. Both decisions are ultimately deliberate. Choices can place the leader's heart in God's hands for shaping as he sees fit. Sometimes leaders' choices can confirm an intention to shape their own hearts apart from God's best designs. The first set of choices enlarges the leader's heart; the other hardens and shrinks it.

The leader's choices carry implications that reach far beyond the life of the leader. What kind of heart you choose to have will limit or increase your impact for God on the world and the people he has created. You will determine what some people come to know about God, his mission, his activity, his heart. You will help them desire or not desire God's heart-shaping activity in their own lives.

Every person on the planet needs spiritual leadership. Because they have been made in the image of God, they are instinctively hungry to discover more of him. They will either find and be guided by leaders who have had their own hearts carefully molded by God for their assignment, or they will be influenced by those whose hearts have been shaped by poor substitutes.

The leader whose heart has been wonderfully and meticulously shaped by God is a magnificent piece of work, a real masterpiece. God has sculpted a life that bears a remarkable likeness to his Son.

You choose how you respond to God's heart-shaping initiatives. These choices are the story of your life.

"As water reflects a face, so a man's heart reflects the man" (Prov. 27:19).

REFERENCES

Clinton, R. *The Making of a Leader.* Colorado Springs: Navpress, 1988.

McNeal, R. *Revolution in Leadership: Training Apostles for Tomorrow's Church.* Nashville, Tenn.: Abingdon Press, 1998.

THE AUTHOR

REGGIE MCNEAL is the director of the Leadership Development Department of the South Carolina Baptist Convention. He draws on his twenty years of local congregational leadership experience as staff member and pastor, plus his work over the last decade with thousands of church leaders as a resource to local churches, denominational groups, seminaries, colleges, and parachurch organizations in their leadership development needs.

He earned his bachelor of arts (1977) in political science from the University of South Carolina and both his master of divinity (1981) and his doctorate (1986) in historical theology from Southwestern Baptist Theological Seminary in Ft. Worth, Texas. He has taught at the college and seminary level as an adjunct faculty member and has served as guest lecturer in leadership issues. He has contributed to a number of religious publications. His *Revolution in Leadership: Training Apostles for Tomorrow's Church* looks at the character and competencies of spiritual leadership at the beginning of the third Christian millennium.

McNeal lives with his wife, Cathy, and their two daughters, Jessica and Susanna, in Columbia, South Carolina.

INDEX

A

Absalom, 28
acceptance of pain, 179–182
accountability, 20, 162
Acts, 92, 103, 105
addictions, 118–119
afterlife, 38–39
ambivalence, 17
American culture, 114–115, 139
American religion, 80–81
Ananias, 40–41
anger, 89
anointment, 24, 110–111
Antioch church, 43
apologetics, 86
apostolic leadership, 102–107, 136
approval, need for, 118–119
architecture for learning communities, 131
attitude, 156–157
authority, relocation of, 82–83

B

Barnabus, 43
Bethany trio, 62–63
boundaries: saying no, 59, 60; setting and maintaining appropriate, 119–120; unresolved issues of, 163
burning bush, 12
burnout issues, 139

C

call to leadership: attendant gifts of, 108–111; call clarification, 57–60, 109, 111–113; calling versus being called, 95, 97–98; challenges to, 58; of Christian leaders, 25; content of the, 100; David's, 22–25, 27; life-changing nature of, 41; meaning of, 97–98; Moses', 12–14; nature/meaning of, 95–96, 107; pattern of God's, 100–101; Paul's, 39–42; questions to consider about, 189; recognizing the, 97–100; serving as leader without the, 99; serving of the, 27–28. *See also* character traits of ministers; leaders; leadership
call transition periods, 106, 160
capitulation, 90
career versus a call, 98
ceremonial cleanliness, 39
chaos theory, 183
character traits of ministers: entrepreneurial, 103–104; kingdom conscious, 103; missional, 102; people developers, 104; schooled by the business culture, 104; spiritual, 105–107; team players, 103; visionary, 104–105. *See also* call to leadership; leaders; leadership
children, 121–122
choice, 144–145
choosing a direction, 157–158
Christian expression, 87
Christian movement, early, 43
Christian values, 90
church culture, 87–88, 133
cleanliness, ceremonial, 39
clergy-laity distinction, 133